iMac

PORTABLE GENIUS
3rd EDITION

iMac

PORTABLE GENIUS
3rd EDITION

by Guy Hart-Davis

WILEY

John Wiley & Sons, Inc.

004. 16S HAR

11/12   4/14

LAD 1/12   LAD 1/14

TC 10   TC 18

iMac® Portable Genius, 3rd Edition

Published by
John Wiley & Sons, Inc.
10475 Crosspoint Blvd.
Indianapolis, IN 46256
www.wiley.com

WILEY

About the Author

Guy Hart-Davis is the author of several other computer books, including *iLife 11 Portable Genius, iWork '09 Portable Genius, Teach Yourself VISUALLY iMac 2nd Edition,* and *Teach Yourself VISUALLY iPhone 5.*

Credits

This book is dedicated to Rhonda and Teddy.

Acknowledgments

My thanks go to the following people for making this book happen:

- Stephanie McComb for asking me to write this edition of the book.
- Chris Wolfgang for shaping the outline and running the editorial side of the project.
- Paul Sihvonen-Binder for reviewing the book for technical accuracy and making many helpful suggestions.
- Lauren Kennedy for copyediting the book with a light touch.
- Jennifer Henry and Andrea Hornberger for laying out the book in the design.
- Evelyn Wellborn for scrutinizing the pages for errors.
- Potomac Indexing, LLC for creating the index.

Contents

chapter 2

How Can I Set Up My iMac for
Multiple Users?

How Can I Use My iMac as an Entertainment Center? 160

chapter 8

How Can I Use My iMac to Get Organized? 240

How Can I Telecommute Efficiently on My iMac? 254

What Are the Best Applications for My iMac? 282

chapter 11

How Can I Run Windows Programs
and Games on My iMac? 300

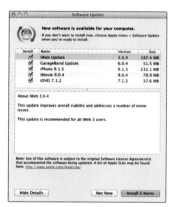

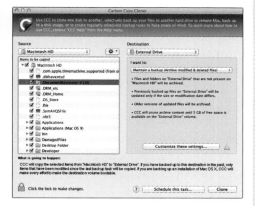

Introduction

Your iMac is a wonderful computer.

Apple keeps improving the iMac, making each generation's screen larger, its hardware faster, its housing sleeker, and its peripherals more attractive — so there's a good chance your iMac is a beautiful monster with a 27-inch screen, more gigabytes of RAM than you have fingers, and a clutter-free wireless keyboard and Magic Mouse or Magic Trackpad.

I need hardly add that your iMac is running Mac OS X Lion, the most powerful and easy-to-use operating system available today. Nor that Mac OS X is gorgeous to look at.

So it's up to you to make the most of your iMac and Mac OS X. To do that, you need the knowledge this book delivers. Here's just a taste of what you'll learn:

- **Make Mac OS X look and feel the way you want it to.** Set up the Dock with the icons for the applications you need, choose where to position it, and teach it how to behave. Choose the desktop picture you want and a suitable screen saver. Make the Magic Mouse or Magic Trackpad work your way, and get Mac OS X to use the sounds you prefer.

- **Set up your iMac up for everyone to use.** Learn about the five types of user accounts Mac OS X offers, and put them to good effect on your iMac. Set up a separate user account for each user, apply Parental Controls to those users who need them, and turn on the Guest account if you require it. Share your song files and photo files easily with other people who use your iMac.

- **Tweak the Finder so that it works your way.** Use the Finder's four different views like a pro, and customize each of the views to suit your needs. Manage application windows, full-screen applications, and extra desktops slickly and smoothly using Lion's new Mission Control feature. Tap the Spotlight search feature so that you can find every file you need within seconds.

- **Network your iMac and other computers to save time and effort.** Use your iMac's built-in Wi-Fi interface to set up a wireless network in moments, or run the cables to create a speedy and trusty Ethernet network. Share files, hardware, Internet access, and music and video on your network.

- **Use your iMac as an entertainment center.** Your iMac plays music, video, and DVDs straight out of the box, but you can also add TV to the list, and can either play shows or record them and play them back later. You can also turn the tables and show your iMac's output on either a television or a video projector.

- **Enjoy your photos and music.** Use iPhoto to import photos from your digital camera and make the most of them, including publishing them online or turning them into Desktop backgrounds or screen savers. Play your songs with iTunes, create compelling playlists from them, and even play your favorite Internet radio stations through your iMac.

- **Keep on top of your email and use chat for business as well as fun.** Set up Apple's Mail application to use each of your email accounts so that you can manage all your email easily. Work with attachments, sort messages automatically using rules and Smart Mailboxes, and squelch spam down to a trickle. Use iChat to chat either on your local network or on the Internet, to transfer files, or even to share movies, slide shows, or presentations.

- **Organize your business, your home life, and everything else.** Take precise control of your time by scheduling your appointments and sharing your calendar not just among all your Macs but also with your iPhone, iPad, iPod, and the web. Track every detail you need to know about your contacts, and carry that valuable information with you everywhere you go.

- **Work efficiently wherever you are.** Connect to your iMac across the Internet and control it via Screen Sharing, or simply connect via File Sharing to pick up the files you forgot to take with you. Take advantage of your iMac's built-in capabilities to do your work for you automatically and effortlessly.

- **Find the best software for your needs.** Your iMac comes with a terrific selection of software, but you may prefer another email application, web browser, or chat client that does things your way. If you create office documents, you'll likely need to add office applications to your iMac — but you may not need to pay for them.

- **Run Windows programs and games on your iMac.** Even if you're a Mac user through and through, you may need to run Windows programs for special tasks — or you may want to play games that run only on PCs. Learn how to use Boot Camp to install Windows directly on your iMac and run it at blazing speed, or use a virtual-machine application to run Windows on top of Mac OS X so that you can use Windows programs alongside your Mac applications.

- **Make your iMac run faster and more reliably.** Maximize your iMac's power by adding as much RAM as it will hold, and keep the hard disk in good order with plenty of space free. Use Software Update to keep your iMac's software up to date, deal with network and Internet issues, and fix problems that crop up with disks and permissions. Create a USB recovery drive or a Mac OS X installation DVD to help you recover from severe problems.

- **Keep your iMac and your files safe.** Secure your iMac against viruses, harden it against attacks through the Internet or other networks, and protect it from the threats that other users can pose. Keep your files safe by backing them up automatically with Time Machine, backing up crucial files to secure locations online, and by backing up your entire iMac so that you can restore it in minutes.

Turn the page, and we'll dive right in.

What's the Best Way to Get Started with My iMac?

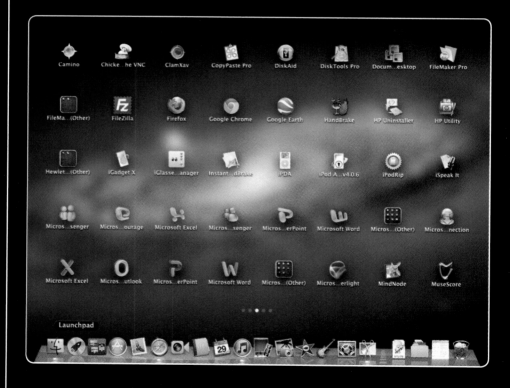

Now that you've unpacked, set up, and started your iMac, you're ready to get to work using Mac OS X. This chapter shows you how to run and manage applications like a pro; connect printers, monitors, and other essential hardware to your iMac; and make your iMac's user interface look, feel, and sound the way you want it to. Finally, the chapter teaches you tricks for using the Apple Remote to control your iMac.

Navigating the Mac Desktop like a Pro

To get anything done — surf the Internet, check your email, or listen to music — on your iMac, you need to run applications. This section shows you how to run applications, arrange applications on your desktop so that you can see what you need to, and quit applications when you've finished using them.

Running an application from the Dock

If the Dock contains an icon for the application you want to run, click that icon to launch the application. The application window appears, and the application's menus appear at the left end of the Mac OS X menu bar.

This is the way you'll probably want to launch most of the applications you use frequently. You can add the applications' icons to the Dock if they're not already there.

Note

If you use an application every time you use your iMac, set the application to launch automatically when you log in. Control+click or right-click the application's icon in the Dock, highlight Options on the shortcut menu, and then click Open at Login. Mac OS X places a check mark next to this item and hereafter opens the application automatically when you log in.

Running an application from Launchpad

When an application's icon doesn't appear on the Dock, you can launch the application from Launchpad instead. Launchpad is Lion's new application launcher and derives its look from the iPad and iPhone Home screens.

To run an application from Launchpad, follow these steps:

1. **Click the Launchpad icon on the Dock to display the Launchpad screen (see Figure 1.1).**

2. **If the application you want doesn't appear on the screen that's displayed, scroll left or right to display another screen.** You can scroll in any of these ways:

   - **Scroll sideways with two fingers on the Magic Mouse or Magic Trackpad.**
   - **Click and drag with any mouse.**
   - **Press Left Arrow or Right Arrow.**
   - **Click one of the dots at the bottom of the screen.** The white dot represents the screen you're currently on.

3. **Click the application you want to launch.** The Launchpad screen disappears, and the application opens.

1.1 Launchpad gives you an easy way to launch any application installed on your iMac for you to use.

Genius

From Launchpad, you can quickly add an icon to the Dock. Simply drag the icon to where you want it on the Dock.

Running an application from Spotlight

If you can't find the application in Launchpad, run it from Spotlight. Click the Spotlight icon at the right end of the menu bar to open the Spotlight search field, and then start typing the application's name. In the search results list, click the application to launch it.

Genius

You can also run an application from the Applications folder if you want, but Launchpad is usually faster and easier. Click the desktop to activate the Finder, choose Go ⇨ Applications from the menu bar to open the Applications folder, and then double-click the application's icon. If you want to close the Applications folder as you open the application, hold down Option as you double-click.

Arranging applications on your desktop

When you have opened several application windows, you may need to resize and rearrange them so that you can see everything you need to. Here's what to do:

- **Switch to another window.** Click the window to which you want to switch. If the window belongs to the same application you're currently using, that application remains active. If the window belongs to another application, that application becomes active.

- **Switch to another application.** Click the application's icon in the Dock. That application's windows come to the front of the display, and that application's menus appear on the menu bar.

Genius

To switch applications quickly using the keyboard, press and hold down ⌘, and then press Tab. A bar appears across the middle of the screen showing an icon for each open application. Press Tab to move the highlight to the application you want, and then release ⌘. While holding down ⌘, you can also press Shift+Tab to move through the applications in reverse order. Also, while holding down ⌘, you can press Left Arrow or Right Arrow to move from application to application.

- **Move a window.** Click a window's title bar and drag it to where you want the window.

- **Resize a window automatically.** Click the green Zoom button at the left end of the window's title bar to resize the window automatically to fit its contents. If Mac OS X chooses an unsuitable size, as sometimes happens, click the Zoom button again to restore the window to its previous size.

- **Resize a window manually.** Move the mouse pointer over one of the window's borders so that it changes to a two-headed arrow, and then drag to change the size. Drag the top or a side to resize only in one dimension. Drag a corner to resize in two dimensions.

- **Minimize a window.** Click the yellow Minimize button at the left end of the window's title bar to minimize the window to an icon on the Dock. Click the minimized icon again to restore the window.

- **Close a window.** Click the red Close button at the left end of the window's title bar.

- **Hide an application.** When you don't need to see an application for the time being, you can hide it by opening the application's menu and choosing the Hide command (for example, Safari ⇨ Hide Safari). The application hides all its windows; you can't choose which windows are hidden and which are visible.

- **Hide all other applications.** When you want to concentrate on one application and ignore all others, open the application's menu and choose the Hide Others command. For example, in Mail, choose Mail ⇨ Hide Others to hide all the other open applications.

Genius

In most applications, you can press ⌘+H to hide the active application, or press ⌘+Option+H to hide all other applications.

Running an application full screen

When you need to devote your attention to a single application, you can run it full screen rather than in a window.

To run an application full screen, click the Full Screen button — the button that shows two arrows pointing north-east and south-west — in its upper-right corner. You can also choose View ⇨ Enter Full Screen or press ⌘+Control+F. Figure 1.2 shows the Safari web browser running in full-screen view.

1.2 Switch an application to full-screen view when you want to concentrate on it.

To make Mac OS X display the menu bar when you're using full-screen view, move the mouse pointer to the top of the screen. The menus slide into view. Similarly, you can display the Dock by moving the mouse pointer to the bottom of the screen. (If you've parked the Dock at the left edge or right edge of the screen, move the mouse pointer to that edge to display the Dock.)

You can switch easily to another application by pressing ⌘+Tab. If the application to which you switch is running in full-screen mode, you go straight from one full screen to another.

When you're ready to return from full-screen mode to a window, choose View ➪ Exit Full Screen or press ⌘+Control+F.

Genius

You can also press Esc twice to return from full-screen view to a window.

Switching applications using Mission Control

Even with your iMac's large screen, once you open a lot of windows, it can become difficult to find the window you need. To help, Mac OS X provides Mission Control, a feature for letting you see all the applications you're running and all the windows you've opened in them.

Note

Older iMacs use the keyboard shortcuts F9 for showing all open applications and windows, F10 for showing the open windows in the current application, and F11 for showing the Desktop.

Mission Control has three main tricks for navigating and managing windows:

- **Show all open windows.** Press F3 or click the Mission Control icon on the Dock to reduce the open windows and arrange them on-screen so that you can see them all at once (see Figure 1.3). Click the window you want to activate, or press F3 after highlighting the window.

Genius

When you have displayed all open windows, you may want to see a window's contents before activating it. Move the mouse pointer over the window to place a blue outline around it, and then press Spacebar to display a preview of the window. Press Spacebar again when you're ready to close the preview.

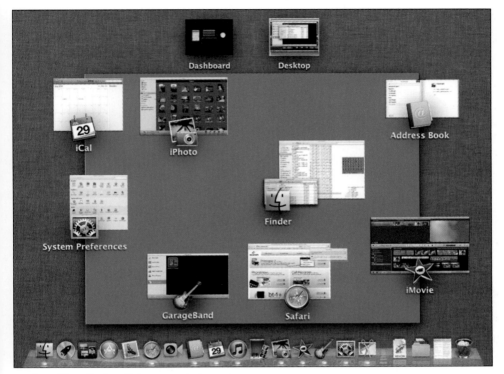

1.3 Press F3 to display all the open windows at once.

Genius

To drag a file to another application (for example, something you want to attach to an email), click and start dragging the file, and then press F3. When you find the window you want, press F3 to make that the active window, and then release the mouse button to drop your file into the window.

● **Show all open windows of the current application.** When you want to focus only on the current application, press Control+F3, or Control+click or right-click the Mission Control icon on the Dock and then click Show Application Windows. Mission Control hides all the other applications, shrinks the current application's windows, and arranges them so that you can see them all at once (see Figure 1.4). Click the window you want to activate, or highlight the window and then press Control+F3 again.

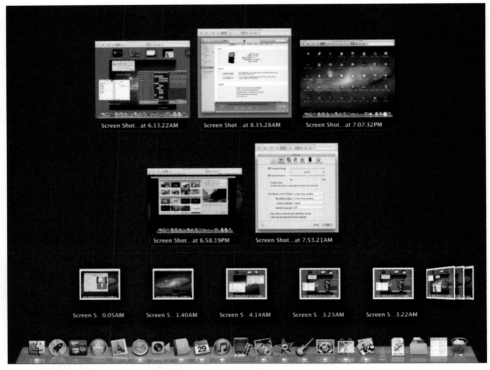

1.4 Press Control+F3 to display all the open windows of the current application at once.

Genius

To copy content from one window to another in the same application, select the content, click, and start dragging it, and then press Control+F3. Find the window you're looking for, press Control+F3 again to activate it, and drag and drop the content to the correct location.

● **Show the desktop.** Press ⌘+F3, or Control+click or right-click the Mission Control icon on the Dock and then click Show Desktop, to slide all the open windows off to the sides of the screen so that you can see the desktop. This is great when you need to open a file or folder on your desktop, but you can also use it to place an item on the desktop: Click and drag the item, and then press ⌘+F3 to reveal the desktop while still holding down the mouse button. Press ⌘+F3 again when you want to restore the windows to their previous positions.

Note

You can see the Mission Control animations in slow motion by pressing Shift as you press the appropriate Mission Control function key.

The keyboard shortcuts and the clicks of the Mission Control icon on the Dock are easy enough, but if you prefer, you can trigger Mission Control in other ways. You can either assign Mission Control to a particular button on a regular mouse (not a Magic Mouse) or make one or more corners of the screen into an active screen corner that runs Mission Control automatically.

Genius

Double-tap the Magic Mouse with two fingers to launch Mission Control. On the Magic Trackpad, swipe up with four fingers.

Quitting an application

When you finish using an application, quit it in one of these ways:

- **Open the application's menu and choose the Quit command.** The application's menu is the menu that has the application's name and appears at the left end of the menu bar; the Quit command also bears the application's name. For example, to quit the TextEdit application, you open the TextEdit menu and choose Quit TextEdit from it.

- **Press ⌘+Q.** This standard keyboard shortcut is the quickest way to quit an application. It works with almost all Mac applications (there are a few exceptions).

- **Use a Dock icon's menu.** Control+click or right-click the application's icon on the Dock, and then choose Quit on the shortcut menu. Not all applications have the Quit command on these menus, but most do.

Resuming work after logging out of, restarting, or shutting down your iMac

When you log out of, restart, or shut down your iMac, Mac OS X gives you the option to resume your applications (see Figure 1.5). If you will want to pick up your computing

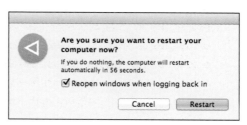

1.5 When logging out of your iMac, restarting it, or shutting it down, you can select the Reopen windows when logging back in check box to make Mac OS X resume your computing session where you left off.

Genius

You don't need to shut down your iMac at the end of each computing session. Instead, you can put your iMac to sleep, or you can allow another user to log in for a session of her own while your session takes it easy in the background, as discussed in Chapter 2. When you wake your Mac, or when you resume your session, all your applications are still running as you left them.

session where you left it, select the Reopen windows when logging back in check box. If not, deselect this check box, and you'll be free to launch whichever applications you want after you log back in.

Connecting Essential Hardware to Your iMac

Your iMac's all-in-one design reduces the number of cables your computer needs, and if you have the wireless keyboard and Magic Mouse or Magic Trackpad as well, the front side of your iMac can be a cable-free zone. But at the back, you'll probably need to connect extra hardware, such as external hard drives and printers.

Pairing the wireless keyboard, Magic Mouse, and Magic Trackpad

To use a wireless device such as a wireless keyboard, Magic Mouse, or Magic Trackpad, you need to pair it with your iMac — telling the iMac and the wireless device that you want the two of them to work together.

If your iMac comes with the Apple wireless keyboard and Magic Mouse or Magic Trackpad, these devices should already be paired with the iMac. Just press the On/Off button on the right side of the keyboard or the Magic Trackpad, slide the On/Off switch on the bottom of the Magic Mouse, and you'll be in business.

If you've added a wireless keyboard or Magic Mouse or Magic Trackpad to an iMac that didn't include them, pair them like this:

1. **Make sure your iMac has Bluetooth turned on.** If the Bluetooth icon appears on the menu bar, click it and make sure that Bluetooth: On appears at the top. If Discoverable: Off appears, click on Discoverable: On, as in Figure 1.6.

   - **If the readout says Bluetooth: Off, click Turn Bluetooth On.**

   - **If the Bluetooth icon doesn't appear on the menu bar, choose Apple menu ➪ System Preferences.** In the Internet & Wireless area of the System Preferences window, click the Bluetooth icon. In Bluetooth preferences (see Figure 1.7), select the On check box, the Discoverable check box, and the Show Bluetooth status in the menu bar check box.

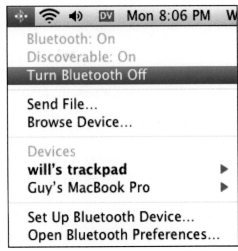

1.6 Using the Bluetooth icon and pop-up menu on the menu bar is the easiest way to turn Bluetooth on and off and to open Bluetooth preferences.

2. **Turn on the mouse, trackpad, or keyboard.** The indicator light glows for a few seconds to indicate that you've got battery power, and then starts flashing to show that the device is in discovery mode.

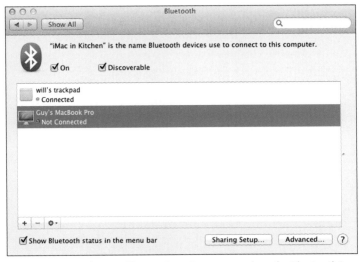

1.7 You may need to use Bluetooth preferences to place the Bluetooth icon on the menu bar.

3. **Choose Apple menu ⇨ System Preferences.** The System Preferences window opens.

4. **In the Hardware section, click the Keyboard icon to open Keyboard preferences, the Mouse icon to open Mouse preferences, or the Trackpad icon to open Trackpad preferences, as appropriate.**

5. **Click the Set Up Bluetooth Keyboard button, the Set Up Bluetooth Mouse button, or the Set Up Bluetooth Trackpad button, and then follow through the steps of the assistant that opens.**

6. **If Software Update opens and prompts you to download an update for the keyboard, mouse, or trackpad, download and install the update.** You may need to restart your iMac after this.

Adding an external hard drive

If your iMac needs extra storage or a separate drive for backup or for transferring files easily, add an external hard drive. Connecting the drive takes only moments, as all you need is the right kind of cable. What may take longer is choosing the best kind of external hard drive for your needs and formatting it with a suitable file system.

Choosing external drives

Current iMac models have three interfaces for connecting external drives:

- **Thunderbolt.** Thunderbolt is a new standard for exceptionally fast devices, such as external drives. Thunderbolt devices can transfer data at up to 10 gigabits per second (Gbps), which means that under ideal conditions, your iMac can transfer around 1.25 gigabytes per second (GBps) to or from a Thunderbolt drive. The upside is the speed; the downside is that Thunderbolt is new, so relatively few devices are available, and those that are available are expensive.

- **FireWire 800.** FireWire 800 can transfer data at up to 800 megabits per second (Mbps), shifting around 100 megabytes (MB) of data per second. This rate is much slower than Thunderbolt, but it's still fast enough for most purposes. Many FireWire external 800 drives are available.

 Note If you have a FireWire 400 drive, you can connect it to your iMac by using a converter cable from FireWire 800 to FireWire 400. At this writing, it's barely worth buying a new FireWire 400 drive, but if you already have one, you can keep using it with your iMac.

● **USB 2.0.** USB 2.0 can transfer data at up to 480 Mbps, which means it moves a maximum of 57MB per second. USB 2.0 external drives are available everywhere. When buying a drive, look for a drive speed of at least 7200RPM (revolutions per minute) and cache of at least 8MB.

Genius

If you need the best performance, get a Thunderbolt external drive — but be prepared to pay extra for it. If you're satisfied with merely high performance instead of blazing performance, go for a FireWire 800 drive. FireWire drives are more expensive than USB 2.0 drives, but they perform better. Both Thunderbolt and FireWire allow you to plug one device into another, with only the first device in the chain actually attached to your iMac.

Connecting an external drive

To add an external drive to your iMac, connect the drive's power supply (if it has one), and then connect the drive to your iMac via a Thunderbolt, FireWire, USB cable.

Mac OS X automatically detects the drive and mounts it, so you can access it from the Devices category in the sidebar of a Finder window. Depending on the Finder preferences you've chosen, an icon for the drive may appear on your desktop.

Formatting an external drive

Most external drives come formatted with the FAT32 file system, but if your drive has a high capacity, you can improve performance by reformatting it using the Mac OS Extended file system.

Caution

Reformatting the drive erases all the data on it, so the best time to reformat the drive is before you start using it. Any time after that, you'll need to copy all the data to another drive, reformat the drive, and then copy the data back. Copying the data is easy enough; the problem is usually finding another drive big enough to hold your capacious external drive's data.

Here's how to reformat an external drive:

1. **Click the desktop and then choose Go ⇨ Utilities.** A Finder window opens showing the contents of the Utilities folder.

2. **Hold down Option and double-click the Disk Utility icon.** Disk Utility opens, and the Finder window closes.

3. **In the list box on the left, click the drive you want to reformat.**

4. **Click the Erase tab to display the Erase pane (see Figure 1.8).**

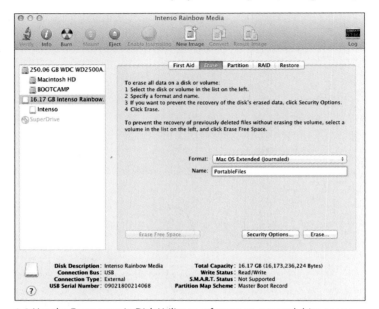

1.8 Use the Erase pane in Disk Utility to reformat an external drive to use Mac OS Extended file system. You can choose among Journaled, Encrypted, and Case-sensitive formats, depending on your needs.

5. **Open the Format pop-up menu and choose the format you want:**

   - **Mac OS Extended (Journaled).** Use this format for drives on which you do not need encryption or case-sensitive filenames. This is the format you will normally want.

   - **Mac OS Extended (Journaled, Encrypted).** Use this format for drives on which you need encryption.

   - **Mac OS Extended (Case-sensitive, Journaled).** Use this format for drives on which you need case-sensitive filenames.

   - **Mac OS Extended (Case-sensitive, Journaled, Encrypted).** Use this format for drives on which you need case-sensitive filenames and encryption.

Genius

Case-sensitive filenames enable you to create different files or folders with the names spelled the same way but using different capitalization. For example, Dog.rtf, dog.rtf, DOG.rtf, and DoG.rtf are different filenames because they have different capitalization. Usually, it's easier not to use one of the case-sensitive formats and simply use a different filename for each file in the same location.

Note If you will share this external drive with Windows PCs, use the MS-DOS (FAT) format. This is the format with which most external drives ship, so you may find that the drive already uses this format.

6. **Type the name for the drive in the Name text box.**

7. **Click Erase.** Disk Utility confirms that you're prepared to delete all the data on the disk (see Figure 1.9).

8. **Click Erase.** Disk Utility erases the disk and reformats it using the format you chose.

9. **Quit Disk Utility.** Press ⌘+Q.

Are you sure you want to erase the disk "Intenso Rainbow Media"?

Erasing a disk deletes all data on all its partitions.

This disk has 1 partition:
"Intenso"

Cancel   Erase

1.9 Disk Utility double-checks that you want to delete all the data on the disk.

Genius If you've already formatted the drive with the Mac OS Extended (Journaled) file system and started using it, you can turn off journaling. In Disk Utility, click the drive in the left list box, hold down Option, and choose File ➪ Disable Journaling.

Connecting a printer

Most consumer-level printers connect via USB, and your iMac includes software drivers for a wide variety of printer models. This means that you can usually install a printer in minutes:

1. **Connect your printer's power supply.**

2. **Connect the printer to your iMac with a USB cable.** The iMac automatically detects the printer and queries it for its model information.

3. **Choose Apple menu ➪ System Preferences.** The System Preferences window opens.

4. **In the Hardware section, click the Print & Scan icon to display Print & Scan preferences.** If the printer appears in the main area of the pane, as in Figure 1.10, it's all set up and ready for use. Skip the rest of this list. Otherwise, carry on.

5. **Click the Add (+) button to open the Add Printer dialog.** If the Default pane (see Figure 1.11) is not displayed at first, click the Default button on the toolbar to display it.

1.10 Use Print & Scan preferences to check if your iMac has recognized the printer. If not, click the Add (+) button under the Printers list box to add the printer.

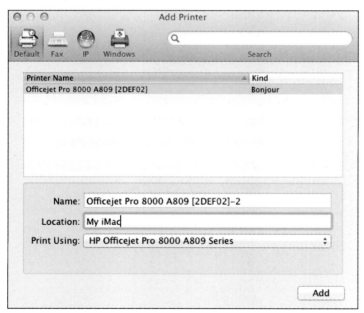

1.11 Use the Add Printer dialog to set up a printer that your iMac has not recognized by itself.

6. **In the Printer Name list box, click the printer.** Your iMac queries the printer and displays its details at the bottom of the dialog.

7. **If necessary, change the name in the Name text box.** For example, you may prefer a descriptive name such as "Color workhorse" to the printer's make and model number.

8. **If you plan to share the printer, make sure the Location text box contains a clear description of where the printer is located.**

Note If you cannot find a driver for your printer in the Printer Software dialog, you may need to download a driver from the printer manufacturer's website. Open the downloaded file and follow the installation procedure, then go back to the Printer Software dialog and select the new driver.

9. **In the Print Using pop-up menu, verify that Mac OS X has chosen a drive that matches the printer model.** If not, do the following:

   - **Open the Print Using pop-up menu and choose Select Printer Software to open the Printer Software dialog (see Figure 1.12).**

   - **Click the driver to use for the printer.** You can narrow the list by typing a search term in the Search box at the top of the dialog.

   - **Click OK.**

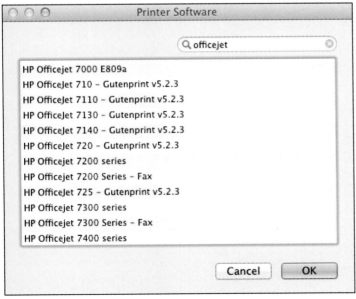

1.12 You can use the Printer Software dialog to tell Mac OS X which driver to use for a printer.

10. **Click Add.** Mac OS X adds the printer.

11. **Choose System Preferences ⇨ Quit System Preferences to quit System Preferences.**

Connecting a scanner

Like printers, most scanners these days connect via USB, with only high-end models connecting via FireWire. Unless you do a lot of scanning, it's usually not worth spending the extra money for a FireWire scanner.

To connect a scanner, you normally plug one end of a USB cable into the scanner and the other end into your iMac. Mac OS X includes a wide variety of scanner drivers, so unless your scanner is a new model or a rare model, Mac OS X will probably recognize it. If not, you will need to download and install a driver from the manufacturer's website.

Note If your scanner includes a custom scanning application for Mac OS X, use it in preference to Image Capture, as it's likely to give both better controls for the scanner's features and better results overall.

To check that your iMac recognizes the scanner, click the Launchpad icon on the Dock, and then click the Image Capture icon. If the scanner appears in the Image Capture window, it's ready for use.

Connecting an additional display

Even though your iMac has a fine large display, you can almost certainly boost your productivity by adding a second monitor. Either the 21.5-inch iMac or the 27-inch iMac can drive an external display up to 27 inches, the size of Apple's Thunderbolt Display or its largest Cinema Display, so you can double the amount of screen space you have. If you have an older iMac, check its capabilities to see how large a display it can handle.

To connect the display, you'll need a suitable connector. Which type of connector you need depends on which graphics port your iMac has and which connection type the display uses.

To connect an external display to the current iMac models, you use the Mini DisplayPort integrated in the Thunderbolt port. On older models, you use the Mini DisplayPort itself or its predecessor, the Mini DVI port.

If your display doesn't have a Mini DisplayPort connector or Mini DVI connector, you'll need to get a suitable connector cable. For example, if the display has a DVI connector, you'll need the Mini DisplayPort to DVI Adapter that the Apple Store sells (or a functional equivalent).

Note Some larger displays use a dual-link DVI connector. For such displays, you'll need the Mini DisplayPort to Dual-Link DVI Adapter (again from the Apple Store) or another adapter that performs the same function.

Once you have the hardware, add the monitor like this:

1. **Connect the monitor to its power supply.**

2. **Connect the monitor to the iMac's Thunderbolt port or Mini DisplayPort, using the adapter if necessary.** The iMac automatically detects the external monitor and starts using it.

3. **Choose Apple menu ⇨ System Preferences.** The System Preferences window opens.

4. **In the Hardware section, click the Displays icon to open Displays Preferences.** Mac OS X opens a Displays window on each screen so that you can set options for each.

5. **In the Display pane, make sure that Mac OS X has chosen the appropriate resolution for each monitor.** Change it if necessary.

6. **Click the Arrangement tab to display the Arrangement pane (see Figure 1.13).**

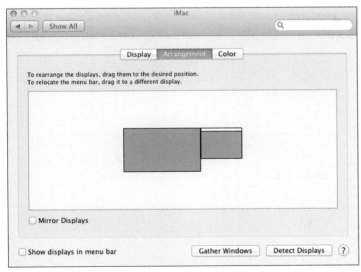

1.13 In the Arrangement pane, click and drag the monitors so that the icons represent their physical position relative to each other.

7. **Click and drag the display icons so that they match the way your monitors are placed.** For example, if you've put the second display above your iMac's screen, click and drag its icon to above the iMac's screen icon. This tells Mac OS X which edges of the monitors match up, so that it works right when you move the mouse from one monitor to the other.

8. **If you want to move the menu bar and Dock to the other monitor, click the white strip and drag it across.**

Note

Select the Mirror Displays check box in the Arrangement pane of Displays preferences if you want both displays to show the same screen. This capability is useful when you are giving presentations or watching TV shows or movies.

9. **Quit System Preferences.** Press ⌘+Q.

Making Your iMac Look and Feel the Way You Want It

Mac OS X looks great right from the first time you turn on your iMac, but you'll probably want to customize the look and feel of the operating system so that it suits your style and the way you work.

This section shows you how to choose General preferences, rearrange the icons in Launchpad, make the Dock look and behave the way you want it to, set up the Desktop and screen saver, make the Magic Mouse or Magic Trackpad (or another mouse) comfortable for you to use, and choose which sounds to use.

Choosing General preferences

Your first step in changing the look and feel of Mac OS X is to choose settings in General preferences. These settings control aspects of the overall look and behavior of windows, so they can make a big difference.

Here's how to change General preferences:

1. **Choose Apple menu ⇨ System Preferences.** The System Preferences window opens.

2. **In the Personal section, click the General icon to display the General preferences pane (see Figure 1.14).**

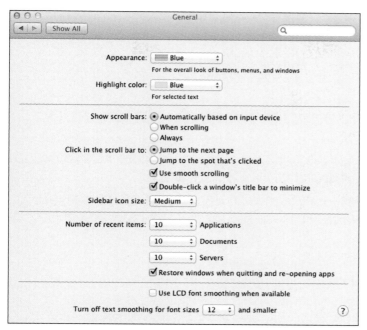

1.14 General preferences let you choose the general appearance of buttons, menus, and windows; decide where to place scroll arrows; and choose whether to display recent items.

3. **To change the overall appearance of Mac OS X buttons, menus, and windows from blue to gray, open the Appearance pop-up menu and choose Graphite instead of Blue.**

4. **To change the color Mac OS X uses for selected text, open the Highlight color pop-up menu and choose the color you want.** To get a color that doesn't appear on the pop-up menu, choose Other, and then click the color in the Colors window.

5. **To control when Mac OS X displays scroll bars in windows whose content is too large for them, select the appropriate option button:**

   ● **Automatically based on input device.** Select this option button to make Mac OS X hide the scroll bars if you're using a device with an alternative form of scrolling. For example, if you're using the Magic Mouse or Magic Trackpad, you can scroll by dragging two fingers across its surface.

   ● **When scrolling.** Select this option button to make Mac OS X display the scroll bars when you start scrolling.

   ● **Always.** Select this option button to make Mac OS X display the scroll bars all the time, as it did in earlier versions.

23

6. **In the Click in the scroll bar to area, choose the way you want the scroll bar to behave:**

   - **Jump to the next page.** Select this option to make Mac OS X display the next page of the document no matter how far down the scroll bar you click.

   - **Jump to the spot that's clicked.** Select this option to make Mac OS X treat the scroll bar as representing the length of the document. When you click a point in the scroll bar, Mac OS X displays the page that point would represent in the document's content. For example, if you click right at the bottom of the scroll bar, Mac OS X displays the last page of the document.

7. **Select the Use smooth scrolling check box if you want to make the windows scroll smoothly rather than in jumps.** This is largely a matter of personal preference.

8. **Select the Double-click a window's title bar to minimize check box if you want to be able to minimize a window by double-clicking its title bar.** This capability is usually helpful unless you're used to double-clicking a window's title bar for another purpose. For example, in Windows double-clicking the title bar toggles the window between a maximized state and a "normal" (nonmaximized) state. If you deselect this check box, double-clicking a window's title bar has no effect.

9. **In the Sidebar icon size pop-up menu, choose the icon size to use in sidebars: Small, Medium, or Large.** Medium is the default.

10. **In the Number of recent items area, choose how many recent items to store on the Apple menu ⇨ Recent Items submenu:**

    - **Applications.** Storing the last 10 or 20 applications you've run can be helpful if you run many applications. But what you'll probably want to do is run most of the applications you use frequently from the Dock and the rest from Launchpad, which makes the Applications part of the Recent Items submenu that much less useful.

    - **Documents.** The Documents part of the Recent Items submenu is great for opening documents you've worked with in the last couple of days. Increase the number of documents to however many easily fit on your iMac's screen — for example, 20, 30, or 50.

    - **Servers.** If you work with many servers, keeping the last 10 or 20 on the Recent Items submenu may be useful. If you normally work with only a few servers, choose None in the Servers pop-up menu to make more space for your recent documents.

11. **Select the Restore windows when quitting and re-opening apps check box if you want Mac OS X to automatically store information about which application windows were open when you quit an application, and to reopen them the next time you launch the application.**

12. **Choose font-smoothing options:**

- **Use LCD font smoothing when available.** Select this check box if you want your iMac to display fonts as smoothly as possible on-screen. Smoothing the fonts is meant to make them look more readable, but you may find you prefer them to have jagged edges.

- **Turn off text smoothing for font sizes *N* and smaller.** In this pop-up menu, choose the smallest type size for which you want to use font smoothing. Smaller fonts are easier to read on-screen without smoothing.

13. **Quit System Preferences.** Choose System Preferences ⇨ Quit System Preferences.

Rearranging the applications in Launchpad

Launchpad is a clever addition to Mac OS X, but if you're like me, you'll find that the Launchpad screens contain way too many icons, and that you often need to scroll from one screen to another to find the application you want to launch.

To fix this problem, you can rearrange the icons in Launchpad to put the applications you launch most frequently from Launchpad on the same screen. You can also put applications into folders, either to keep related applications together or simply to get the applications you seldom or ever use out of the way.

Genius

If you've used an iPad, iPhone, or iPod touch, you're likely already familiar with the techniques for rearranging Launchpad icons because they're the same as the techniques you use for rearranging the icons on the iOS home screens.

Moving an application to a different location

To move an application to a different location, click it and drag it to where you want it. Mac OS X moves the other applications out of the way. In Figure 1.15, you can see I am dragging the Camino icon.

If you want to move the application's icon to a different Launchpad screen, drag to the left edge or right edge of the screen. Wait until the next screen appears, drag the icon to its destination, and drop it there.

1.15 Click and drag an icon in Launchpad to move it to a different location.

Creating a folder for Launchpad icons

To create a folder, follow these steps:

1. **Move the icons you want to put in the folder to the same screen.** This step is optional, but it's usually helpful.

2. **Click one of the icons and drag it on top of one of the others.** Launchpad creates a folder, as shown in Figure 1.16, and dims the other icons.

3. **Release the icon you dragged.** Launchpad puts the icon in the folder.

4. **Double-click the folder's default name to select it.**

5. **Type the new name for the folder (see Figure 1.17), and then press Return to apply it.**

6. **Click outside the folder to close the folder.** The other Launchpad icons appear again.

Now that you have created the folder, you can add other icons to it by dragging them onto the folder and dropping them there.

1.16 In Launchpad, drag one icon on top of another icon to create a folder containing both icons.

1.17 Select the folder's default name, and then type the new name over it.

Taking an application out of a Launchpad folder

To take an application out of a Launchpad folder, follow these steps:

1. **Open Launchpad.** For example, pinch in with five fingers on the Magic Trackpad.

2. **Click the folder to open it.**

3. **Click the application's icon, and then drag it out of the folder.** The icon appears on the Launchpad screen again.

Note   If a folder contains only two items, and you remove one of them, Mac OS X gets rid of the folder. The remaining item (the one you didn't remove from the folder) appears on the Launchpad screen under its own name.

Making the Dock behave the way you prefer

In Mac OS X, the Dock enables you to launch applications, switch to running applications, open folders or files, and put files or folders in the Trash.

It takes only a moment to get the hang of the Dock's main features:

● **Launch an application.** Click the application's icon on the left side of the Dock. A blue light appears below the application's icon to indicate that it's running.

Note If no blue light appears below a running application's icon on the Dock, this feature is switched off. You'll learn how to turn it on shortly.

● **Switch to a running application.** Click the application's icon on the Dock.

● **Open a file or folder.** Click the item's icon on the right side of the Dock.

● **Put a file or folder in the Trash.** Click and drag the file or folder to the Trash icon at the right end of the Dock.

To work quickly and smoothly in Mac OS X, set up the Dock to work the way you prefer. That means choosing its positioning and behavior, making it contain the icons you need, and learning how to use its hidden features.

Positioning and resizing the Dock

Start by opening Dock preferences and choosing the settings you want for the Dock, like this:

1. **Control+click or right-click the Dock divider bar and choose Dock Preferences to open Dock preferences (see Figure 1.18).**

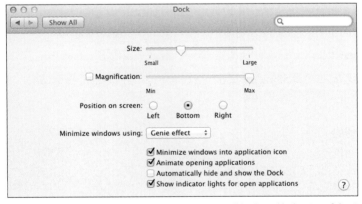

1.18 Use Dock preferences to quickly set the overall look and behavior of the Dock.

2. **If you want to resize the Dock, drag the Size slider to the left or the right.** Mac OS X shrinks the Dock's icons as needed to fit on the screen, so if the Dock is full, you may not be able to make the icons larger.

3. **If you want to magnify the Dock icons when you move the mouse pointer over them, select the Magnification check box.** Click and drag the slider to set the degree of magnification. Magnification can help you find the right icon when the Dock is jammed full of tiny icons.

4. **In the Position on screen area, choose the Left option, the Bottom option, or the Right option to control which side of the Desktop the Dock appears on.**

5. **In the Minimize windows using pop-up menu, choose the effect you want to use when minimizing a window to the Dock.** Genie effect is visually cooler, but Scale effect is faster.

Genius

You can hold down Shift while minimizing a window or restoring it from the Dock to see the effect in slow motion.

6. **Select the Minimize windows into application icon check box if you want Mac OS X to minimize a window to the application's icon on the Dock rather than to its own icon on the right side of the Dock.** This feature is great when the Dock is full and you have no more room for extra icons.

7. **Select the Animate opening applications check box if you want the Dock to bounce the icon for an application that's opening.** Deselect this check box if you want the application to open calmly.

8. **Select the Automatically hide and show the Dock check box if you want the Dock to hide at the edge of the screen until you move the mouse pointer over it.** This feature is useful when you need every square inch of screen space or you prefer an uncluttered look.

9. **Select the Show indicator lights for open applications check box if you want the Dock to display a blue light below the icon for each application that's running.** This light lets you see at a glance which applications are running, so many people find it useful.

10. **Quit System Preferences.** Press ⌘+Q.

When you want to change the Dock's position or behavior quickly, you don't need to open Dock preferences. Instead, Control+click or right-click the Dock divider bar and choose the command from the shortcut menu (see Figure 1.19). For example, to move the Dock to the right side of the screen, choose Position on Screen ➪ Right.

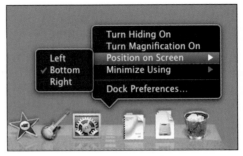

1.19 Use the Dock divider bar's shortcut menu to make instant changes to the Dock.

If you choose to minimize windows into their application icons rather than to separate icons of their own, you can restore a minimized window one of two ways:

- **Restore a single minimized window.** If the application has only one window, and that window is minimized, click the application's icon to restore the window.

- **Restore one of several minimized windows by name.** If you've minimized several windows, Control+click or right-click the application's icon, and then click the name of the window on the shortcut menu (see Figure 1.20).

Putting the applications you want on the Dock

Your next move is to make sure the Dock contains the applications you want. Apple populates the Dock with a selection of widely used applications, such as Mail, Safari, and iTunes, but you'll likely want to customize the selection.

1.20 Use an application's shortcut menu to restore a minimized window by name.

You can add an application's icon to the Dock in any of these ways:

- **Add an application from Launchpad.** Open Launchpad by clicking its icon on the Dock, and then click and drag each application you want to the Dock.

- **Add a running application.** When you start an application, Mac OS X adds its icon to the Dock. Control+click or right-click the application's icon and choose Options ⇨ Keep in Dock from the shortcut menu to keep the application in the Dock.

- **Add an application from the Applications folder.** Open the Applications folder by clicking the desktop and choosing Go ⇨ Applications. Then click and drag each application you want to the Dock.

To remove an application's icon from the Dock, click the icon and drag it off the Dock toward the center of the screen. Drop the icon, and it vanishes in a puff of smoke.

To rearrange the icons on the Dock, click an icon and drag it to where you want it to appear.

Setting up the folders on the Dock

To the right side of the Dock divider bar appear shortcuts to folders and files, and the Trash.

Mac OS X starts you off by putting the Documents folder and the Downloads folder on the Dock. You can create a shortcut to any other folder by clicking and dragging the folder's icon from a Finder window to the Dock. In the same way, you can add shortcuts to individual files you need to open frequently.

You can display each folder shortcut either as a folder or as a stack; to change, Control+click or right-click the shortcut and then click Folder or Stack in the Display as section of the shortcut menu. Displaying the shortcut as a folder makes it show a folder icon, while displaying it as a stack makes it show the icon of the topmost icon in the stack of objects it contains. For example, if you display the Documents folder shortcut as a stack and sort it by name, the shortcut shows a preview of the first file in the folder alphabetically.

Whether you choose folder or stack, you can display the folder's content as a fan, a grid, or a list. To change, Control+click or right-click the shortcut and then click Fan, Grid, or List in the View content as section of the shortcut menu. Choose Automatic if you want Mac OS X to decide how best to display the folder's contents depending on the number of items and what they are.

The fan arrangement displays a gently curving line of items (see Figure 1.21). This works well for folders that contain just a few items, but if there are more, you may need to click the More in Finder icon to reach the full list of items.

The grid arrangement shows the folder's contents as large icons arranged on a grid. If there are more icons that fit on the grid at once, as in Figure 1.22, you can scroll up or down to see the others.

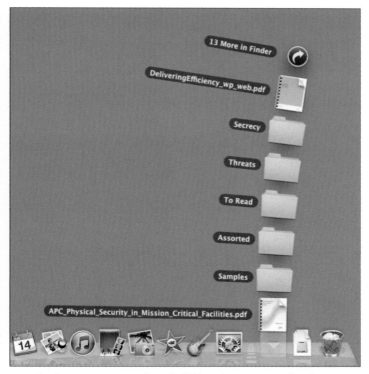

1.21 The fan arrangement is best for folders that contain only a few items.

1.22 The grid arrangement is good for picking an item from a moderately busy folder.

Genius

If you want to customize the Dock beyond the options Apple gives you, download TinkerTool (free; http://bresink.com/osx/TinkerTool.html). TinkerTool provides a whole pane of Dock-related options, including putting the Dock at the beginning or end of the screen edge rather than the middle, locking the Dock so that users can't change its size or contents, and turning off the Dock's three-dimensional glass effect.

The list arrangement (see Figure 1.23) shows a list of the folder's contents. This is good for folders that contain many items. You can highlight a subfolder to display its contents.

Controlling the Dock with keyboard shortcuts

You can bring out additional features on the Dock by using keyboard shortcuts along with the mouse, like this:

- ⌘+Option+drag a file onto a Dock icon to force the file to open in that application.

- To hide all applications except the one you're clicking, ⌘+Option+click the chosen application's icon in the Dock.

- When you're using an application's Dock menu, press Option to change the Quit command to Force Quit.

- To reveal a Dock item's location in the Finder, ⌘+click its Dock icon.

1.23 The list arrangement is good for a folder that contains many items.

- If you ⌘+click and drag an icon from the Dock, you'll copy the icon's original file to the new location.

- Shift+click and drag the Dock divider bar to move the Dock to the left, bottom, or right side of your screen.

- **To restrict the Dock to its best-looking sizes as you resize it, press Option as you click and drag the Dock divider bar.**

- **To temporarily toggle Dock magnification on or off, press ⌘+Shift while you move the mouse pointer over the Dock.**

Sending text to other applications via the Dock

You can also use the Dock to move text from one application to another. Just select the text, click and drag it to a Dock icon, and release the mouse button to drop the text into that application. Table 1.1 shows what happens in several applications when you try this neat little trick.

Table 1.1 How Applications Handle Dragged Text

Dock Icon	What You Drag	What It Does
Safari	URL	Opens the web page.
Safari	Text	Performs a Google search using the text as the search term.
TextEdit	Text	Creates a new document containing the selected text.
Mail	Text	Creates a new Mail message containing the selected text.
Stickies	Text	Creates a new sticky note containing the selected text.

Genius If you're having trouble dragging text out of a Safari window, slow down a little. Click and drag to select the text, then click the selection and hold the mouse button down for a second before you start dragging.

Setting up the desktop and screen saver

Your desktop's overall look depends on the background picture you choose. Mac OS X includes a selection of attractive pictures, but you can easily use your own pictures or photos instead.

For when you leave your iMac without putting it to sleep or turning it off, you can set a screen saver to play. A screen saver is not necessary to protect your iMac's screen from damage (as was the case in the old days), but it can hide your work and provide visual entertainment.

Choosing the desktop background

Here's how to change the desktop background:

1. **Control+click or right-click the desktop and choose Change Desktop Background from the pop-up menu.** Mac OS X opens Desktop & Screen Saver preferences with the Desktop pane (see Figure 1.24) at the front.

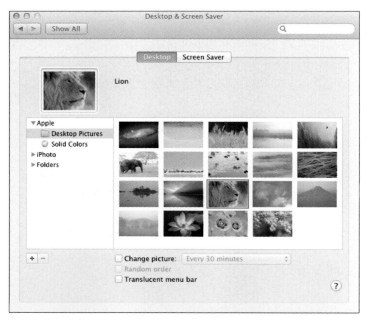

1.24 In the Desktop pane of Desktop & Screen Saver preferences, choose the picture or sequence of pictures you want to use on the desktop.

2. **In the left pane, click the folder or collection of pictures you want to use.** For example, click the Desktop Pictures folder in the Apple category. You can expand and collapse the three categories (Apple, iPhoto, and Folders) by clicking the disclosure triangle to the left of the name.

3. **In the main area, click the photo or picture to use on the desktop.** Mac OS X applies it to the desktop so that you can see how it looks.

4. **If you're using a photo or picture rather than one of Apple's desktop pictures, a pop-up menu appears above the pictures.** Open this pop-up menu and choose how to fit the pictures to the screen: Fill Screen, Fit to Screen, Stretch to Fill Screen, Center, or Tile.

5. **Select the Translucent menu bar check box if you want the desktop to show through the Mac OS X menu bar.**

6. **Quit System Preferences.** Choose System Preferences ⇨ Quit System Preferences.

Note If you have connected an extra monitor to your iMac, you can choose a different picture for its desktop background. Just use the controls in the Secondary Display preferences window that System Preferences displays on that monitor.

Note If you want the desktop picture to change periodically, click the folder or collection of pictures. Then select the Change picture check box and choose when to change in the pop-up menu: When logging in, When waking from sleep, Every 5 seconds, Every minute, Every 5 minutes, Every 15 minutes, Every 30 minutes, Every hour, or Every day. Select the Random order check box if you want to mix up the order rather than go from first to last.

Choosing a screen saver

Here's how to set up your screen saver:

1. **Control+click or right-click the desktop and choose Change Desktop Background from the pop-up menu.** Mac OS X opens Desktop & Screen Saver preferences with the Desktop pane at the front.

2. **Click the Screen Saver tab to display the Screen Saver pane (see Figure 1.25).**

1.25 In the Screen Saver pane of Desktop & Screen Saver preferences, pick the screen saver you want and set any options for it.

3. **In the Screen Savers list, click the screen saver you want to use.** The Preview box shows a preview of the screen saver.

Note

To get more screen savers, click the Add (+) button below the Screen Savers list box and then click Browse Screen Savers. Mac OS X opens a Safari window to a page on the Apple website from which you can download screen savers, icons, and other items.

4. **If the Options button is available, click it to display a dialog in which you can choose options for the screen saver.** If the Options button is grayed out, the screen saver has no options you can set.

5. **For a screen saver in the Pictures category, choose the display style by clicking one of the three Display Style buttons:**

   - Click the Slideshow button (left) to make a slide show of the pictures.

   - Click the Collage button (middle) to make each picture spiral down to form a collage on a background.

   - Click the Mosaic button (right) to display miniature versions of the pictures tiled in a mosaic.

6. **Click and drag the Start screen saver slider to set the length of time Mac OS X waits before starting the screen saver.**

7. **Select the Use random screen saver check box if you want Mac OS X to pick a screen saver automatically.**

8. **Select the Show with clock check box if you want the screen saver to include a clock readout.**

9. **If you have connected an extra monitor, select the Main screen only check box if you want to display the screen saver on only the primary screen (the screen on which the menu bar appears).** Mac OS X blanks out the secondary screen when the screen saver runs. Deselect this check box to have the screen saver appear on both screens.

10. **Click Test to see how the screen saver looks when running.** Move the mouse to end the test.

11. **If you want to trigger or cancel the screen saver by using an active screen corner, click Hot Corners.** Mac OS X displays the Active Screen Corners dialog (see Figure 1.26). Open the appropriate pop-up menu and choose Start Screen Saver or Disable Screen Saver as needed, and then click OK.

1.26 In the Active Screen Corners dialog, you can set a screen corner to start the screen saver and another to stop the screen saver.

12. **When you have set up the screen saver to your satisfaction, quit System Preferences.** Press ⌘+Q.

Genius

You can also create slide shows of your photos to use as screen savers. See Chapter 6 for details.

Making the Magic Mouse or Magic Trackpad comfortable for you to use

Apple recommends the Magic Mouse or the Magic Trackpad as the pointing device for the iMac, so there's a good chance that you'll have one or the other. I'll cover adjusting the settings for both in this section.

Setting up the Magic Mouse the way you want it

If you use Apple's Magic Mouse, configure it to suit the way you work. Follow these steps:

1. **Choose Apple menu ➪ System Preferences.** The System Preferences window opens.

2. **In the Hardware section, click the Mouse icon to display Mouse preferences.** Figure 1.27 shows the Point & Click pane of Mouse preferences for a Magic Mouse.

1.27 In the Point & Click pane of Mouse preferences for a Magic Mouse, choose whether to scroll with your finger movements, how to perform secondary clicks, whether to use smart zoom, and how fast to track.

3. **Select the Scroll with finger direction check box if you want the mouse to scroll content to follow the movement of your fingers on the Magic Mouse.**

4. **Select the Secondary click check box if you want to be able to perform right-clicks on the Magic Mouse.** This is usually helpful. Open the pop-up menu and choose Click on right side or Click on left side, as needed.

5. **Select the Smart zoom check box if you want to be able to zoom in on the current item by double-tapping with one finger.** This movement mimics the iOS movement for zooming in. Double-tap again to zoom out.

6. **Drag the Tracking Speed slider to set the tracking speed.** Move the mouse to test the current tracking speed.

7. **Click the More Gestures tab to display its contents (see Figure 1.28).**

8. **Select the Swipe between pages check box if you want to be able to swipe between the pages of a document.** Open the pop-up menu and choose the means of swiping: Scroll left or right with one finger, Scroll left or right with two fingers, or Swipe with one or two fingers.

1.28 In the More Gestures pane of Mouse preferences for a Magic Mouse, choose whether to swipe between pages and full-screen apps, and decide whether to launch Mission Control from the Magic Mouse.

9. **Select the Swipe between full-screen apps check box if you want to be able to swipe left or right with two fingers to switch between full-screen applications.** This movement can be a great time-saver.

10. **Select the Mission Control check box if you want to be able to display Mission Control by double-tapping with two fingers.** This movement too is usually helpful.

11. **Press ⌘+Q to quit System Preferences.**

Note If you use a regular mouse instead of a Magic Mouse, open Mouse preferences and adjust the tracking speed, scrolling speed, and double-click speed. You can also choose whether the left mouse button or the right mouse button is the primary button. If your mouse has a scroll wheel, you can choose whether to use the wheel to zoom.

Setting up the Magic Trackpad to work your way

If you use a Magic Trackpad to control your iMac, spend a few minutes adjusting its settings so that it's comfortable for you to use. Here's what to do:

1. **Choose Apple menu ⇨ System Preferences.** The System Preferences window opens.

2. **In the Hardware section, click the Trackpad icon to display Trackpad preferences.**
   Figure 1.29 shows the Point & Click pane of Trackpad preferences.

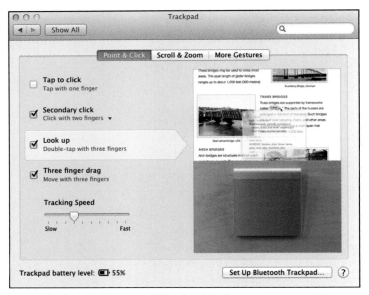

1.29 In the Point & Click pane of Trackpad preferences, choose which tap, click, and drag movements to use. You can also adjust the tracking speed.

3. **Select the Tap to click check box if you want to be able to click by tapping with one finger.** This movement can be useful if you have a delicate touch, but usually the Magic Trackpad's built-in click mechanism is easier to use.

4. **Select the Secondary click check box if you want to be able to perform right-clicks on the Magic Trackpad.** This is usually helpful. Open the pop-up menu and choose Click with two fingers, Click in bottom right corner, or Click in bottom left corner, as needed.

5. **Select the Look up check box if you want to be able to look up a word or phrase by double-tapping it with three fingers.**

6. **Select the Three finger drag check box if you want to be able to drag objects by moving the mouse pointer over them and then dragging with three fingers.** This option is turned off by default, but it's well worth a try.

40

7. **Drag the Tracking Speed slider to set the tracking speed.** Move your fingers across the Magic Trackpad to test the current tracking speed.

8. **Click the Scroll & Zoom tab to display its contents (see Figure 1.30).**

9. **Select the Scroll direction: natural check box if you want to scroll content to follow the movement of your fingers on the Magic Trackpad.**

10. **Select the Zoom in or out check box if you want to be able to zoom in by pinching two fingers outward or zoom out by pinching two fingers inward.** These movements are usually helpful.

11. **Select the Smart zoom check box if you want to be able to zoom in on the current item by double-tapping with two fingers.**

12. **Select the Rotate check box if you want to be able to rotate objects by placing two fingers on the Magic Trackpad and then rotating them.** For example, you can rotate a photo in iPhoto.

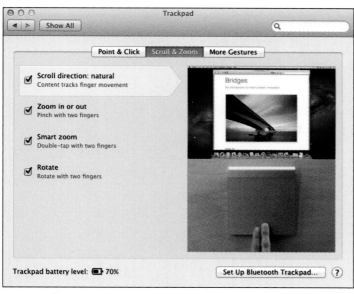

1.30 In the Scroll & Zoom pane of Trackpad preferences, choose which of the scroll, zoom, and rotate moves to use.

13. **Click the More Gestures tab to display its contents (see Figure 1.31).**

14. **Select the Swipe between pages check box if you want to be able to swipe between the pages of a document.** Open the pop-up menu and choose Scroll left or right with two fingers, Swipe left or right with three fingers, or Swipe with two or three fingers.

15. **Select the Swipe between full screen apps check box if you want to be able to swipe left or right to switch between full-screen applications.** Open the pop-up menu and choose Swipe left or right with three fingers or Swipe left or right with four fingers.

16. **Select the Mission Control check box if you want to be able to display Mission Control by swiping up.** Open the pop-up menu and choose Swipe up with three fingers or Swipe up with four fingers, as needed.

17. **Select the App Exposé check box if you want to be able to reveal the windows of the active application by swiping down.** Open the pop-up menu and choose Swipe down with three fingers or Swipe down with four fingers, as needed.

18. **Select the Launchpad check box if you want to be able to open Launchpad by pinching with your thumb and three fingers.** Pinching with your thumb and four fingers works too, which is useful if you're as clumsy as I am.

1.31 In the More Gestures pane of Mouse preferences for a Magic Trackpad, choose whether to swipe between pages and full-screen apps, whether to launch Mission Control from the Magic Trackpad, and which other gestures to use.

19. **Select the Show Desktop check box if you want to be able to display the desktop by pinching outward (*paunching*) with your thumb and three fingers.** Again, the thumb and four fingers works too.

20. **Press ⌘+Q to quit System Preferences.**

Choosing Sound preferences

When Mac OS X needs your attention, it plays an alert sound. You can change the alert sound and its volume — or turn off the sound altogether — in the Sound preferences pane like this:

1. **Choose Apple menu ⇨ System Preferences.** The System Preferences window opens.

2. **In the Hardware section, click the Sound icon to display Sound preferences.**

3. **Click the Sound Effects tab to display the Sound Effects pane (see Figure 1.32).**

1.32 In the Sound Effects pane of Sound preferences, choose your preferred alert sound and the volume at which to play it.

4. **In the Select an alert sound list box, click the sound you want to use for alerts.** To help you decide, Mac OS X plays the sound when you click it.

5. **If you have connected external speakers to your iMac, open the Play sound effects through pop-up menu and choose which speakers to use.** Choose Selected sound output device to use the speakers, or choose Internal Speakers to use your iMac's speakers.

6. **Click and drag the Alert volume slider to set the volume level at which to play the alerts.** This slider sets the relative sound level within the master volume level set by the Output volume slider. For example, you may want to play the alerts at half volume so that they don't interfere with the audio. When you move the slider, Mac OS X plays the sound so that you can judge the volume.

7. **Select the Play user interface sound effects check box if you want Mac OS X to play sound effects to give audio feedback to actions you take.** For example, Mac OS X plays a crunching sound when you put a file in the Trash.

Genius Even if you have connected external speakers to your iMac, you may find it handy to play the alert sounds through your Mac's internal speakers so that they're easier to distinguish from the audio you're playing.

8. **Select the Play feedback when volume is changed check box if you want Mac OS X to beep when you change the volume.**

9. **Click and drag the Output volume slider to set your iMac's overall output volume.** Select the Mute check box if you want to mute the sound at its current volume so that you can restore it to the same volume when not muted.

10. **Select the Show volume in menu bar check box if you want the menu bar to include a Volume pop-up menu that you can use to adjust the volume using the mouse.**

11. **Quit System Preferences.** Press ⌘+Q.

Using the Apple Remote to Control Your iMac

If you have an Apple Remote, you can use the Remote to control playback.

First, you need to pair the Remote with your iMac. Here's how to pair it:

1. **Choose Apple menu ⇨ System Preferences.** The System Preferences window opens.

2. **In the Personal section click the Security & Privacy icon to display Security & Privacy preferences.**

3. **If the General pane is not already displayed, click the General tab to display it.**

4. **If the padlock icon is closed, click the icon, and then type your username and password in the Authentication dialog.** The padlock opens.

5. **Click Pair.** Mac OS X displays a dialog with instructions.

6. **Hold the Remote close to the iMac, and then hold down the Menu button and the Next button until a graphic appears on screen showing two chain links.** Release the buttons, and the Remote is paired with the iMac.

7. **Quit System Preferences.** Choose System Preferences ⇨ Quit System Preferences.

Once the Apple Remote is paired, its buttons are easy to use — but the Remote also has a few hidden tricks you'll probably want to play with.

- **In iPhoto, press the Previous button or the Next button to navigate among slides in a slide show.** Press the Play/Pause button to toggle Pause on and off.

- **Hold down the Play/Pause button for a few seconds to put your iMac to sleep.**

- **Press any button on the Remote to wake up your iMac from sleep.**

- **When booting your iMac, hold down the Menu button on the Remote to display the System Picker.** This has the same effect as holding down Option on the keyboard. You can then press Forward or Previous to move among the available startup disks, and then press Play/Pause to start your Mac using the startup disk you've selected.

- **You can disable the Apple Remote from controlling your iMac or another Mac.** This can be useful when you want to use the Apple Remote to operate an Apple TV instead, or when other Macs are responding to the Apple Remote when you don't want them to. Here's what to do:

  1. **Choose Apple menu ⇨ System Preferences.** The System Preferences window opens.

  2. **In the Personal section, click the Security & Privacy icon to display Security & Privacy preferences.**

  3. **If the General pane is not already displayed, click the General tab to display it.**

  4. **Select the Disable remote control infrared receiver check box.**

  5. **Quit System Preferences.** Choose System Preferences ⇨ Quit System Preferences.

Genius When you face the sticky problem of a disc that won't eject — maybe your iMac says something on the disc is still in use, or maybe it just ignores your Eject commands — you can get the disc out using the Apple Remote. Press Menu as you boot your iMac to open the Startup Manager, choose a CD or DVD in the Startup Manager, and then press Volume Up to eject the disc.

Checking and Replacing the Apple Remote's Battery

If your Apple Remote seems to stop working, the battery may have run out. Here's how to check:

1. **Launch iChat.** If the iChat icon appears on the Dock, click it. Otherwise, click the Desktop, choose Go ⇨ Applications, and double-click iChat.

2. **Choose Video ⇨ Video Preview.** The video preview window opens. (This window has a name such as My Built-in iSight.)

3. **Point the Apple Remote at the camera, and press any button.** If the Apple Remote sends a signal, you will see a flash of white light from the top end of the Apple Remote. This flash isn't visible to the naked eye, but it appears clearly on-camera.

4. **Quit iChat.**

The Apple Remote uses a standard replaceable coin-size battery, a CR2032. You can buy these at any good electronics store or drugstore, but you'll get better deals online at sites such as eBay.

To open the Apple Remote, press on the indented circle on the base with the end of a straightened paper clip. The battery compartment slides right out. You can then slip in a new battery (positive side up, so the writing is showing) and slide the battery compartment back in.

How Can I Set Up My iMac for Multiple Users?

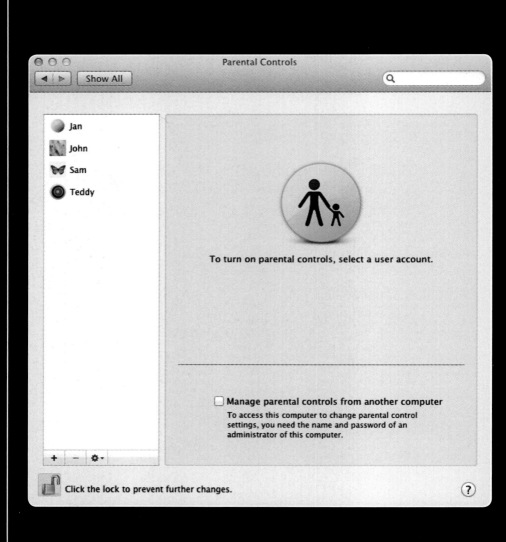

You may well want to keep your iMac's bright screen and sleek keyboard to yourself, but chances are you will need to let other people use the iMac at least some of the time. Thanks to Mac OS X's smart design, you can easily create user accounts for other people that give them exactly the privileges they need without surrendering control of your iMac to them. For children or less-experienced users, you can use Mac OS X's Parental Controls to limit what they can do and help them avoid dangers and temptations online. And you can even share some of your files with other people without letting them investigate your personal documents or sensitive data.

Planning Which User Accounts to Create

The first step to making your iMac user-friendly for multiple people is to work out which user accounts you need to create. In this section, I explain Mac OS X's five account types and what they're for, and then show you how to decide which accounts you need.

Understanding Mac OS X's five types of user accounts

Mac OS X provides five types of user accounts:

- **Administrator.** An Administrator user has the run of the computer. This means an Administrator can change all system settings in Mac OS X; install applications; and view, move, delete, or modify any file on the iMac. You need an Administrator account to run your iMac — but you'll be wise to create Administrator accounts only for those you absolutely trust with your most precious files. (This may well be nobody other than you.)

- **Standard.** A Standard user can install software in his own home folder and change his own settings, but not systemwide settings.

Note

The first account you create when setting up Mac OS X on your iMac is an Administrator account. In this chapter, I'm assuming that your user account is this account (or another Administrator account that this account has created). If you're using a non-Administrator account instead, you won't be able to set up other user accounts.

Genius

For security, don't use your Administrator account for your everyday tasks. Instead, keep it for administering your iMac, and create a Standard user account for yourself that you use the rest of the time. To be honest, most people don't do this — but if you want to keep your iMac secure, it's a great idea.

- **Guest.** The Guest user account is for users who need to use the iMac temporarily rather than regularly. Mac OS X automatically creates this account but leaves it inactive until you enable it in System Preferences. When a user logs in as the guest user, she can run applications and create and save documents — for example, she can write a letter, surf the web, or use Mail to access her email — but she can't touch any of the files in other users' folders, and she can't change system preferences. The Guest user account has no password and no security. Enable the Guest user account only when you need it for a guest, and disable it when you no longer need it.

Caution

To keep the Guest user account pristine, Mac OS X deletes everything in the Guest user account's home folder when the guest user logs out. Make sure each guest user understands this — a warning appears at logout, but it may come as a surprise — and that guest users have a means of keeping the files they've created. For example, a guest user can save documents to a USB key drive or email them to safety before logging out.

- **Managed with Parental Controls.** A Managed account is an account to which an Administrator has applied specific restrictions. To apply these restrictions, the Administrator uses the confusingly named Parental Controls — confusing not only because they're applied by parents rather than to parents but also because the Administrator can apply them to any account that needs them (no parents or children need be involved). Parental Controls enable you to restrict which applications users can run and what they can do on the Internet. I show you the details of Parental Controls later in the chapter.

- **Sharing Only.** A Sharing user can access your iMac only across a network in order to exchange files with you. The user can't log in to your iMac like other users and doesn't have a home folder on the iMac.

Deciding which user accounts your iMac needs

You will want to create a separate user account for each person who regularly uses the iMac. Don't be tempted to have users share an account — it's a recipe for lost files, struggles over settings, and needless discontent.

The only user account you should share is the Guest account. If other people use the iMac only occasionally, have them use the Guest account rather than setting up a huge number of separate user accounts. For example, if a friend stops by and needs to check her email, have her use the Guest account rather than setting up a separate account for her.

On your list of the user accounts needed, also note which of them will be Standard accounts and which will be Managed with Parental Controls. For the Managed with Parental Controls accounts, you may want to write down the details of the Parental Controls you apply.

Genius

If you need another user to administer the Mac, create an Administrator account for him. But it's clearest and easiest to have a single Administrator account for the Mac. That way, you can be certain that nobody has changed vital settings or installed unsuitable (or pirated) software. You can also be sure that nobody else has accessed your private files.

Creating the User Accounts

With your plan in place, you can create the user accounts. You can create an account in moments, as you'll see shortly. To keep your data secure, you will need to know how to choose secure passwords, and you may want to turn on Mac OS X's FileVault encryption. You can set Mac OS X to allow quick switching among user accounts, and you can create sharing accounts for users who need only access your iMac's files across the network.

Here are the basic steps for creating a user account:

1. **Choose Apple menu ➪ System Preferences to open the System Preferences window.**

2. **In the System area, click the Users & Groups icon to display the Users & Groups pane (see Figure 2.1).**

2.1 In the Users & Groups pane in System Preferences, you will normally need to unlock the padlock before you can create a user account.

3. **Click the padlock icon, type your username and password in the Authentication dialog, and then click OK.** The padlock opens.

4. **Click the Add (+) button below the list of accounts to display the New Account dialog (see Figure 2.2).**

5. **Open the New Account pop-up menu, and then choose the account type: Administrator, Standard, Managed with Parental Controls, or Sharing Only.**

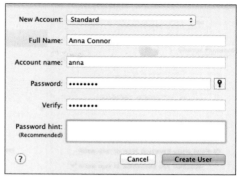

2.2 Choose the account type in the New Account pop-up menu, and then type the details for the account.

6. **In the Full Name text box, type the user's name.** For example, type Anna Connor.

7. **In the Account name text box, check the account name Mac OS X suggests, and change it if necessary.** Mac OS X derives an account name by removing spaces and periods from the full name — for example, anna.

8. **Type a password for the user in the Password text box and the Verify text box.** The next section explains ways of choosing strong passwords.

9. **If necessary, type a hint in the Password hint text box.**

10. **Click Create Account.** Mac OS X closes the New Account dialog, creates the account, and adds it to the list of accounts.

You can then choose settings for the new account, as discussed later in this chapter.

Choosing secure passwords

Nobody has yet invented foolproof but convenient ways of using biometrics (such as fingerprints or retina scans) or tokens (such as smart cards) with computers, so passwords are still our main means of keeping our secrets secure and authenticating ourselves (proving our identity) to computers and websites. That means it's vital to know how to choose secure passwords — and plenty of them.

You need plenty of passwords because of the first rule about passwords: Use a different password for each computer or account. For example, even if you share your iMac's login password with someone else — and you shouldn't — you probably don't want to share the passwords for your credit cards or bank accounts with that person.

Genius

There's an exception to the first rule about passwords: For low-priority situations, such as websites where you don't have any important information stored, it's safe enough to share a password among different accounts. The downside is that if you suspect someone else has learned your password, you then must change it for all the accounts that use it.

Always use at least eight characters for your passwords, because longer passwords are harder to crack: Every extra character you use makes the password many times harder to break by a brute-force attack that tries to guess the password.

To create a password, you can rely on your own ingenuity or use Mac OS X's Password Assistant, a utility that generates secure passwords for you. For best results, you may want to think of a password and then use Password Assistant to see how strong it is.

To create a password that'll stick in your mind but will be impossible for anyone else to guess, follow these steps:

1. **Start with a phrase that's memorable to you, but not something that will occur to other people.** For example, choose a few words from a song, advice that has always stuck in your mind, or something unforgettably embarrassing you once said.

2. **Add numbers and symbols.** Replace some of the characters with numbers or symbols that look or sound similar (so you can remember them).

3. **Use both uppercase and lowercase letters.** Almost all passwords are case sensitive, so a capital letter is considered a different character than its lowercase counterpart. By mixing uppercase and lowercase characters, you make your password that much harder to break.

Genius

Avoid typing your password on a keyboard that someone else is looking at. If someone's hanging over your shoulder, ask them to look away. No matter how swiftly you type, it's possible for someone to watch your fingers and work out the characters.

Mac OS X makes Password Assistant available whenever you need to choose an account password, but you can also open it manually at other times. In the dialog for creating a new account or changing a password, click the key button to the right of the New Password field to open Password Assistant. If you've already typed a password in the New Password field, Password Assistant's Quality indicator shows the password's strength.

Genius

Password Assistant is part of the Keychain Access utility, which you can launch by using Launchpad or by clicking the desktop, choosing Go ⇨ Utilities, and then double-clicking the Keychain Access icon. To open Password Assistant, choose File ⇨ New Keychain, specify the name for the keychain, and then click the key button. For even easier access, download the Password Assistant utility (www.code poetry.net/products/passwordassistant), which enables you to call up the Password Assistant whenever you want.

After opening Password Assistant (see Figure 2.3), do the following to create a password or check a password's strength:

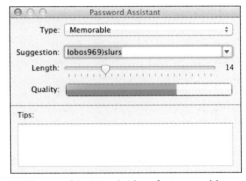

2.3 Password Assistant's idea of a memorable password may not agree with yours, but keep trying until you get something that will stick in your head.

1. **Open the Type pop-up menu and choose the type of password you want.**

   - **Memorable is usually the best place to start, but you may also want to try Letters & Numbers if you prefer not to type symbols.**

   - **Choose Manual if you want to test one of your own passwords.**

Caution

Numbers Only passwords are relatively weak, because there are fewer combinations of numbers than of numbers, letters, and symbols (given the same number of characters). Random passwords tend to be exceptionally hard to remember. The FIPS-181-compliant setting produces passwords that meet Federal Information Processing Standard 181 (FIPS-181); these passwords contain only lowercase letters and are not particularly strong.

2. **For any password type except Manual, drag the Length slider till the Suggestion box shows the length of password you want.**

3. **Open the Suggestion pop-up menu and choose one of the suggestions, or click More Suggestions to see others.** If you chose Manual, type your password.

Note After picking a suggested password from the Suggestion pop-up menu, you may need to type a character after it to make the Quality indicator register. You can then delete the extra character if you don't want it.

4. **Look at the Quality indicator to see how strong the password is.** The indicator uses red, amber, and green coding to indicate dangerously weak, okay-ish, and strong passwords. Play around with the options until the indicator is well in the green.

5. **Type the password in the password fields of the dialog.**

6. **Click the Close button to close Password Assistant.**

Managing passwords with Keychain Access

Creating a memorable password using the technique just described is easy enough. What's much harder is coming up with another memorable password. And then another. And so on for all your different accounts. How do you remember all these complicated passwords?

The good news is that you don't have to. Instead, you use the Mac OS X keychain.

Your keychain is a secure file on your iMac that stores usernames and passwords for you, as well as any other information you want to keep safe, such as credit card numbers. When you have stored a particular password, your Mac inserts it for you when it's needed. All you have to remember to keep your keychain safe is the keychain's password. Mac OS X sets your keychain's password to your login password at first, but you can change it to any password you want.

Here's how to add passwords to your keychain:

- **When connecting to a network server.** Type your account name and the password, and then select the Remember this password in my keychain check box just below the Password text box.

- **When using an application that uses passwords.** Look for a keychain check box in the Login dialog; if you don't find one, try looking in the application's preferences. Not all applications use keychains, but you'll find that most email and FTP applications do use the keychain to store your passwords.

● **When logging into a secure website.** Make sure that your web browser's preferences are set to use autofill for web forms. For example, in Safari, follow these steps:

1. **Choose Safari ⇨ Preferences to open the Preferences window.**

2. **Click the AutoFill button on the toolbar to display the AutoFill pane.**

3. **Select the User names and passwords check box.**

4. **Click the Close button to close the Preferences window.**

By default, Mac OS X stores these passwords in a keychain called Login, which it automatically unlocks when you log in and locks again when you log out. You can also lock the keychain yourself, and you can set it to lock when your iMac's been idle for a specified length of time.

Here's how to lock the keychain or set it to lock itself automatically:

1. **Open Keychain Access (see Figure 2.4).** Click the desktop, choose Go ⇨ Utilities to open a Finder window showing the Utilities folder, and then hold down Option as you double-click the Keychain Access icon.

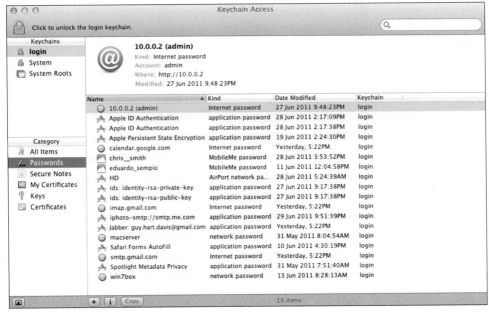

2.4 The closed padlock icon indicates that the login keychain is locked; before the system can use it again, the user must type the keychain password to unlock it.

2. **In the Keychains pane on the left, click the keychain you want to lock, and then click the padlock icon in the upper-left corner to lock it.**

3. **To set a keychain to lock automatically when you leave your iMac, follow these steps:**

   - Control+click or right-click the keychain in the Keychains pane, and then choose Change Settings for Keychain from the pop-up menu. The Keychain Settings dialog opens (see Figure 2.5).

   2.5 You can set Keychain Access to automatically lock a keychain for you after a period of inactivity or when your iMac is asleep.

   - Select the Lock after N minutes of inactivity check box, and then type the number of minutes.

   - Select the Lock when sleeping check box if you also want to lock the keychain when your iMac goes to sleep.

   - Click Save to save the changes.

The keychains Mac OS X gives you are a good start, but you can take tighter control over your passwords by creating additional keychains. These keychains remain locked until you specifically unlock them.

Genius

If you're constantly locking and unlocking your keychains, start Keychain Access and choose Keychain Access ⇨ Preferences. In the General tab, select the Show keychain status in menu bar check box. This gives you a handy menu, marked with that familiar padlock icon, from which you can lock and unlock keychains.

Here's how to create a keychain:

1. **In Keychain Access, Control+click or right-click in the Keychains pane and choose New Keychain from the shortcut menu.** You can also choose File ⇨ New Keychain from the menu bar. The New Keychain dialog opens (see Figure 2.6).

2.6 In the New Keychain dialog, name your keychain and choose whether to store it in the Keychains folder or elsewhere.

2. **Type the name for the keychain in the Save As text box.**

3. **If necessary, choose where to store the keychain.** The New Keychain dialog suggests the Keychains folder in your Library folder, which is normally the best place.

4. **Click Create.** Keychain Access prompts you to type a password.

5. **Type the password in the New Password text box and the Verify text box.** The Password Strength indicator shows whether the password is weak, fair, good, or excellent. You can also click the key button and use Password Assistant to choose a password.

6. **Click OK to close the dialog and create the keychain.** Keychain Access adds the keychain to the Keychains pane.

Note If you type a password that's too short, Keychain Access stops you with a warning and displays the password dialog again. If you're determined to use that password, leave it in place, and then click OK again. This time, Keychain Access accepts the password.

You can also use Keychain Access to change a password, decide which applications can use a password, and control whether you're asked for a keychain password when you invoke the keychain. Here's what to do:

1. **In the Keychains pane, click the keychain that holds the password.** Keychain Access displays the list of passwords.

2. **Control+click or right-click the password, and then choose Get Info from the shortcut menu.** Keychain Access displays the information window.

3. **To change the password, follow these steps:**

   • **Click the Attributes tab to display the Attributes pane (see Figure 2.7).**

2.7 Use the Attributes pane for a password in Keychain Access to see where the password is used or to change the password.

- **Select the Show password check box.** In the authentication dialog that opens, type your password for this keychain and click the Allow button.

- **Type the new password in the text box (to use Password Assistant, click the key button), and then click Save Changes.**

4. **To control access to the password, follow these steps:**

   - **Click the Access Control tab to display the Access Control pane (see Figure 2.8).**

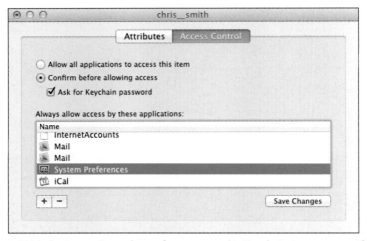

2.8 Use the Access Control pane for a password in Keychain Access to specify which applications may use the password.

- **If you want to make the password available to all applications, select the Allow all applications to access this item option.**

- **Otherwise, to limit the password to certain applications, select the Confirm before allowing access option, and then build a list of applications in the Always allow access by these applications list box.** To add an application, click the Add (+) button, choose the application in the resulting dialog, and then click the Add button. To remove an application, click it in the list, and then click the Remove (–) button. Select the Ask for Keychain password check box if you want Mac OS X to prompt you for the keychain password each time one of these applications uses the password.

- **Click Save Changes.**

5. **Click the Close button to close the information window.**

Genius

To add custom information to your keychain, open Keychain Access and click Secure Notes in the Category section. Click the Add (+) button to add a note, and then type your data and a name for the note. If you've locked the keychain with a strong password, Secure Notes is safe enough for sensitive information such as credit card numbers.

Encrypting your iMac's hard disk with FileVault

Under ordinary circumstances, using separate user accounts is enough to keep other people from messing with your files. But a really determined user can get around this precaution in a number of ways, such as mounting your iMac in Target Disk mode or booting it with a CD or DVD containing a "live" operating system (such as Linux). Encryption offers a higher level of security against such attacks.

Mac OS X's FileVault feature encrypts all the data on your iMac's hard disk. When you log in, FileVault decrypts your files so that you can use them. When you log out, FileVault reencrypts your files, protecting them again.

Caution

You have to really log out, not just use fast user switching, to make FileVault reencrypt your data. To log out, press ⌘+Shift+Q, or choose Apple menu ➪ Log Out.

When you set up FileVault, you specify which users can decrypt the hard disk. You may prefer only some of your iMac's users to be able to decrypt it, so that you or one of your trusted users always has to start the iMac before others can use it.

Using FileVault is a good idea for MacBook Pros or Airs, especially for those users who travel or work remotely with their laptops, put them at risk of theft or loss. But using FileVault is also vital if you have sensitive data on your iMac and keep it in a public area. FileVault uses Advanced Encryption Standard with 128-bit keys (AES-128), which is a U.S. government standard approved for encryption of secret materials, so the encryption is plenty strong enough for private use. (For top-secret materials, the government uses AES with 192-bit or 256-bit keys.)

To make sure you and other users of your iMac don't lose files by encrypting them and then forgetting your password, FileVault automatically creates a recovery key for you. This key can decrypt the encrypted file even after a user has forgotten his or her FileVault password. It's vital that you store the recovery key safely, as you will need it to access your data if you forget your login password. For additional security, you can store the recovery key online with Apple if you want.

Note

Even if you're backing up your iMac's important files and folders regularly (as discussed in Chapter 13), it's a good idea to back them up again before turning on FileVault, just in case something goes wrong with the encryption process.

Setting up FileVault

To start using FileVault, follow these steps:

1. **Save any open documents, and close all the applications you're using.** FileVault has to restart your iMac in order to encrypt its files.

2. **Choose Apple menu ⇨ System Preferences to open the System Preferences window.**

3. **In the Personal area, click Security & Privacy to open the Security & Privacy preferences.**

4. **If the padlock icon is closed, click it, type your username and password in the authentication dialog, and then click OK.**

5. **Click the General tab to display the General pane (see Figure 2.9), and then set two settings to close holes that someone could use to get around FileVault:**

    - **Select the Require password after sleep or screen saver begins check box, and then choose Immediately, 5 seconds, or 1 minute in the pop-up menu.** For tight security, choose Immediately.

    - **Select the Disable automatic login check box to prevent your iMac from logging you in automatically.**

6. **Click the FileVault tab to display the FileVault pane (see Figure 2.10).**

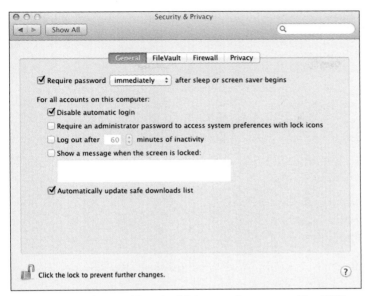

2.9 In the General pane of Security & Privacy preferences, set Mac OS X to require a password after sleep or the screen saver, and disable automatic login.

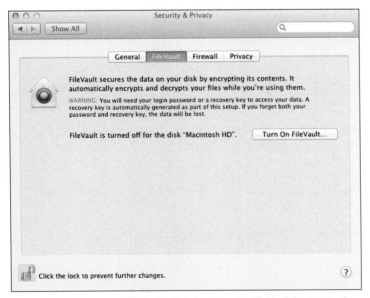

2.10 To start setting up FileVault, click the Turn On FileVault button in the FileVault pane of Security & Privacy preferences.

7. **Click Turn On FileVault.** If your iMac has two or more user accounts set up, Mac OS X displays the dialog shown in Figure 2.11 so that you can choose which users to allow to decrypt the disk.

8. **For each user you want to let decrypt the disk, click Enable User, type the user's password in the dialog that opens, and then click OK.**

9. **Click Continue.** Mac OS X displays the Recovery Key dialog (see Figure 2.12).

10. **Write down the recovery key and keep it somewhere safe.** You may want to keep the recovery key on paper rather than in a computer file.

2.11 In this dialog, choose which users can decrypt the disk. Click the Enable User button for a user, then type the user's password and click OK.

11. **Click Continue. Mac OS X displays the Apple can store the recovery key for you dialog (see Figure 2.13).**

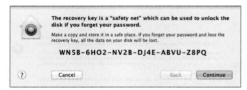

2.12 Write down the recovery key Mac OS X displays in the Recovery Key dialog and keep it safe.

2.13 In the Apple can store the recovery key for you dialog, choose whether to store the recovery key with Apple for extra security.

12. **Select the Store the recovery key with Apple option or the Do not store the recovery key with Apple option, as needed.** If you select the Store the recovery key with Apple option, the dialog expands to reveal the Answer these security questions section (see Figure 2.14). Select a question in each of the three pop-up menus, and fill in the corresponding answer you want to use.

13. **Click Continue.** Mac OS X displays a dialog telling you that you must restart your iMac (see Figure 2.15).

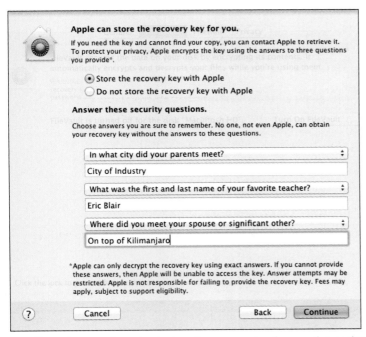

Apple can store the recovery key for you.

If you need the key and cannot find your copy, you can contact Apple to retrieve it. To protect your privacy, Apple encrypts the key using the answers to three questions you provide*.

- ● Store the recovery key with Apple
- ○ Do not store the recovery key with Apple

Answer these security questions.

Choose answers you are sure to remember. No one, not even Apple, can obtain your recovery key without the answers to these questions.

In what city did your parents meet? ↕

City of Industry

What was the first and last name of your favorite teacher? ↕

Eric Blair

Where did you meet your spouse or significant other? ↕

On top of Kilimanjaro

*Apple can only decrypt the recovery key using exact answers. If you cannot provide these answers, then Apple will be unable to access the key. Answer attempts may be restricted. Apple is not responsible for failing to provide the recovery key. Fees may apply, subject to support eligibility.

(?)   Cancel   Back   Continue

2.14 If you choose to have Apple store the recovery key for you, choose three security questions and fill in your answers in the expanded Apple can store the recovery key for you dialog.

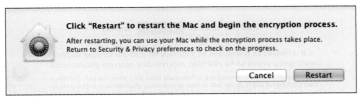

Click "Restart" to restart the Mac and begin the encryption process.

After restarting, you can use your Mac while the encryption process takes place. Return to Security & Privacy preferences to check on the progress.

Cancel   Restart

2.15 Click the Restart button to restart your iMac and begin the encryption process.

14. **Click Restart.** Mac OS X restarts your iMac.

15. **When Mac OS X displays the login screen again, log back in as normal.**

Mac OS X then starts encrypting your iMac's hard disk in the background. Mac OS X tries to handle the encryption sensibly rather than hogging the processor, but even so you may find your iMac runs more slowly than usual while the encryption is taking place. If you want to see how the encryption is progressing, open the FileVault pane in Security & Privacy preferences and look at the Encrypting readout (see Figure 2.16).

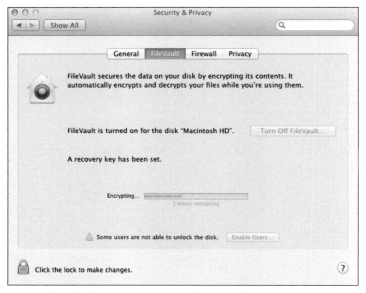

2.16 Look at the Encrypting readout in the FileVault pane in Security & Privacy preferences to see how the encryption is progressing.

Note FileVault may take several hours to encrypt your iMac's hard drive, depending on how fast your iMac is and how much data the drive contains. But after that, your iMac will run nearly as fast as before. FileVault will slow it down a little, but normally not enough to notice.

Logging in while FileVault is on

When FileVault is on, only the names of users allowed to decrypt the disk appear on the login screen after you boot your iMac. Before a user who is not allowed to decrypt the disk can log in, one of the allowed users must log in. This login decrypts the disk. The allowed user can then log out, and the nonallowed users appear on the login screen.

Genius

If you set your iMac to use Fast User Switching, as discussed next, you can quickly switch from the allowed user to a nonallowed user by using the Fast User Switching menu.

Adding other users to FileVault

If you chose to allow only some of your iMac's users to unlock the disk, you may need to give other users this power. To do so, open the FileVault pane in Security & Privacy preferences and click the Enable Users button. You then use the same dialog shown in Figure 2.11, which appeared earlier in this chapter.

Turning off FileVault

If you decide you don't want to use FileVault anymore, follow these steps:

1. **Open the FileVault pane in Security & Privacy preferences.**

2. **Click the padlock icon and authenticate yourself.**

3. **Click the Turn Off FileVault button.** Mac OS X displays a confirmation dialog (see Figure 2.17).

4. **Click Turn Off Encryption**. Mac OS X starts decrypting the disk, displaying a Decrypting readout in the FileVault pane as it does so.

2.17 Click Turn Off Encryption to confirm that you don't want to use FileVault anymore.

Deciding Whether to Use FileVault

FileVault isn't for everyone because it's not completely safe. Every time you (or another allowed user) start a computing session by logging in, FileVault decrypts your iMac's hard disk, and every time you shut down your iMac, it re-encrypts it. If this process is interrupted, or skipped due to a crash, FileVault's data can be corrupted — possibly to the extent that you can't open any files or log in to your own account.

If you feel that your data is sensitive enough to warrant using FileVault, set up a comprehensive backup system, as discussed in Chapter 13. At the very least, turn on Time Machine to create automated backups.

Switching users quickly

When you're the only person who uses your iMac, you may prefer to stay logged in the whole time so that you can start work the moment you sit down at the keyboard. But when you share your iMac with other people, each user needs to log in using his or her own user account.

Logging in can take anywhere from a few seconds to a couple of minutes (if you have many login items for the iMac to load), but you can save time by using fast user switching. After you log in as usual, fast user switching lets you and the other users switch from one account to another in moments without logging out or logging in.

Fast user switching adds a menu to the right-hand end of your menu bar, next to the Spotlight menu (see Figure 2.18). To switch to a different account, you just click on it in the menu and then type the account password. The desktop appears to rotate to the left to display the other user's desktop. Switching back to your account works the same way.

2.18 Fast user switching enables you to switch quickly to another account by using the menu at the right end of the menu bar.

Here's how to set up fast user switching:

1. **Choose Apple menu ⇨ System Preferences to open the System Preferences window.**

2. **In the System area, click Users & Groups to open Users & Groups preferences.**

3. **If the padlock icon is closed, click it, type your username and password, and then click OK.**

4. **At the bottom of the accounts list on the left, click Login Options to display the Login Options pane (see Figure 2.19).**

5. **Select the Show fast user switching menu as check box.**

6. **Open the Show fast user switching menu as pop-up menu, and then click Name, Short Name, or Icon to control how the menu appears on the menu bar.** Name is usually clearest but takes up the most space. Short name shows the account name, which is often shorter than the full name. Icon displays just a head-and-shoulders icon with no username.

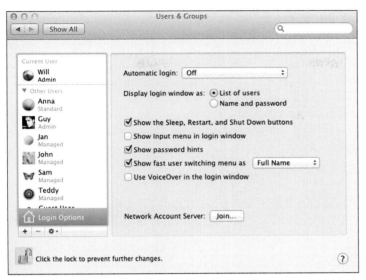

2.19 To turn on fast user switching, select the Show fast user switching menu as check box, and choose Name, Short Name, or Icon in the pop-up menu.

Now, when you're ready to leave your iMac, open the fast user switching menu and choose Login Window. Mac OS X leaves your applications running, but displays the login window so that another user can log in.

Genius

When you display the login window or another user logs in, Mac OS X handles your running applications as smartly as possible. Tasks that involve only your account keep running. For example, Mail keeps checking for new email (if you've set it to do so), and downloads in Safari keep running. But applications such as iTunes and DVD Player stop playback because the other user may need the sound and video hardware.

If that user is still logged in when you return, but has left the iMac, you can switch to your account by opening the fast user switching menu, clicking your account on it, and then typing your password when prompted. You don't need to log out the other user, nor do you need to display the login window.

Caution

Everything that's happening in your account, even while another account is in use, is using computing resources. So if you leave your iMac for an extended time, or if the other user just needs every ounce of power your iMac has, either close your documents and applications, or log out of the iMac entirely.

Setting up Sharing Only users

Fast user switching is great for people who need to use your iMac directly. But if someone needs only to access your iMac across a network to share files, you don't need to give her a full user account to log in via the login window. Instead, you can set up a Sharing Only account that permits access to files but not changes to system settings.

Genius

If several people need sharing access to your iMac, you'll probably want to make each of them a shared folder to which no one else has access. If you only have one or two sharing-only users, it may make more sense to just use the Public folder in your home folder.

Genius

A Sharing Only account is a lot like offering guest access to your shared folders, except that you can specify the folders to which each sharing user has access.

To set up a Sharing Only user account, first create the user account like this:

1. **Choose Apple menu ⇨ System Preferences to open the System Preferences window.**

2. **In the System area, click Users & Groups to open Users & Groups preferences.**

3. **If the padlock icon is closed, click it, type your username and password, and then click OK.**

4. **Click the Add (+) button below the list of accounts on the left to display the New Account dialog.**

5. **Open the New Account pop-up menu and choose Sharing Only.**

6. **Type the full name, account name, and password as usual.**

7. **Click Create User.** The dialog closes, and Mac OS X creates the account.

Now you need to set up shared folders for your Sharing Only user. Still in System Preferences, follow these steps:

1. **Click the Show All button at the top of the System Preferences window.**

2. **In the Internet & Wireless section, click the Sharing icon to display the Sharing preferences (see Figure 2.20).**

3. **In the Service list on the left, select the File Sharing check box to turn on file sharing.**

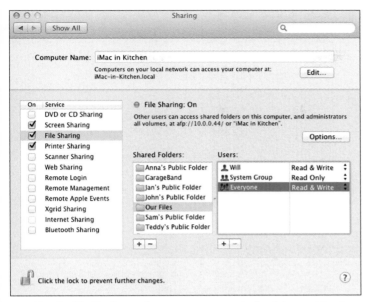

2.20 Use the File Sharing preferences to set exactly the right combination of access privileges for each folder your iMac is sharing.

4. **In the Shared Folders list box, click the folder you want to share.** If the folder doesn't appear in the list, click the Add (+) button and use the resulting dialog to add it.

5. **In the Users list box, click the user or group you want to affect, and then use the pop-up menu to set the access privileges.**

   - **If the user or group isn't in the list, click the Add (+) button and use the resulting dialog to add them.**

   - **To control access, you can choose Read & Write, Read Only, Write Only (Drop Box), or No Access.** Read & Write gives full access, while Write Only (Drop Box) enables users to copy files into that folder but not to see its contents.

Setting Up Accounts for Children and Less-experienced Users

For children, less-experienced computer users, or anybody you don't trust to act responsibly, you can set up a Managed user account rather than a Standard user account. By choosing the right Parental Controls settings, you can make your iMac bombproof while giving each user access to the items he needs.

71

Creating a Managed user account

Here's how to set up a new Managed user account to which you can apply Parental Controls:

1. **Choose Apple menu ⇨ System Preferences to open the System Preferences window.**

2. **In the System section, click Users & Groups to open the Users & Groups preferences.**

3. **If the padlock icon is closed, click it, type your username and password, and then click OK.**

4. **Click the Add (+) button to display the New Account dialog.**

5. **Open the New Account pop-up menu and choose Managed with Parental Controls.**

6. **Fill in the other required user information: Name, Account Name, and Password.**

7. **Click Create User.** Mac OS X closes the New Account dialog, adds the account to the account list, and displays its preferences (see Figure 2.21). Because you chose Managed with Parental Controls, the Enable parental controls check box is selected; you can apply Parental Controls to an existing Standard account by selecting this check box.

2.21 After creating a Managed user, click Open Parental Controls to open the Parental Controls preferences.

8. **Click Open Parental Controls to display the Parental Controls preferences.** If the Apps pane (see Figure 2.22) isn't at the front, click the Apps tab to bring it to the front.

2.22 Start applying Parental Controls using the Apps pane in Parental Controls preferences.

Note When you quit System Preferences, all of your preference panes are automatically locked again; this prevents others from being able to change user account settings without having to type an administrator password.

Making a user use Simple Finder

For a Managed user who's just starting with the Mac (or with computers in general), you can strip down the user interface to its essentials by applying Simple Finder. To do so, select the Use Simple Finder check box in the Apps pane in Parental Controls preferences.

As you can see in Figure 2.23, Simple Finder reduces the Dock to a Finder icon and folders for My Applications (the Applications folder), Documents, and Shared (the /Users/Shared folder). To open an application, the user clicks the My Applications folder, and then clicks the application in the My Applications folder window that opens. Each of these folders displays only in Icon view; List, Column, and Cover Flow view are not available in Simple Finder.

Note The My Applications folder shows only the applications you choose to make available to the user, as described later in this chapter.

2.23 Simple Finder greatly simplifies the user interface and can help new or less-confident users come to grips with Mac OS X.

If you need to switch back to the regular Finder while your iMac is in Simple Finder mode, choose Finder ⇨ Run Full Finder. You'll need to type your administrator name and password; then you'll be able to see all your files, change Finder preferences, and run disallowed applications (by once again typing your administrator password). When you're done, switch back to Simple Finder by choosing Finder ⇨ Return to Simple Finder.

Caution One menu command still available in Simple Finder is Help, but there's no edited version of Mac Help that's customized for Simple Finder. You'll probably want to warn Simple Finder users that choosing Help might not turn out to be so helpful to them.

Restricting access to applications

Simple Finder is a drastic change that you'll need to use only for some users. But most of the Parental Controls are useful for many Managed users.

First, you may need to let a Managed user use most apps but prevent her from running certain applications — for example, a Managed user can use only Safari for browsing rather than other browsers, only Mail for email rather than other email applications,, and only iChat for instant messaging rather than other instant-messaging software — to ensure that he or she cannot use other applications to bypass the web and People controls you set (as discussed later in this chapter). Or you may want to take the opposite approach and make only a handful of your iMac's applications available to the user. Providing only a few applications can be useful for new users, especially when you combine it with Simple Finder.

Genius For Managed users, you will probably want to restrict most of the utilities in the / Applications/Utilities folder. If you choose to restrict only some of these, restrict Terminal, Console, and Disk Utility.

To restrict a user's access to applications, first select the Limit applications check box in the Apps pane in Parental Controls preferences. You can then open the Allow App Store Apps pop-up menu and choose which apps from the App Store to allow. Your choices are Don't allow, up to 4+, up to 9+, up to 12+, up to 17+, or All.

Note You can temporarily override the restriction on an application by providing your administrator's name and password.

Next, select and deselect check boxes in the Allowed Apps list box as needed. The list breaks up the applications into the categories App Store, Other Apps, Widgets, Utilities, and Developer. You can select or deselect the check box for an entire category, or expand a category so that you can select or deselect the check boxes for individual applications and utilities.

For example, you may want to deselect the check box for the Utilities category to remove all the contents of the /Applications/Utilities folder from the user's reach. And even if you allow the user to run particular utilities, you'll almost certainly want to deselect the Developer check box to prevent the user from running any developer tools.

Note

The App Store category contains the applications you've downloaded from the App Store. The Other Apps category contains applications you've installed from CDs, DVDs, or files from sources other than the App Store. Other Apps includes the apps that come with Mac OS X; System Preferences and Dashboard also appear here.

Preventing the user from modifying the Dock

If each user has his or her own user account, you'll probably want to select the Allow User to Modify the Dock check box in the Apps pane to allow users to customize the Dock. Most users find customizing the Dock helpful, but you may want to turn it off if a user tends to drag icons off the Dock (and into oblivion) by accident.

Note

If you turn on Simple Finder, the Allow User to Modify the Dock check box is not available.

Restricting web access

It's all too easy to run into unsuitable, unsavory, or downright unpleasant items on the web, so chances are you'll want to use the web pane settings in Parental Controls to restrict what a Managed user can access on the web.

Here's how to restrict web access:

1. **Click the Web tab in Parental Controls preferences to display the Web pane (shown in Figure 2.24 with the Allow access to only these websites option selected).**

2. **To cut off access to adult websites, select the Try to limit access to adult websites automatically option, and then follow these steps:**

   - **Click Customize to display the dialog shown in Figure 2.25.**

   - **In the Always allow these websites list box, build a list of permitted sites.** To add a site, click the Add (+) button, type the website's address in the edit box that Mac OS X adds to the list box, and then press Return. To remove a site, click it in the list box, and then click the Remove (−) button.

   - **In the Never allow these websites list box, build a list of forbidden sites.** Use the Add (+) button and Remove (−) button as described in the previous paragraph.

   - **Click OK to close the dialog.**

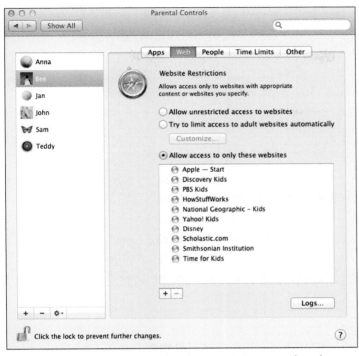

2.24 In the Web pane, choose which website restrictions to apply to the user account.

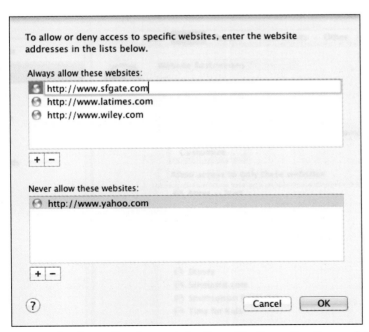

2.25 Use the Always allow these websites list and the Never allow these websites list in this dialog to customize the list of permitted and blocked websites.

3. **To restrict the user to only those websites you approve, select the Allow access to only these websites option.** A list box of child-friendly websites appears, which you can then customize like this:

- **To add a site to the list, click the Add (+) button, and then choose Add Bookmark from the pop-up menu.** In the dialog that appears, type in the website title text box the name under which you want the website to appear in the list of sites, and then type the URL in the Address text box. Click OK to add the site.

- **To remove a site from the list, click it, and then click the Remove (–) button.**

Restricting the people the user can email and chat with

To set restrictions on the people a Managed user can contact via email, follow these steps:

1. **Click the People tab in the Parental Controls preferences to display the People pane (see Figure 2.26).**

2.26 The People pane in Parental Controls preferences enables you to restrict a Managed user to communicating with contacts whom you approve.

2. **Select the Limit Mail check box.**

3. **Add permitted contacts to the Allowed Contacts list box like this:**

   - Click the Add (+) button below the list box to display the dialog shown in Figure 2.27.

   - If the contact is in your Address Book, click the disclosure button to the right of the Last name text box. The dialog expands to show your Address Book. Click the contact, and then click Add.

2.27 You can add a permitted contact either by typing the information, as shown here, or by picking him or her from your Address Book.

   - If the contact isn't in your Address Book, type the first name, last name, and email address in the dialog. You can add extra email addresses by clicking the Add (+) button in the Allowed accounts box. Select the Add person to my address book check box if you want to add this contact to your Address Book. Then click Add.

4. **To remove a contact, click the contact's entry, and then click the Remove (−) button.**

5. **To have Mac OS X email you asking permission for the Managed user to contact an unapproved contact, select the Send permission request to check box.** Type your email address in the text box.

If the user tries to email someone who's not on the list, Mac OS X automatically sends you an email notifying you of the fact and asking whether you'll give permission.

Caution

The People restrictions in Parental Controls work only with Apple Mail and iChat, not with other email and instant-messaging applications. To prevent Managed users from using other applications, click the Apps tab, select the Limit Applications check box, and then clear the boxes for the applications you don't want the user to run. Then click the web tab and block web mail sites such as Yahoo! Mail and Gmail.

Restricting chat usage and contacts

To choose which contacts a Managed user can chat with, select the Limit iChat check box in the People pane in Parental Controls preferences. You can then add the contacts to the list in the Allowed Contacts list box by using the technique described in the previous section. The only difference is that, in the pop-up menu in the Allowed accounts box, you need to choose AIM as the address type rather than Email.

iChat does not have an option for notifying you if the Managed user tries to chat with an unap-proved contact. This problem doesn't arise because the Managed user can chat only with contacts you've added to the buddy list.

Setting time limits for computer use

To control how long Managed users use the iMac, and the times at which they can use it, follow these steps:

1. **Click the Time Limits tab in Parental Controls preferences to display the Time Limits pane (see Figure 2.28).**

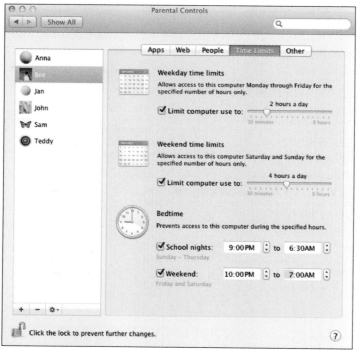

2.28 In the Time Limits pane, choose how many hours a Managed user may use your iMac on weekdays and weekends, and decide which hours are off limits.

2. **To restrict weekday usage, select the upper Limit computer use to check box, and then drag the slider to choose the number of hours (or minutes).**

3. **To restrict weekend usage, select the lower Limit computer use to check box, and then drag the slider to choose the number of hours (or minutes).**

4. **To mark off a block of time on Sunday through Thursday nights when the user may not use the iMac, select the School nights check box.** Use the upper pair of time boxes to set the beginning and ending times — for example, from 8:00 PM to 7:00 AM.

Genius

You can use the Bedtime settings to prevent Managed users from using the iMac during the daytime if necessary. For example, you could set School nights of 9:00 PM to 6:00 PM to allow a Managed user to use the iMac only between 6 and 9 p.m., leaving it free for your use the rest of the time.

5. **To mark off a block of time on Friday and Saturday nights when the user may not use the iMac, select the Weekend check box.** Use the lower pair of time boxes to set the beginning and ending times.

Fifteen minutes before a user's time is up, a dialog appears showing the remaining time and enabling the user to request more time. To authorize the additional time, you (or another administrator) must type your password.

Similarly, if a Managed user tries to log in during the bedtime period, a dialog appears explaining that the user's computer time has expired and again offering the option of persuading an administrator to authorize extra time (see Figure 2.29). If the request is denied, the iMac returns to the login screen. The login screen adds a no-entry icon to any users who are currently within their bedtime periods so they can see when it's not worth even trying to log in.

2.29 As an administrator, you can determine the amount of extra time you're willing to give a Managed user.

Note

Each Managed user's clock keeps running while his or her account is logged on and active, even if the iMac is idle at the time. So remind users to log out, display the login window, or put the iMac to sleep when they leave it.

Applying Other Parental Controls to an account

To choose other parental control settings, click the Other tab in the Parental Controls window and work in the Other pane. Here, you can choose these four settings:

- **Hide profanity in Dictionary.** Select this check box to bowdlerize the Mac OS X Dictionary as much as possible. Mac OS X then removes inappropriate content from the dictionary, thesaurus, and Wikipedia content presented through the Dictionary application. Any content the user accesses in other applications comes through unfiltered.

- **Limit printer administration.** Select this check box to prevent the user from changing settings on a printer. You will probably want to select this check box for most Managed users. The user can still print using the printer.

- **Limit CD and DVD Burning.** Select this check box if you want to prevent the user from burning items to optical discs. Usually, burning discs is mostly harmless, but it can raise issues of copyright infringement.

- **Disable changing the password.** Select this check box to prevent the user from changing his password. Normally, allowing the user to change a password helps him set a memorable password. The reason you might turn this off is because the user may set a password that is too weak to provide adequate protection.

Note Even if you allow managed users to change their own passwords, you still retain control over those passwords. You can reset them in the Password pane of Users & Groups. If you change passwords, the old passwords no longer work.

Genius After setting up Parental Controls for one user, you can copy those settings to another user's account. Select the first user's account in the Parental Controls preferences, then click the Action button (the gear icon) at the bottom of the user list and choose Copy Settings from the Action pop-up menu. Then switch to the other account you're configuring, click the Action button again, and choose Paste Settings from the pop-up menu.

Using the Parental Control logs to see what a user does

When you turn on Parental Controls for a user's account, Mac OS X keeps track of everything that happens while that account is logged in. To see how the Parental Controls are working and decide whether you need to change them, click the Logs button on the Apps tab, web tab, or People tab, and then review the information in the Log dialog that opens (see Figure 2.30). Here's what it includes:

- **Websites Visited.** This list shows you what sites the user has visited on the web. Review it to see if the user has visited unsuitable sites. To check a site, click it, and then click Open. To add a site to the blocked list, click it, and then click Block.

2.30 The log shows all the applications used and sites visited, grouped either by site or by date.

- **Websites Blocked.** This list shows the sites the user tried to view but was unable to reach because of your settings on the Content tab of the Parental Controls preferences. Review this list to identify sites that the user should be able to reach. When you find one of these sites, click it, and then click Allow.

- **Applications.** Here you see when and for how long users were active in any of the applications to which they have access. You can click Open to open the application if you're not familiar with it, or simply click Restrict to prevent the user from using the application in the future.

- **iChat.** This log shows when, with whom, and for how long users were actively working in iChat. You can click Open to open a transcript of a text chat or click Restrict to block a contact.

To focus on the information you're interested in, open the Show activity for pop-up menu and choose the length of time — from Today or One Week to One Year or All. Then open the Group by pop-up menu and choose whether to group the data by date or by website, application, or chat contact (depending on the log).

Managing Parental Controls from another Mac

If you and your kids have separate Macs, you can manage their user accounts from your iMac without having to sit down at theirs. You need to have an administrator account on the other Mac, but you should have this already.

On the Mac you want to manage, take these steps:

1. **Log in using your administrator account.**
2. **Choose Apple menu ⇨ System Preferences to open System Preferences.**
3. **Click the Parental Controls icon to display the Parental Controls preferences.**
4. **Click the Action button (with the gear icon) and choose Allow Remote Setup from the pop-up menu.**
5. **Quit System Preferences and log out.**

Choosing a Kid-Safe Browser

If you use the Content options in Parental Controls, you can make Safari pretty safe for kids to use — but you may find it hard to strike a balance between allowing them to freely access fun or educational content and preventing them from running into any of the adult or unpleasant material on the web.

Instead of putting Safari in a straitjacket, you can give your kid a kid-safe browser to use. These browsers are designed to keep kids safe on the web and make sure they're not exposed to content you don't want them to see. Safety is about keeping them away from places where they might run into predators and preventing them from providing personal information that could put them in danger.

At this writing, kid-safe browsers for Mac OS X is a small field, and the best entrant is BumperCar ($30, www.freeverse.com). It automatically turns on "safe search" filters for search engines, blocks profanity and obscenity, blocks ads and cookies, disables typing of any personal data that you specify, and uses a customizable whitelist and blacklist to allow and block particular sites. BumperCar can also read sites' self-assigned content ratings and use them to allow or block those sites.

If you're concerned about the amount of time kids spend using the web, you can have BumperCar enforce time limits as well as blackout hours. The design and included links on BumperCar's start page are determined by the user level you choose. You have three choices: Young Children, Older Children, or Preschool.

Now, on your own Mac, follow these steps:

1. **Choose Apple menu ⇨ System Preferences to open System Preferences.**

2. **Click the Parental Controls icon to display the Parental Controls preferences.**

3. **In the Other Computers section of the left list box, click the Mac you just primed for remote management.**

4. **In the Password Required dialog, type your administrator username and password for the other Mac, and then click OK.** The Parental Controls pane shows a list of the user accounts on the other Mac.

5. **Click the account you want to manage, and then work with it as described earlier in this chapter.**

Making Files Available to All Users

As well as a home folder and subfolders for each user, Mac OS X automatically creates a Shared folder in the Users folder. You and the other users of your iMac can place files in this folder to share them with each other.

To reach this folder, click the Finder button on the Dock to open a Finder window, and then choose Go⇨Computer from the menu bar. Double-click your iMac's hard drive in the Devices list (the default name is Macintosh HD), and you'll see the Users folder. Open the Users folder to display its contents, and then open the Shared folder.

Note
To give yourself instant access to the Shared folder, click and drag it to the Favorites list in the sidebar.

If you need to share only a few files, putting them directly in the Shared folder will probably work fine. But if you share many files, create subfolders in the Shared folder to help keep the files straight. For example, you might create a Documents folder, a Music folder, and a Photos folder.

Sharing your song files

If you love music, it's easy to find song files taking up a large chunk of your iMac's hard drive. If the other people who use your iMac also have large music libraries that overlap with yours, you may want to place the song files in the Shared folder so that each of you can access them.

Caution
Don't create a shared music library file. It's technically possible to do this, but it tends to cause headaches both inside Mac OS X and between users. Having a separate music library file for each user is much better, as each person can decide which songs to include and how to play them back.

The best time to set up a shared folder of songs is before each person creates his or her own music library — so if you're planning to create new user accounts, decide whether you also want to share songs. If you do, follow these steps to move your music library to the Shared folder:

1. **Open iTunes if it's not running.**

2. **Choose iTunes⇨Preferences to open the Preferences dialog.**

3. **Click the Advanced tab to display the Advanced pane (see Figure 2.31).**

2.31 Click Change in the Advanced pane of iTunes Preferences to change the folder that contains your iTunes Media file.

4. **Click Change to open the Change iTunes Media Folder Location dialog.**

5. **Navigate to the /Users/Shared folder.** For example, click the Shared folder in the Favorites list.

6. **Click the New Folder button to open the New Folder dialog, type the name iTunes, and then click Create.** You now have the folder /Users/Shared/iTunes.

7. **Click the New Folder button to open the New Folder dialog again, type the name iTunes Media, and then click Create.** You now have the folder /Users/Shared/iTunes/iTunes Media.

8. **With this folder still selected, click Choose.** iTunes closes the Change iTunes Media Folder Location dialog and inserts the new path in the iTunes Media folder location box in the Advanced pane.

9. **Still in Advanced preferences, select the Keep iTunes Media folder organized check box and the Copy files to iTunes Media Folder when adding to library check box.**

87

10. **Click OK to close the Preferences dialog.**

11. **Choose File ⇨ Library ⇨ Organize Library to display the Organize Library dialog (see Figure 2.32).**

12. **Select the Consolidate files check box.**

13. **Click OK.** iTunes copies all your song and other media files (including movies) to the folder you chose a moment ago.

2.32 Select the Consolidate files check box in the Organize Library dialog to make iTunes move your media files to a different folder.

Now that you have copied the media files to the /Users/Shared/iTunes/iTunes Media folder, you can just use iTunes as normal. When you rip a CD, the songs go into the shared folder.

Each of the other users needs to give iTunes the new location of her iTunes Media folder by following Steps 1 through 8 of the previous list, with the exception that she must select the /Users/Shared/iTunes/iTunes Media folder rather than create it. Users can then use the File ⇨ Add to Library command to add to their library such songs as they want from the folder. (Alternatively, they can open a Finder window to the shared folder, and then click and drag songs or folders across to the upper-left corner of the iTunes window.)

Note

When any user deletes a song from your music library, iTunes asks whether to move the song to the Trash or keep it in the iTunes Media folder. The user must click the Keep File button to keep the file in the folder so that other users can still play the song in their music libraries.

Sharing your photo files

Like songs, photos can take up a huge amount of space — and if you share your iMac with people close to you, chances are that you'll want to share your photos, too. You can share the photos for viewing by using iPhoto's built-in sharing features, as discussed in Chapter 6, but what you may want to do is share the photos themselves so that each person can create a separate photo library containing the photos he or she wants. Each person can then edit the photos (for example, cropping them and improving the color balance), and create their own albums, web slide shows, and so on.

The problem with sharing your photo files is that iPhoto stores the photos in a big file called a package. You can't separate the photos themselves (which you probably want to share) from the details of what you've done to the photos (which you probably don't want to share).

It is possible to create a single photo library in the /Users/Shared folder and share it with other users, but it's seldom a good idea. Only one person can open the photo library at a time, which tends to be restrictive.

For sharing photos, the easiest way to proceed is normally like this:

1. **Import your photos using the Finder rather than iPhoto.** Instead of using iPhoto to grab the photos off the camera and import them directly, use the Finder to put the photos in a shared folder. For example, you could create a folder named Photos in the /Users/Shared folder, and then create subfolders in it, naming them by date or event.

2. **Add the photos to iPhoto manually.** Choose File ➪ Import to Library to display the Import Photos dialog, navigate to the folder in which you put the photos, select the photos you want, and then click Import. Alternatively, open a Finder window to the folder that contains the photos, and then click and drag them to the Library area of the iPhoto sidebar.

Sharing photos this way works pretty well but has two disadvantages:

- **First, you and the other users need to communicate about photos you've added to the /Users/Shared folder.** The photos won't just appear in iPhoto; you need to add them.

- **Second, your iMac ends up containing multiple copies of the same photos: One in the /Users/Shared/Photos folder, and then another copy in each of the photo libraries into which you and the other users import the photo.** You can delete or archive folders from the /Users/Shared/Photos folder after everyone's imported the ones they want, but the other multiple copies remain. Having extra copies reduces the chance that you'll lose precious photos, but it takes up much more disk space than having single copies.

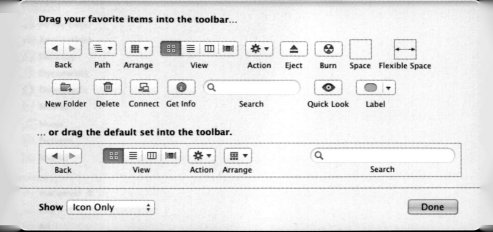

The Finder — Mac OS X's application for managing files and folders — may appear straightforward, but you can save time and effort by learning its ins, outs, and secrets. In this chapter, you learn how to make the Finder show the information you need to see and hide the information you don't need to see; spread out your work with multiple windows and desktops, and navigate among them quickly and easily with Mission Control; find all the files you need by searching with Mac OS X's powerful Spotlight feature; and burn files and folders to CDs and DVDs.

Making the Finder Show the Information You Need

To work quickly and efficiently in the Finder, you need to know how to make the most of the four views it offers and how to preview a file without opening it. You'll also want to customize the Finder toolbar to show the buttons you need and customize the Finder's sidebar so that it contains the items you use rather than the default items. Last, you should set up the Mission Control feature so that you can flip quickly from window to window as you work.

Using the Finder's four views effectively

To create, find, and identify files quickly, you'll need to exploit the four views the Finder offers for looking at files and folders. The views have different strengths and weaknesses, so you'll probably want to use each of them at different times.

This section makes sure you know when to use each view, how to switch among them, and ways to make the most of each view.

Icon view

Icon view (see Figure 3.1) displays each file or folder as an icon with its filename under it.

Genius

When working in Icon view, you can adjust the icon size as needed. Choose View➪ Show View Options to display the View Options window, then drag the Icon size slider to the right to zoom in or to the left to zoom out. The maximum icon size is 512×512 pixels; the minimum is 16×16 pixels.

In Icon view, you can arrange the icons any way you want them. Unless the Finder is automatically arranging the icons for you (as discussed in a moment), you can click and drag the icons to where you want to position them. If you position icons so that they overlap, you can make the Finder separate them by choosing View➪ Clean Up and then clicking an option on the Clean Up submenu: Name, Kind, Date Modified, Date Created, Size, or Label.

Or you can have the Finder arrange the icons by one of the properties shown in Table 3.1. Choose View➪ Arrange By, or Control+click or right-click in open space in the viewing area and choose Arrange By, and then click the command you want on the submenu.

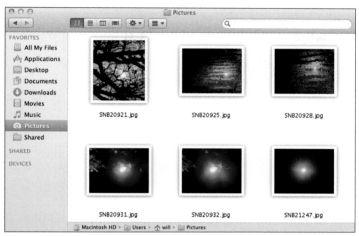

3.1 Icon view is good for working with graphics and other files you can identify visually.

Note After opening the View Options window, you can navigate to another folder as needed, so that you can set view options for as many folders as you want without closing the View Options window.

Table 3.1 Commands and Keyboard Shortcuts for Arranging Icon View

Arrange By	Keyboard Shortcut	Explanation
Name	⌘+Ctrl+1	The filename
Kind	⌘+Ctrl+2	The file's type — for example, Folders, Images, Documents
Application	—	The default application for the file
Date Last Opened	⌘+Ctrl+3	The date you last opened the file (with or without modifying it)
Date Added	⌘+Ctrl+4	The date you added the file to the folder
Date Modified	⌘+Ctrl+5	The date you last changed the file
Date Created	—	The date you created the file
Size	⌘+Ctrl+6	The file's size
Label	⌘+Ctrl+7	The color of the file's label
None	⌘+Ctrl+0 (zero)	Removes the existing arrangement

If you want the Finder to automatically arrange the icons for you in your preferred way, here's how to do that:

1. **Choose View ➩ Show View Options.**
   The View Options window for the current folder opens (see Figure 3.2), showing the folder's name in the title bar.

2. **If you want the Finder to always use Icon view when displaying this folder, select the Always open in icon view check box.**

3. **If you want to browse this folder in Icon view, select the Browse in icon view check box.**

4. **Open the Arrange By pop-up menu and choose the property to arrange the icons by.**

   - Choose Name, Kind, Application, Date Last Opened, Date Added, Date Modified, Date Created, Size, or Label to arrange the icons by that property.

   - Choose None to turn off automatic arranging.

5. **Open the Sort By pop-up menu and choose the property to sort the icons by.**

   - Choose None to turn off automatic sorting.

   - Choose Snap to Grid to make the Finder keep the icons arranged on an invisible grid so that they don't overlap, but you can still choose their arrangement.

   - Choose Name, Kind, Date Last Opened, Date Added, Date Modified, Date Created, Size, or Label to sort the icons by that property.

3.2 In the View Options window for Icon view, you can change the icon size, alter the grid spacing, and reposition the labels. If you select None in the Arrange By pop-up menu, you can use the Background option buttons to change the window background.

6. **If you want to use these settings for other Finder windows by default, click Use as Defaults.**

7. **When you finish choosing view options, click the Close button or choose View ⇨ Hide View Options to close the View Options window.**

Note   To see which folder Icon view is displaying, make sure the Finder window is displaying the path bar at the bottom of the window; if it's not, choose View ⇨ Show Path Bar to display it. This shows the path of folders to the folder you're viewing. To jump to another folder, double-click its icon.

Genius   In the View Options window, you can click and drag the Grid Spacing slider to make the grid tighter or looser. You can also change the text size (in the Text size pop-up menu), choose whether to position icon labels below icons or to their right, and choose whether to show information about items (select the Show item info check box) as well as their names.

When you plan to continue working in the same folder for a while, or if you want to have the most space possible in the viewing area of the Finder window, Control+click or right-click the Finder window's title bar and then click Hide Toolbar on the context menu to hide the sidebar and the toolbar (see Figure 3.3). Repeat this move when you want to bring back the sidebar and the toolbar.

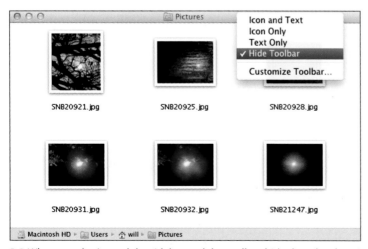

3.3 When you don't need the sidebar and the toolbar, hide them by choosing Finder ⇨ View ⇨ Hide Sidebar.

Note

Hiding the sidebar and the toolbar works in any view, but it's usually most helpful in Icon view. You can also hide them by choosing View ⇨ Hide Toolbar and reveal them by choosing View ⇨ Show Toolbar; you can also press ⌘+Option+T. If you want to hide only the sidebar, press ⌘+Option+S or choose View ⇨ Hide Sidebar; choose View ⇨ Show Sidebar when you want to display the Sidebar again.

List view

List view (see Figure 3.4) shows your files and folders as a list. Double-click a subfolder to display its contents in the window. You can then click the Back button to go back to the previous folder.

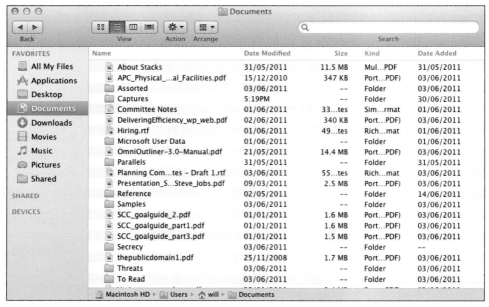

3.4 In List view, you see the contents of the current folder as a list of subfolders and files.

List view is great for sorting your files quickly. Click a column heading once to sort it in the default order. Click again to reverse the sort order. For example

- **Name.** Click the Name column heading once to sort in alphabetical order. Click again to sort in reverse alphabetical order.

- **Date Modified.** Click the Date Modified column heading once to sort in reverse date order, so the most recently modified files appear first. Click again to sort in date order.

Here's how to customize List view so that it shows the columns you want:

1. **Choose View ⇨ Show View Options.** The View Options dialog opens (see Figure 3.5).

2. **If you want the Finder to always use List view when displaying this folder, select the Always open in list view check box.**

3. **If you want to browse this folder in List view, select the Browse in list view check box.**

4. **Open the Arrange By pop-up menu and choose the property to arrange the icons by.**

   - Choose Name, Kind, Application, Date Last Opened, Date Added, Date Modified, Date Created, Size, or Label to arrange the icons by that property.

   - Choose None to turn off automatic arranging.

5. **If you chose Kind, Application, or Label in the Arrange By pop-up menu, open the Sort By pop-up menu and choose the property to sort the icons by: Name, Kind, Date Last Opened, Date Added, Date Modified, Date Created, Size, or Label.** The Sort By pop-up menu isn't available for other arrangements.

6. **In the Show Columns area, select the check box for each column you want to display.** Clear the check box for each column you want to remove. You can't remove the Name column, so it doesn't have a check box.

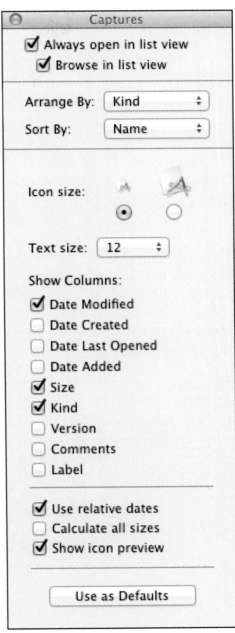

3.5 You can customize List view to show exactly the columns you need.

7. **Select the Use relative dates check box if you want the Finder to show recent dates such as Today and Yesterday rather than using regular dates for every item.**

8. **Select the Calculate all sizes check box if you want to see the size of every file and folder.** If you deselect this check box, Mac OS X doesn't immediately compute the size of folders, which means the Finder can display the list faster, especially with folders that contain many items.

9. **Select the Show icon preview check box if you want each item to have an icon.** You can increase the icon size by selecting the right option button in the Icon size area. You can also increase or decrease the text size by using the Text size pop-up menu.

10. **If you want to use these settings for other Finder windows by default, click Use as Defaults.**

11. **When you finish choosing view options, click the Close button or choose View ⇨ Hide View Options to close the View Options window.**

Column view

Column view (see Figure 3.6) shows your files and folders in separate columns. When you click an item in the sidebar, the first column in the viewing area displays a list of the item's contents. Click a folder in the first column, and the second column shows its contents. You can continue clicking subfolders to display their contents in further columns. When you reach a file, click it to display its details, including a preview.

You can change the width of any column by clicking and dragging its dividing bar. Double-click this dividing bar to resize the column to fit its contents. Click and drag the bar to the right of the preview to change the size of the preview; if you drag past the right border of the Finder window, you widen the window as well.

Note

To customize Column view, choose View ⇨ Show View Options. In the View Options window, select the Always open in column view check box to make the Finder always use Column view for this folder at first. You can also change the text size; choose whether to show icons, icon previews, and the preview column; and choose the properties by which to arrange and sort files and folders.

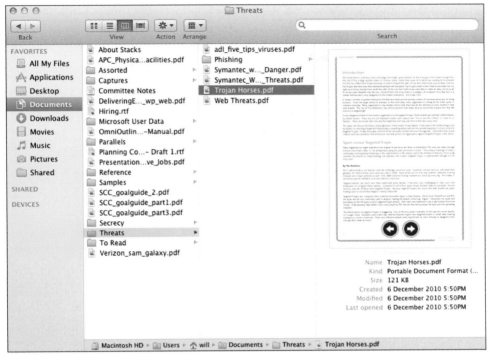

3.6 In Column view, you can navigate quickly through the folders and subfolders on your drives. To move through the preview of a file such as the PDF shown here, hold the mouse pointer over the preview, and then click the arrow buttons that appear.

Cover Flow view

With the fourth and last view, Cover Flow view (see Figure 3.7), you can browse your files and folders much as you browse album covers in iTunes or on an iPhone or iPad.

- **In the list at the bottom of the window, click the file you want to view.** The preview area shows a preview of the file, with smaller previews of the files before it to its left and the files after it to its right.

- **Click one of the other previews to display it.**

- **Scroll left or right by swiping two fingers on the Magic Mouse or Magic Trackpad to move quickly through the previews.**

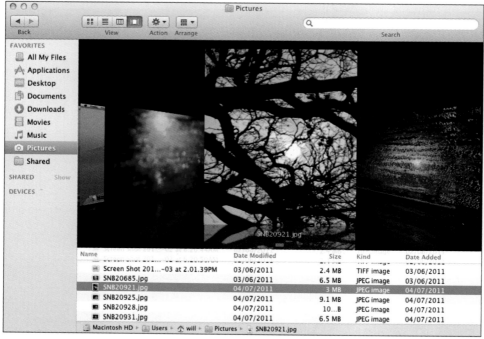

3.7 Cover Flow view is great for browsing through file previews.

Note

To change the division of the window between the previews and the file list, click and drag the handle on the bar between them.

Use Cover Flow view when you need to identify a document by sight — for example, picking out a picture from a stack with sequential names, or choosing a PDF by its title page when you've forgotten its name.

Genius

You can customize Cover Flow view by choosing View ➪ Show View Options and then working in the View Options window. Apart from the Always open in Cover Flow check box and the Browse in Cover Flow check box, the controls are the same as for List view, discussed earlier in this chapter.

Changing views

You can switch views instantly in any of these ways:

- **Click the View buttons on the Finder toolbar.** These buttons appear by default from left to right: Icon view, List view, Column view, and Cover Flow view. This is usually the easiest way to change views unless your hands are on the keyboard at the time.

- **Press the ⌘ key shortcuts.** Press ⌘+1 for Icon view, ⌘+2 for List view, ⌘+3 for Column view, and ⌘+4 for Cover Flow view.

- **Open the View menu on the menu bar.** Choose View ➪ as Icons, View ➪ as List, View ➪ as Columns, or View ➪ as Cover Flow.

- **Open the View submenu on the shortcut menu.** Control+click or right-click open space in the document area of the Finder window, and then choose View ➪ as Icons, View ➪ as List, View ➪ as Columns, or View ➪ as Cover Flow from the shortcut menu. Usually, it's hard to find open space in Cover Flow view.

Previewing a file without opening it

In the old days, you had to open a file to see its contents. For example, to see what a Microsoft Word document contained, you needed to open it in Word or another application that could read Word files.

Mac OS X's Quick Look feature enables you to preview a file quickly in the Finder without opening the file. To preview a file in Quick Look, take one of these actions:

- **Keyboard.** Select the file, and then press the spacebar or ⌘+Y.

Genius

If you want to be able to give the Quick Look command easily with the mouse, choose View ➪ Customize Toolbar. Drag the Quick Look button to the toolbar, and then click Done. You can then click a file and click the Quick Look button (the button with the eye icon) on the Finder toolbar.

- **Shortcut menu.** Control+click or right-click the file, and then choose Quick Look.
- **Menu bar.** Click the file, and then choose File ➪ Quick Look.

When you give one of the Quick Look commands, Mac OS X opens a window showing the contents of the file along with controls for viewing the file full screen, playing it (for a file with contents such as music or video), opening it in an application, scrolling through its pages if it has them, and closing the Quick Look window (see Figure 3.8).

Quick Look works with an impressive range of document types — picture files, PDFs, text documents, Excel spreadsheets, Word documents, and many more types. Some movie types (such as MOV files) and audio files (such as AAC files) play in the Quick Look window.

If you select multiple files and open the Quick Look window, you can click the Next button and Previous button or use the arrow keys to view each document in turn. You can see the thumbnails of all the files in a grid by clicking the Index Sheet button, and then clicking the file you want to display. This is great when you need to jump from one file to another.

3.8 Use Quick Look to see the contents of a file without opening the file in an application.

To view the current file full screen, click the Full Screen button. The control buttons then appear on a pop-up bar near the bottom of the screen. To return to viewing the current file in a window, click the Exit Full Screen button, the button with two diagonal arrows pointing toward each other.

Genius

On the Magic Trackpad, you can switch from a Quick Look window to full screen by pinching outward (*paunching*) with two fingers. To switch back from full screen to a window, pinch in with two fingers.

To open the current file, click the Open In button. This button's name shows the application in which the file will open. For example, the Open in Preview button in Figure 3.8 indicates that the file will open in the Preview application.

To close the Quick Look window, press the spacebar or ⌘+Y or click the Close (the X) button. But you can also leave the Quick Look window open so that it displays whatever document you click on as you move around the Finder.

Note

You can also close the Quick Look window by Control+clicking or right-clicking the file and choosing Close Quick Look or by choosing File ➪ Close Quick Look.

Customizing the toolbar

The Finder window's toolbar contains a handful of widely used buttons, but you can easily add the buttons you need and remove the buttons you never use.

Genius

To change the Finder toolbar instantly, ⌘+click and drag a button to a new position. To remove a button from the toolbar, ⌘+click and drag the button off the toolbar into the Finder window.

Here's how to customize the toolbar:

1. **Click the Finder icon on the Dock to open a Finder window.**

2. **Choose View ➪ Customize Toolbar to display the Customize Toolbar dialog.** You can also Control+click or right-click the toolbar and choose Customize Toolbar from the shortcut menu.

3. **Click and drag any buttons you don't want off the toolbar.** They disappear in a puff of smoke.

4. **From the selection of buttons, click and drag any buttons you want to add to the toolbar.**

   - You can add buttons wherever you want, and you can add as many as you want.

   - If you add a button that's already on the toolbar, the original button disappears so that there is only one instance.

5. **Click and drag to rearrange the buttons' order on the toolbar.**

6. **Add spaces and separators as needed:**

   - To add a standard-size space between buttons, click and drag the Space button there.

   - To create an adjustable space, click and drag the Flexible Space button. The space adjusts its width when you drop buttons on it.

   - To add a dotted vertical line between toolbar buttons, click and drag the Separator button between them.

7. **If you decide to revert to the original toolbar, click and drag the default set of buttons onto the toolbar.**

8. **Click Done.**

Genius

By default, toolbar buttons show only icons, but you can add text labels to the buttons or show only text with no icons. Open the Show pop-up menu at the bottom of the Customize Toolbar dialog and choose Icon & Text or Text Only, as needed. To change quickly, Control+click or right-click the menu bar in a Finder window and then click Icon & Text, Icon Only, or Text Only on the context menu.

Customizing the sidebar

The sidebar on the left side of a Finder window (see Figure 3.9) contains links to locations you're likely to visit frequently. The sidebar divides the locations into three categories:

- **Favorites.** This section contains the All My Files view; various widely used folders, including your Documents folder, your Desktop folder, and the Applications folder; and any saved searches you choose to add to the Sidebar (as discussed later in this chapter). You can add other items, as you'll see in a moment.

- **Shared.** This section contains computers that are sharing folders on your network.

- **Devices.** This section contains your iMac, its hard drive, and each external drive you connect — for example, a FireWire drive, a USB key drive, or a digital camera. If you have a MobileMe subscription, your iDisk also appears here.

3.9 The sidebar in the Finder window provides instant access to locations you often use.

You can collapse and expand each of these sections as needed. To collapse a section that's displayed, move the mouse pointer over its heading, and then click the word Hide that appears to the right of the heading. To expand the section again, move the mouse pointer over the heading, and then click the word Show.

Genius

Add the files and folders you're currently working on to the sidebar. If the names are too long to appear in full, click and drag the right border of the sidebar to widen it.

You can quickly customize the sidebar like this:

- **Remove a location you've added.** If you don't use a location, click and drag it out of the sidebar. The location vanishes in a puff of smoke. This affects only the shortcut to the location, not the folder or other item. (To remove the items Mac OS X adds to the sidebar, see the following numbered list.)

- **Rearrange the locations.** Click and drag the locations into the order you find most useful. You can't rearrange the locations in the Shared section.

- **Add a location.** Click the file, folder, or application you want to add, and then drag it to the Favorites section. You can also select the item and press ⌘+T or choose File ⇨ Add To Sidebar.

Here's how to control which categories of items appear in the sidebar:

1. **Click the desktop, and then choose Finder ⇨ Preferences.** The Finder Preferences window opens.

2. **Click the Sidebar tab to display the Sidebar pane (see Figure 3.10).**

3. **Deselect the check box for any item you want to prevent from appearing in the sidebar.** For example, if you don't want your iPhone showing up in the sidebar every time you plug it in, deselect the box next to CDs, DVDs, and iPods. If you remove all the items in a category, the Finder removes that category from the sidebar.

4. **Click the Close button to close the Finder Preferences window.**

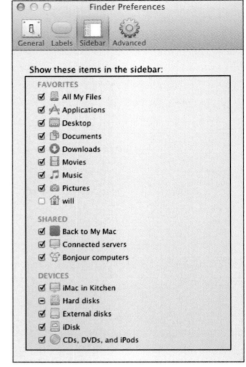

3.10 In the Sidebar pane in Finder Preferences, deselect the check box for any item you want to remove from the sidebar.

Managing Windows and Desktops with Mission Control

Even with your iMac's large screen, once you open a lot of windows, it can get hard to find the window you need. When you run one or more applications full screen, navigating among applications becomes harder still, because each full-screen application is running in its own desktop space. To help, Mac OS X provides Mission Control, a feature for organizing windows and desktops easily so you can find what you're looking for.

Understanding what Mission Control does

Mission Control has four tricks for navigating and managing windows:

- **Show all open windows and desktops.** Press F3 to reduce the open windows and desktops and arrange them on-screen so that you can see them all at once (see Figure 3.11). Click the window or desktop you want to activate, or press F3 after highlighting it. This feature is called Mission Control, but the name tends to apply to the other three features discussed next.

Note Older iMacs use the keyboard shortcuts F9 for showing all open windows, F10 for showing the open windows in the current application, and F11 for showing the Desktop.

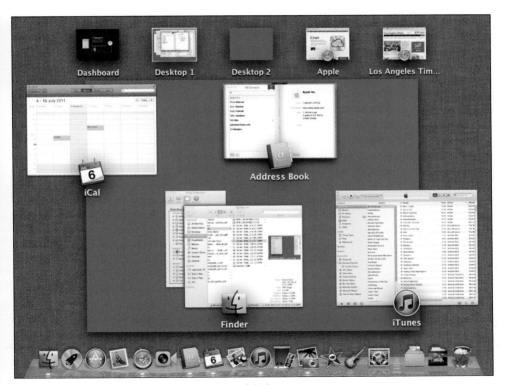

3.11 Press F3 to display all the open windows and desktops at once.

Genius

To drag a file to another application (for example, something you want to attach to an email), click and start dragging the file, and then press F3. When you find the window you want, press F3 to make that the active window, and then release the mouse button to drop your file into the window.

- **Show all open windows of the current application.** When you want to focus only on the current application, press Control+F3. Mission Control hides all the other applications, shrinks the current application's windows, and arranges them so that you can see them all at once (see Figure 3.12). Click the window you want to activate, or highlight the window and then press Control+F3 again. This feature is called App Exposé.

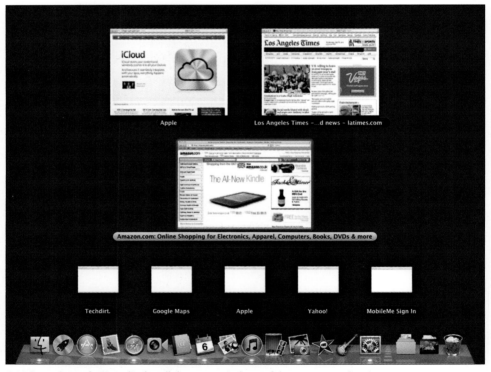

3.12 Press Control+F3 to display all the open windows of the current application at once.

Genius With the Magic Trackpad, swipe up with four fingers to launch Mission Control. Swipe down with four fingers to launch App Exposé. Place your thumb and three fingers and spread them apart to show the Desktop. With the Magic Mouse, double-tap with two fingers to launch Mission Control.

Genius To copy content from one window to another in the same application, select the content, click and start dragging it, and then press Control+F3. Find the window you're looking for, press Control+F3 again to activate it, and drag and drop the content to the correct location.

- **Show the desktop.** Press ⌘+F3 to slide all the open windows off to the sides of the screen so that you can see the desktop. This is great when you need to open a file or folder on your desktop, but you can also use it to place an item on the desktop: Click and drag the item, and then press ⌘+F3 to reveal the desktop while still holding down the mouse button. Press ⌘+F3 again when you want to restore the windows to their previous positions. This feature is called Show Desktop.

- **Show Dashboard.** Press F12 to display Dashboard so that you can work with the widgets it contains. Press F12 again when you're ready to hide Dashboard. This feature is called Show Dashboard.

Note You can see the Mission Control animations in slow motion by pressing Shift as you press the appropriate Mission Control function key or combination.

Running Mission Control with a regular mouse or hot corners

The keyboard shortcuts, Magic Trackpad swipes, and Magic Mouse double-tap described previously are easy enough, but you can also assign Mission Control to buttons on a regular mouse (not a Magic Mouse) or make one or more corners of the screen into an active screen corner for running Mission Control automatically.

Here's how to set up a button or hot corner to run Mission Control:

1. **Press Option+F3 to open Mission Control preferences (see Figure 3.13) in System Preferences.** You can also choose Apple menu ⇨ System Preferences, and then click the Mission Control icon in the Personal section.

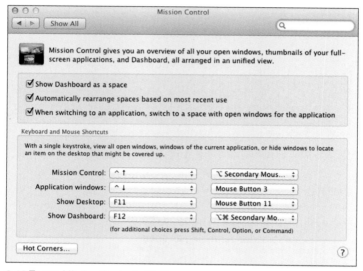

3.13 To run Mission Control with the mouse, set up an active screen corner or a mouse-click.

2. **In the box at the top of the pane, choose from these options for Mission Control:**

   - **Show Dashboard as a space.** Select this check box if you want Dashboard to appear as its own space on the Mission Control screen. If you use Dashboard, this option is usually helpful.

   - **Automatically rearrange spaces based on most recent use.** Select this check box if you want Mac OS X to try to rearrange your spaces so that those you've used most recently are right to hand. Try using Mission Control with this option and see if it suits you. If not, deselect this check box.

   - **When switching to an application, switch to a space with open windows for the application.** Select this check box if you want Mac OS X to automatically display a space containing open windows for the application to which you switch. This behavior is usually helpful.

3. **In the Keyboard and Mouse Shortcuts section, use the four pairs of pop-up menus to set the keyboard and mouse shortcuts you want to use:**

- The left Mission Control pop-up menu shows the keystroke assigned to displaying all windows and desktops — for example, Control+Up arrow. This shortcut is in addition to any shortcut built into your iMac's keyboard, and you may not need to change it. The right Mission Control pop-up menu lets you assign a mouse button or mouse combination (for example, Option+Secondary Mouse Button).

Genius

To add one or more modifier keys (⌘, Shift, Option, or Control) to one of the Mission Control keyboard shortcuts or mouse-clicks, hold down the key or keys as you open the pop-up menu. Then click the combination you want to use.

- Similarly, the two Application windows pop-up menus enable you to change the keystroke and assign a mouse button or mouse combination to display all the windows from the current application.

- Likewise, the two Show Desktop pop-up menus give you control over the keystroke and mouse button or mouse combination for hiding all open windows and displaying the desktop.

- And the two Show Dashboard pop-up menus let you choose the keystroke and mouse button or mouse combination for showing the Dashboard and then hiding it again.

4. **Click the Hot Corners button to display the Active Screen Corners dialog (see Figure 3.14).**

5. **Open the pop-up menu for each screen corner you want to use, and then choose the Mission Control action: Mission Control itself, Application Windows, Desktop, or Dashboard.**

3.14 Use the Active Screen Corners dialog to set up hot corners for triggering Mission Control, the screen saver, display sleep, or other actions.

- The menu also offers other options: Launchpad, Start Screen Saver, Disable Screen Saver, and Put Display to Sleep.

- The – option at the bottom of each menu means that the active screen corner does nothing.

6. **When you finish setting up Mission Control, quit System Preferences.** For example, press ⌘+Q.

Moving windows among your desktops

After displaying all your open windows and desktops using Mission Control, you can click a window on its current desktop and then drag it to the desktop on which you want to place it.

Genius Press Shift as you drag a window to a new space in the Spaces overview to bring along all the other windows from that application.

Finding the Files You Need

Keeping your files organized neatly into folders is a great way of keeping what you need ready at hand, but chances are that your iMac will contain so many files and so much data that you'll often need to search for items. Mac OS X's Spotlight search technology builds a comprehensive index of everything on your iMac — not just the files and folders you create but the email messages you send and receive, the web pages you visit, and the song files you download in iTunes — and enables you to search for them in several handy ways.

Searching quickly with the Spotlight menu

When you need to search all your iMac's contents quickly by one or two terms, use the Spotlight menu like this:

1. **Press ⌘+spacebar or click the Spotlight icon (the magnifying glass) at the right end of the menu bar to open the Spotlight menu.**

2. **Type your search terms.** As you type, the Spotlight menu displays search results, narrowing them down as you continue to type.

3. **Hold your mouse pointer over an item to preview it and see if it's what you're looking for.** Figure 3.15 shows an example.

4. **If the item you want appears on the Spotlight menu, click the item to open it.** If you want to see the full range of search results so that you can sort them or refine them, click the Show All in Finder button at the top of the menu to open a Search window (see Figure 3.16). You can then use the techniques explained in the next section.

3.15 Use the Spotlight menu to search quickly for information on your iMac. Hold the mouse pointer over an item to preview it.

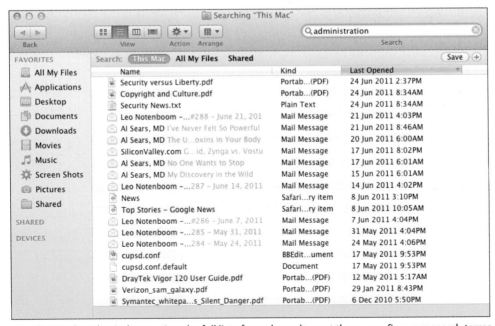

3.16 Open a Search window to view the full list of search results, sort them, or refine your search terms.

Searching in a Search window

When you need to perform a more-focused search, start off in a Finder window rather than with the Spotlight menu.

Genius

Searching from a Finder widow restricts the search to individual documents and leaves out larger databases such as your Address Book, your iCal information, and your Safari browsing and bookmarks.

Here's how to search from a Finder window:

1. **Open a Finder window to the folder from which you want to start the search.** For example

   - **Search your home folder.** Click the desktop and choose Go ⇨ Home to open a Finder window to your home folder.

   - **Search the Documents folder.** If you think the file is in a folder contained by your Documents folder, click the desktop and choose Go ⇨ Documents to open a Finder window showing your Documents folder.

2. **Click in the search field or press ⌘+F to move the focus there.**

3. **Type your search term or terms in the search field.** When you start typing, the Finder window changes to a Search window, and Spotlight displays matching results as you continue typing.

4. **If you want to search in the names of files rather than in their contents, click the Filename contains item that appears on a pop-up menu from the search field.**

5. **On the left side of the Search bar below the toolbar, click the button bearing the name of your starting folder (for example, "Documents") if you want to restrict the search to that folder.** By default, Spotlight searches your entire iMac and selects the This Mac button to indicate that it is doing so.

6. **If you need to add another search criterion, follow these steps:**

   - **Click the Add (+) button at the right end of the Search bar to add another line of search controls (see Figure 3.17).**

   - **Open the first pop-up menu and choose an item from it: Kind, Last opened date, Last modified date, Created date, Name, Contents, or Other.** If you choose Other, select the search attribute in the Select a search attribute dialog (see Figure 3.18), and then click OK.

- **Use the controls on the same line to fill in the details.** For example, if you choose Kind in the first pop-up menu, specify the kind of file by choosing an item such as Document, Music, Movie, or PDF. If you choose Created date from the first pop-up menu, choose the date or the date range — for example, "Created date is yesterday" or "Created date is within last 3 months."

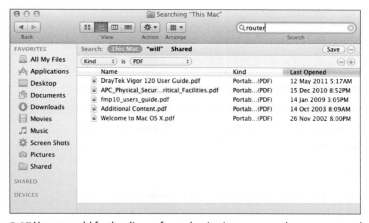

3.17 You can add further lines of search criteria to narrow down your search to exactly the files you need.

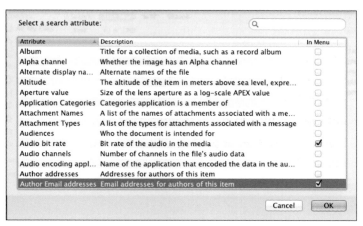

3.18 To zero in on the files you need, you can select from a wide range of search attributes in the Select a search attribute dialog.

7. **Repeat Step 6 to add as many criteria as needed.**

Genius

You can set up a group of conditions so that a file meeting any one of them is included in the search results. Instead of clicking + to add search criteria, Option+click the button, which changes from a plus sign to an ellipsis when you hold down Option. Choose Any, All, or None from the pop-up menu, and then set your criteria and run your search.

8. **As soon as you find the file you need, go ahead and open it.** But if you need to sift through your search results to find the right file, try these moves:

- **See where a file is.** Look at the path bar at the bottom of the Finder window. Even if the path bar was hidden before you started the search, the Finder displays it during the search.

- **Preview a file with Quick Look.** You can use Quick Look on your search results. Move the highlight to the file, and then press spacebar.

- **Preview a file with Cover Flow view.** Click the Cover Flow button in the View group on the toolbar or choose View ⇨ as Cover Flow to switch to Cover Flow view. You can then browse through the search results visually.

- **Sort the search results.** Click the List button in the View group on the toolbar or choose View ⇨ as List to switch to List view. You can then click a column heading to sort in ascending order by that item, or click again to sort in descending order. For example, click the Kind column to sort the files by their type — HTML Document, JPEG Image, Portable Document Format (PDF), and so on.

- **Open the folder that contains the file.** Control+click or right-click the file and choose Open Enclosing Folder, or click the file and choose File ⇨ Open Enclosing Folder or press ⌘+R.

9. **When you finish using the search results, click the Close button or choose File ⇨ Close Window to close the Search window.**

Saving a search as a Smart Folder for future use

After performing a search that finds items you'll need to find again in the future, you can save the search as a Smart Folder. Here's how to create a Smart Folder:

1. **After creating and refining your search, click the Save button at the right end of the Search bar.** The Specify a name and location for your Smart Folder dialog opens (see Figure 3.19).

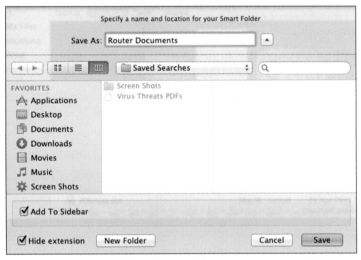

3.19 You can save a search as a Smart Folder so that you can use it again instantly in the future.

2. **In the Save As text box, type the name for the search.** Make the name as brief and descriptive as possible so that you can easily identify the search.

3. **In the Where pop-up menu, choose the folder in which to save the search.** The default location, the Saved Searches folder, is usually the best choice unless you have a reason for saving the search elsewhere — for example, because you want to share it with other users of your iMac.

4. **Select the Add To Sidebar check box if you want to add the Smart Folder to the Favorites category in the sidebar.** This puts the search right at your fingertips whenever you need it, so it's a good choice for searches you'll need often.

5. **Click Save to save the search.**

Searching Smarter with the Spotlight Menu

To make your searches in the Spotlight menu more effective, you can type keywords and criteria to restrict the search. Spotlight lets you use any of the search attributes you can use in a Search window, but many of these are so highly specialized (and difficult to type) that it's best simply to use the Search window interface.

These are the search attributes that are most widely useful in the Spotlight menu:

- **Kind.** To restrict a search to a particular file type, use the kind keyword followed by the kind — for example, kind:pdf or kind:Microsoft Word. You can use any of the kinds that appear in the Kind column of a Finder window in List view, including Alias, Application, Folders, JPEG Images, and MP3 Audio Files.

- **Last modified date.** To restrict a search to files last modified on a particular date, use the date keyword followed by the date — for example, date:yesterday or date:12/18/10-12/20/10.

- **Created date.** To restrict a search to files created on a specific date, use the created keyword followed by the date — for example, created:today or created:>5/24/10 (created after May 24, 2010).

- **Author.** If you know who created the file, use the author keyword and the name — for example, author:chris. Only some applications save the Author attribute, but Pages, Numbers, Word, Excel, iChat, and Mail are among them, so it's useful for those document types.

Burning CDs and DVDs

When you need to share large amounts of files or folders with other people or copy them for safety, you can burn them to CD or DVD. Your iMac's optical drive can burn both CDs and DVDs, and you can choose between recordable discs (to which you can burn data only once) and rewritable discs (to which you can burn data multiple times).

Mac OS X lets you create burn folders — folders in which you store the files until you are ready to burn them to disc. For example, you can create a burn folder of the files and folders you want to take on a trip, add the files and folders as you remember them, and then burn the disc just before you leave.

Making a burn folder

Here's how to make a burn folder:

1. **Open a Finder window to the folder in which you want to create the burn folder.**
   For example, click the desktop and choose Go ⇨ Home to open your home folder.

Note If you choose File ⇨ New Burn Folder with no folder open in a Finder window, Mac OS X creates the burn folder on the desktop. This is often a handy place to put a burn folder, as you can access it easily, and its presence will remind you to remove it when you have finished using it.

2. **Choose File ⇨ New Burn Folder.** Mac OS X creates a folder named Burn Folder and highlights the name. Type the name you want, and then press Return to apply the name.

3. **Click and drag files and folders to the burn folder.**

4. **When you're ready to burn the disc, open the folder and double-check its contents to make sure it contains the items you want and no others.** You can then burn the disc as described later in this chapter.

Caution Only the top-level folders that you see in a burn folder's window are aliases and can be deleted with impunity; if you double-click one of these folders, you're actually opening the real folder. So be careful!

Adding files and folders to a CD or DVD

Creating a burn folder ahead of time can be convenient, but at other times you may prefer simply to insert a CD or DVD in your iMac, add files to it, and then burn the disc. For this, you actually use a burn folder, too, but Mac OS X hides the fact from you.

When you insert a blank CD or DVD in your iMac's optical drive, Mac OS X displays the dialog shown in Figure 3.20. Open the Action pop-up menu and choose Open Finder, and then click OK.

Mac OS X then creates a burn folder on your desktop and links it to the disc. The burn folder is named Untitled CD or Untitled DVD,

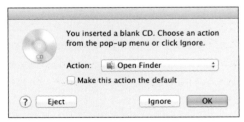

3.20 To load a blank CD or DVD so that you can add files to it, choose Open Finder in the Action pop-up menu in this dialog.

119

but you can rename it like any other folder — for example, select the folder, press Return to select the current name, type the new name, and then press Return to apply it.

Click and drag files and folders to the burn folder, and then burn the disc as described next.

Note

If you always want to use the Finder when you insert a blank disc of this type, you can select the Make this action the default check box before clicking OK, but in many cases it's better to leave your options open for when you want to use iTunes, Disk Utility, or another application instead.

Burning the disc

After creating a burn folder in one of the two ways just described, you can burn the disc like this:

1. **Give the Burn command in one of the following ways to display the Burn dialog (see Figure 3.21):**

   • **Select the burn folder, and then choose File ⇨ Burn from the menu bar.** This command is always available.

   • **Control+click or right-click the burn folder, and then choose the Burn command from the shortcut menu.**

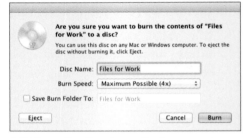

3.21 Name the disc, choose the burn speed, and decide whether to save the burn folder for future use.

   • **If the burn folder appears as a disc icon on your desktop, click and drag it to the Trash.** The Trash icon changes to a burn icon as you drag.

2. **If necessary, change the name in the Disc Name text box.** Mac OS X suggests the burn folder's name.

3. **In the Burn Speed pop-up menu, choose the speed at which to burn the disc.** Usually, it's best to start with the Maximum Possible speed, test the resulting disc, and then reduce the speed only if you get errors. But you may prefer to play it safe and burn at a lower speed anyway.

4. **Select the Save Burn Folder To check box if you want to save the burn folder for future use.** Change the name in the text box if necessary.

5. **Click Burn.** Mac OS X displays a Burn dialog to show the burn's progress. When the burn completes, Mac OS X mounts the disc so that it appears in the sidebar in the Finder.

6. **Open a Finder window, click the disc in the sidebar, and verify that its contents are all present and correct.** Open some of the files to make sure they're okay.

7. **Click the Eject button next to the disc's name in the sidebar to eject the disc.** Label the disc and store it safely.

How Do I Set Up a Local Network?

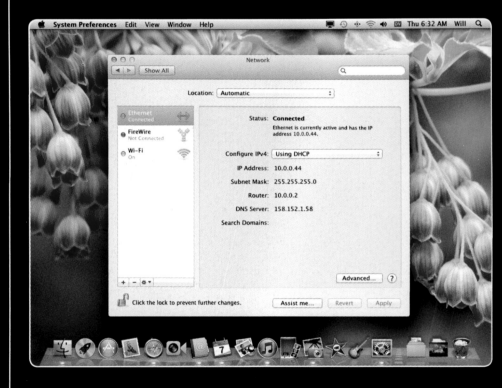

An iMac is great, and an iMac with an Internet connection is even better. But best of all is your iMac connected to a local network so you can share everything from files to hardware with other people — while keeping your personal and sensitive files strictly to yourself. This chapter shows you how to set up either a wireless or a wired network if you don't already have one, how to connect your iMac to the network, and how to set up sharing. And if you've wondered how to create a temporary network when you need one, you'll find out how to do so using any networking technology, from Wi-Fi to FireWire.

Making the Network Connection

The first step in networking your Macs is to connect them, either wirelessly or via cables. This section covers creating a permanent network using either a wireless access point or network cables. See the end of the chapter for instructions on setting up temporary networks using wireless, Ethernet cables, or FireWire.

Setting up a wireless network

A wireless connection is ideal if you want to set up a network quickly and easily or if you want to be able to move your iMac from room to room without trailing a cable. You can also create a network that mixes both wired and wireless parts, as in Figure 4.1.

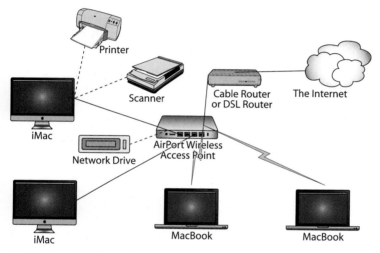

4.1 Whether wired or wireless, a network lets you quickly share data, music, and more.

To set up a permanent wireless network, you need

- **A wireless access point.** This device connects the computers and other devices to the network. Apple's AirPort range of wireless access points is designed for use with Macs but also works well with PCs, so it's often the best choice.

- **A wireless network card in each computer.** This card lets the computer connect to a wireless network. All current and recent Macs include wireless network cards except for the Mac Pro, on which a wireless network card is a build option. Apple used to refer to the wireless cards as AirPort cards, but now (in Mac OS X 10.7, Lion) refers to them simply as Wi-Fi.

Genius

If you need both a wireless access point and a backup drive, look at Apple's Time Capsule. This is an AirPort Extreme with a built-in hard drive. You can use Time Capsule to back up either a single Mac or all the Macs on your network.

Checking your iMac's Wi-Fi capabilities

If you're not sure which type of Wi-Fi card your iMac has, follow these steps to find out:

1. **Choose Apple menu ⇨ About This Mac.** The About This Mac window opens.

2. **Click the More Info button.** The System Information utility launches and displays a larger About This Mac window, which contains an Overview tab, a Displays tab, a Storage tab, and a Memory tab.

3. **On the Overview tab, click the System Report button.** You can also choose File ⇨ Show System Report or press ⌘+N. System Information displays a larger window whose title bar shows your iMac's name (for example, iMac).

4. **In the left pane, expand the Network category if it is collapsed.** To expand the category, click its disclosure triangle.

5. **In the Network category, click Wi-Fi.** The details for the Wi-Fi card appear.

6. **Look at the Card Type readout.** See whether it says AirPort Extreme or simply AirPort.

7. **Quit System Information.** Press ⌘+Q.

How Fast Will Your Wireless Network Be?

Wireless network connections are typically slower than wired network connections, but the latest wireless networks are fast enough for all but the heaviest-duty tasks.

Networking speeds are measured in bits per second: gigabits (billions of bits), megabits (millions of bits), and kilobits (thousands of bits). Each byte of data normally contains 8 bits, so the maximum number of bytes the network can transfer is one-eighth that of the "headline" speed. For example, Gigabit Ethernet's 1 gigabit per second (Gbps) can transfer up to 125 megabytes (MB) per second, 802.11n network's 600 megabits per second (Mbps) up to 75 MB per second, Fast Ethernet's 100 Mbps up to 12.5 MB per second, and 802.11g network's 54 Mbps up to 6.75 MB per second. In practice, speeds are usually substantially slower, especially when many computers are using the network.

continued

continued

How fast your wireless network is depends on the networking standard your wireless network equipment meets. At this writing, four wireless network standards are widely used:

- **802.11n.** This standard provides the fastest wireless network speeds available — up to 600 Mbps.

- **802.11g.** This standard, often called Wireless G, has a maximum speed of 54 Mbps and is widely used.

- **802.11b.** This standard, called Wi-Fi, has a maximum speed of 11 Mbps. It is still widely used worldwide, especially in hotspot networks such as those in coffee shops and airports, but the transfer speeds are too low for large files (for example, video).

- **802.11a.** This standard has a maximum speed of 54 Mbps but is not widely used outside corporate networks.

If you want the highest wireless network speeds for your iMac, the best choice is an Apple AirPort wireless access point, which is guaranteed to work well with your iMac's wireless network card.

Apple has used the names AirPort Extreme and AirPort Express for both 802.11g and 802.11n equipment. The latest models from the Apple Store are 802.11n. For example, the AirPort Extreme Base Station with Gigabit Ethernet and AirPort Express Base Station with 802.11n are the 802.11n models and include compatibility with 802.11g, 802.11b, and 802.11a wireless equipment. But if you buy used, double-check that you're getting the 802.11n model rather than the 802.11g model.

Setting up an AirPort wireless access point

After you unpack your AirPort, choose a suitable location for it. Depending on the AirPort model, you need to juggle three or four criteria here, so you will probably have to compromise a bit.

- **Network or Internet connection.** You will need to connect your AirPort to your network switch or hub, or to your cable or DSL router. You can use an Ethernet cable up to 300 feet long to make the connection.

- **Wireless network coverage.** Position the AirPort as near as possible to the center of the area you want the wireless network to cover. All other things being equal, the coverage reaches the same distance in each direction horizontally, and a shorter distance up and down. You'll get less coverage in any directions blocked by extra-thick walls or areas of shielding.

- **Power.** The AirPort must be near an electrical outlet.

- **Speakers.** If you have AirPort Express, you'll want to connect it to your main speakers so that you can play music through it from iTunes on any computer.

Connect the AirPort as follows:

- **Network or Internet connection.** Use an Ethernet cable to connect the AirPort's wide area network Ethernet port either to your network switch or hub, or to your cable or DSL router. (If your cable or DSL router has a built-in switch, you're effectively making both these connections at once.)

- **Wired computers and printers.** Use an Ethernet cable to connect any computers or printers directly to the AirPort. These computers will get higher network speeds than the ones that connect wirelessly, so it's a good idea to use these ports for computers that you don't mind having tethered. This step doesn't apply to the AirPort Express, which has only one Ethernet port.

- **Networked printer or networked drive.** Use a USB cable to connect the printer or external hard drive to the AirPort's USB port. If you need to connect more devices than the number of USB ports on your AirPort, connect a USB hub to the AirPort and then connect the devices to the hub.

- **Speakers (AirPort Express only).** Connect your speakers or home stereo to the AirPort Express's stereo mini-jack via either an analog audio cable or a digital audio cable.

- **Power.** If you have an AirPort Express, plug it directly into a socket. For other AirPort models, connect the power supply to a socket, and plug the connector into the AirPort.

Note If AirPort Utility automatically checks for updates on launch, allow it to do so, and install any available updates to make sure you have the latest version of the software. The latest version may have extra features, fewer bugs, or both.

With the AirPort connected, configure it as follows from your iMac:

1. **Click the Finder on the Dock, choose Go ⇨ Utilities, and then double-click AirPort Utility.** AirPort Utility opens, searches for available AirPorts, and displays a list of those it finds (see Figure 4.2).

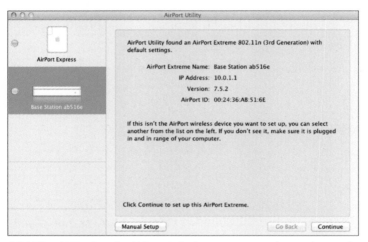

4.2 AirPort Utility lists the AirPorts it finds on your network or within wireless range of your iMac.

2. **In the left pane, click the AirPort you want to configure, and then click Continue.**

3. **If AirPort Utility prompts you for the AirPort's password, type the password, and then click OK.** Some AirPort models have a default password that you can find in the user manual. Other models have no password until you set one. The first configuration screen then appears.

4. **Type the name you want to give the AirPort, type a password, and then click Continue.** If you have more than one AirPort, use descriptive names so that you can identify them easily.

5. **On the second configuration screen (see Figure 4.3), select the I want to create a new wireless network option, and then click Continue.** At this point, you'll normally want to create a new network, as in this example. However, this screen also lets you add the AirPort to an existing network or use it to replace an existing base station.

Note When setting up an AirPort, you create two passwords. The first password is for accessing the AirPort using AirPort Utility; you'll want to keep this password to yourself. The second password is for connecting a computer to the AirPort network. You share this password with anyone who will set up a computer's wireless network connection.

128

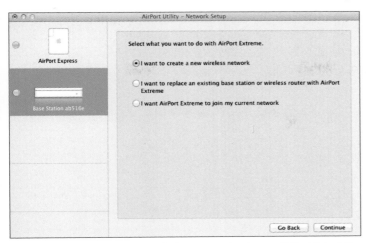

4.3 The easiest way to set up a wireless network using an AirPort is to follow the wizard.

6. **On the third configuration screen (see Figure 4.4), choose security settings, type a password, and click Continue.** See the sidebar for advice on choosing the best security for your needs.

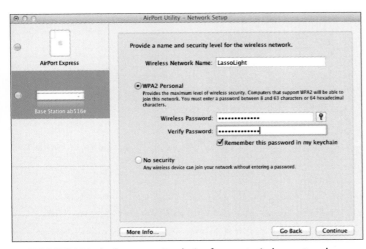

4.4 WPA/WPA2 is the best security choice for most wireless networks.

Note

When setting up an AirPort Extreme, you also have the option to create a *guest network* — a wireless network that enables guests to connect to the Internet but not to your network. Creating a guest network is often a good idea. Select the Enable guest network check box, choose the security type in the Guest Network Security pop-up menu, and type a password in the Guest Network Password box and the Verify Password box.

7. **On the Select how you connect to the Internet screen, choose how the AirPort connects to the Internet, and then click Continue.** Normally, you'll want to select the I use a DSL or cable modem with a static IP address or DHCP option, the I use a DSL or cable modem using PPP over Ethernet (PPPoE) option, or the I connect to my local area network option.

8. **On the Summary screen, check the details of the settings you've selected, and then click Update.**

9. **When the wizard finishes configuring the AirPort, click Quit to quit AirPort Utility.**

Using third-party equivalents

Apple's AirPort access points are hands down the best wireless network hardware to use when you network Macs, because you can be sure that the access points will work with the Macs' Wi-Fi cards and deliver full speed. Even better, Mac OS X includes tools for setting up and configuring AirPort access points, so you don't need to install other configuration tools or struggle with them.

When you buy network hardware from other vendors, you may run into compatibility issues. This was a problem during the seven years that the 802.11n standard was being drafted, as different manufacturers' implementations of the standard didn't always work together at full speed. Now that the standard is finalized, this should be less of an issue — but if you have the chance to test the equipment before you buy it, you should do so.

If you're buying a wireless access point, buy 802.11n. But if someone offers you an old 802.11g wireless access point after upgrading to 802.11n, grab it with both hands. Used with either 802.11g AirPort Extreme cards or 802.11n AirPort Extreme cards, an 802.11g access point should give 54 Mbps speeds, which is plenty for most current networking needs.

How you set up a wireless access point that's not an AirPort varies, but usually you have two choices:

- **Use a Windows-based tool.** The Set Up a Wireless Router or Access Point Wizard in Windows 7 and Windows Vista, and the Wireless Network Setup Wizard in Windows XP let you select settings for a wireless network, save the settings to a USB flash drive, and then apply them to the wireless access point and each PC in turn by connecting the flash drive.

- **Configure the wireless access point through your web browser.** This is easy enough to do, but it takes a little more effort to connect each computer to the network. You may need to connect the access point to your Mac via an Ethernet cable to configure it. Check the manufacturer's site for setup instructions if you don't have a manual. You may need to use a browser other than Safari, which sometimes doesn't agree with Windows-centric access points; Firefox and Camino generally do better.

Choosing the Best Wireless Encryption Method

The most important choice you make for your wireless network is which type of encryption to use. AirPorts offer two or three choices, depending on the model:

- **WPA/WPA2 Personal.** Wi-Fi Protected Access (WPA) or Wi-Fi Protected Access 2 (WPA2) is the best choice for securing a wireless network unless you need to let older devices that cannot use WPA or WPA2 access the network.

- **128-bit WEP.** Wired Equivalent Privacy (WEP) is an older and less-effective means of securing a wireless network. Despite the name suggesting the equivalent privacy of a wired network, WEP has known flaws that allow an attacker who targets your network to learn the password. Use WEP only if you have devices that cannot use WPA or WPA2, and always use 128-bit WEP rather than 40-bit WEP. At this writing, some AirPort Express models offer WEP, but the AirPort Extreme does not.

- **No security.** This choice creates a wireless network that is completely unsecured. Any wireless-enabled computer or device within range of the AirPort can connect to the network. Creating a completely open network like this is never wise.

Connecting your iMac to the wireless network

When the wireless access point is up and running, you can connect your Mac to it quickly:

1. **Click the Wi-Fi menulet at the right end of the menu bar and choose Turn Wi-Fi On if the menu says Wi-Fi Off.**

2. **Click the Wi-Fi menulet again, and then click the network you want to join (see Figure 4.5).** If the network's name doesn't appear, see the next list of steps. Mac OS X prompts you for the password.

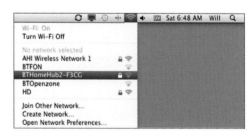

4.5 Select the wireless network from the Wi-Fi menulet.

131

3. **Type the network's password.** Select the Show password check box if you want to see the characters you're typing — for example, if you find you get a complex password wrong. Make sure the Remember this network check box is selected (see Figure 4.6), and click Join. Your iMac connects to the network. The Wi-Fi menulet icon shows the strength of the connection, from one bar (weak) to four bars (strong).

4.6 Normally, you want to tell Mac OS X to remember the network so that you can connect to it again.

Note If the Wi-Fi menulet doesn't appear on the menu bar, open System Preferences and click Network to display the Network preferences. In the left list box, click Wi-Fi. Select the Show Wi-Fi status in menu bar option, and then quit System Preferences.

If the network you want to join doesn't appear on the Wi-Fi menulet, it's probably closed, which means it is configured not to broadcast its presence. To join, you must tell Mac OS X the network's name and security type as well as the password. Follow these steps:

1. **Open the Wi-Fi menulet and click Join Other Network.** The Find and join a Wi-Fi network dialog appears (see Figure 4.7).

2. **Type the network's name in the Network Name box.**

3. **Open the Security pop-up menu and choose the security type, and then type the password in the Password box.** Select the Show password check box if you want to see the letters you're typing.

4.7 Use the Find and join a Wi-Fi network dialog to join a wireless network whose name doesn't appear in the Wi-Fi menulet.

4. **Select the Remember this network check box if you plan to use this network again.**

5. **Click Join.** The dialog closes, and your iMac connects to the wireless network. The Wi-Fi menulet icon shows the strength of the connection, from one bar (weak) to four bars (strong). You can now start using the wireless network.

Networking with Ethernet cables

As you've just seen, wireless networks are easy to set up. But if you need a permanent network, a wired network using Ethernet cables may be a better choice, as it can give you better performance and greater security.

Ethernet is the general term for networking computers via eight-wire cables. Figure 4.8 shows a diagram of an Ethernet network. Most networks use one of the three main Ethernet standards, which offer different networking speeds:

- **Gigabit Ethernet.** This provides the fastest affordable data-transfer speeds — up to 1 gigabit per second (Gbps). All current Macs apart from the MacBook Air include Gigabit Ethernet network cards, as do most Macs with Intel processors. If you're buying new network equipment, Gigabit Ethernet is the best choice. It's a bit more expensive than Fast Ethernet equipment, but the extra speed is well worth having.

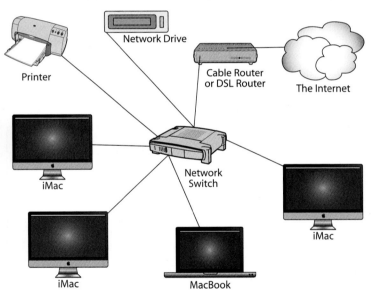

4.8 An Ethernet network's logical layout is a star shape with the switch or hub at the center, but you can position the devices wherever you need them in the physical world.

Genius

At this writing, 10 Gigabit Ethernet equipment is available, but it's painfully expensive, and Macs don't have 10 Gigabit Ethernet ports, so they can't make the most of it. For these reasons, Gigabit Ethernet is currently a better buy than 10 Gigabit Ethernet.

- **Fast Ethernet.** This provides data-transfer speeds of up to 100 Mbps. If you already have Fast Ethernet equipment, continue using it until you find that your network isn't fast enough. Similarly, if one of your friends is upgrading his or her network to Gigabit Ethernet and offers you the "old" Fast Ethernet equipment, don't turn it down.

- **Ethernet.** This provides data-transfer speeds of up to 10 Mbps. Standard Ethernet equipment is outdated at this writing, but it's still viable if you need only a low-speed network and either already have the equipment or can pick it up for nothing.

Note An Ethernet network typically forms a logical star shape, with the switch in the middle and the other devices connected to it. Logical means the way in which the information is routed rather than the actual physical layout of the network cables and equipment. The physical layout of the network may look like a circle or even a straight line rather than a star.

Buying the best cables

If you're putting in the effort of building a wired network, you'll want it to be fast, long lasting, and reliable. Choose cables as follows:

- **For a new Ethernet network, use either Category 5 enhanced (Cat 5e) or Category 6 (Cat 6) cables.** These grades of cable can carry Gigabit Ethernet or faster signals. If you already have Category 5 (Cat 5) cable, by all means use it, as it can manage Gigabit Ethernet as well. But if you're buying new, go for one of the higher grades.

- **Buy good-quality cables rather than bargain-basement cables.** A cable that's poorly made, or that has been stressed by stretching or twisting, can degrade the performance of the whole network.

- **Consider making your own cables.** If you need just a few cables, it's usually easiest to buy ready-made cables; you may also want to buy a selection of different-colored cables so that you can easily tell one from another. But if you need many cables, buying a roll of cable, RJ-45 jacks, and a crimping tool lets you create cables of exactly the lengths you need, and may work out to be less expensive overall.

Using network switches and hubs

As you can see in Figure 4.8 (earlier in this chapter), the central connecting point of an Ethernet network is the network switch or hub.

A network hub is a simple connection box into which you plug the network cables. When a signal comes along one cable to the hub, the hub repeats it along each of the other cables. The computer for which the signal is marked picks the signal off the wire, while the other computers ignore it. In a network built around a hub, only one computer can transmit data at a time.

A network switch is a more sophisticated form of connection box. The switch listens to the broadcasts from the computers connected to the network and makes a map of which computer is connected to which cable. When a signal comes along one cable to the switch, the switch determines which cable the destination computer is connected to and sends the signal along only that cable rather than sending it along all the cables. Cutting out unnecessary signaling greatly improves network performance and allows multiple computers to transmit data at once.

Unless you have a hub already, buy a switch rather than a hub. Gigabit Ethernet switches are now the best choice, as they cost only a little more than Fast Ethernet switches but deliver up to ten times the performance.

Here's how to set up the physical parts of an Ethernet network:

1. **Decide where to locate the switch or hub.** The switch or hub requires a power supply and a connection to each computer or other network device, including your cable router or DSL router.

2. **Connect the switch or hub to each computer or device via an Ethernet cable.** If all your computers and devices are in the same room, this may take only moments. But if you need to run cables all over your home, it will take considerable time and effort.

3. **Connect the switch or hub to its power supply, and turn it on.** If the switch includes a cable router or DSL router, follow its setup instructions. Having the router act as a DHCP server, providing IP addresses to each device on the network automatically, is usually the easiest way to set up the network.

4. **Turn on any of your computers or devices that were turned off, and configure them if necessary.**

When you connect a Mac to an Ethernet network, Mac OS X attempts to detect suitable network settings. If you need to change the settings, follow these steps:

1. **Choose Apple menu ⇨ System Preferences.** The System Preferences window opens.

2. **In the Internet & Wireless section, click the Network icon to display Network preferences.**

135

3. **Click Ethernet in the left list box if it's not already selected.** The Ethernet status and preferences appear (see Figure 4.9).

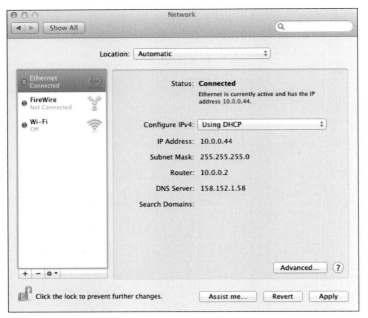

4.9 You may need to change the Ethernet settings in the Network preferences.

4. **From the Configure IPv4 pop-up menu, choose how you want your Mac to get an IP address and network configuration:**

   ● **Using DHCP.** Requesting an IP address and network configuration from a DHCP server (for example, your cable router or DSL router) is usually the easiest way of assigning IP addresses.

   ● **Using DHCP with manual address.** This option requests the network configuration from the DHCP server but lets you set the IP address manually. Use this when you need to make sure a Mac has a particular IP address (for example, because you will configure your router to forward incoming requests to that address).

   ● **Using BootP.** This option is normally used in corporate networks rather than home networks.

   ● **Manually.** This option lets you set the IP address, subnet mask, and router manually. You may need to do this if your network has no DHCP server.

   ● **Off.** This option turns the Ethernet interface off altogether.

5. **Click Apply to apply the configuration.**

You can connect two or more switches or hubs together via an Ethernet cable if necessary. For example, if you put one switch in the family room and one in the study, you will need only one cable running between the two rooms, no matter how many computers and devices each room contains.

Sharing Access and Data

After you set up the network, you can use it to share files, your Internet connection, printers, scanners, and more.

Sharing files

To share files, you share the folders that contain them. Mac OS X comes equipped with the following shared folders for you to use, but you may need to set up extra shared folders of your own (as discussed next):

● **Public folder.** Each user account has a Public folder (in the Home folder) that is accessible to all users of your Mac. Each user can see the files in each other user's Public folder and copy them, but not create files; only the user whose Public folder it is can create files.

● **Drop Box folder.** Each user's Public folder contains a Drop Box folder that other users can place files in to give them to that user. Nobody but the user can see the contents of his or her Drop Box.

● **/Users/Shared folder.** Each user of the Mac can access this folder freely for sharing files. This shared folder doesn't appear on the network.

For example, if you want to pass some files to Bill, copy them to his Drop Box folder; you can't see what's in Bill's Drop Box folder (although if you try to copy to the folder a file it already contains, you'll receive a message telling you that a file of that name already exists). Similarly, Bill can share files with you by copying them to your Drop Box folder, but he can't see the contents of your Drop Box folder. And if you, Alice, and Bill all need to work on some files together on the same Mac, you can place them in the /Users/Shared folder (or one of its subfolders).

Sharing specified folders

You can share any of the shared folders discussed in the previous section with other users of your network by turning on File Sharing. You can also share other folders of your choosing.

Here's how to set up File Sharing and choose the folders you want to share:

1. **Choose Apple menu ⇨ System Preferences.** The System Preferences window opens.

2. **In the Internet & Wireless section, click the Sharing icon to open Sharing preferences.**

3. **In the left list box, select the File Sharing check box.** The File Sharing controls appear (see Figure 4.10).

4. **In the Shared Folders box, select the shared folder you want to affect.** The Users box shows the users with whom the folder is shared and the permissions they have. If the folder doesn't appear, click the Add (+) button below the Shared Folders box, select the folder in the dialog that appears, and then click the Add button.

5. **In the Users box, click the user you want to affect.** If the user doesn't appear, click the Add (+) button below the Users box, select the user in the dialog that appears (or click New Person and set up a new user), and then click the Add button. Click Everyone if you want to make the folder available to anyone with Guest access to your iMac.

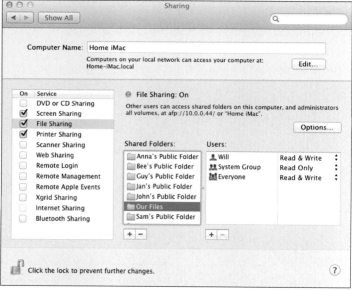

4.10 The File Sharing controls let you control which users can access which folders and which actions they can take with the files in the folders.

6. **Choose the level of permissions you want the user to have for the folder:**

    ● **Read Only.** This permission lets the user view the files in a folder but not change them.

    ● **Write Only (Drop Box).** This permission lets the user add files to a folder but not see its contents, as with the Drop Box folder in each user's Public folder.

    ● **Read & Write.** This permission lets the user view, create, and delete files in a folder. (The Write permission includes deletion.)

    ● **No Access.** This permission prevents the user from accessing the folder at all.

7. **To choose the networking protocols your Mac uses to share files, click Options.** The Options dialog appears (see Figure 4.11):

- **Share files and folders using AFP.** Select this check box when sharing folders with Macs. AFP is Apple Filing Protocol and gives the best performance with Macs.

- **Share files and folders using SMB (Windows).** Select this check box when you need to share files with Windows PCs or Linux machines. Select the check box for the user

4.11 You can choose which networking protocols your Mac uses to share files.

account with whom you want to share, type the password for the user in the Authenticate dialog that appears, and then click OK.

- Click Done when you've made your choices.

8. **Quit System Preferences.** Choose System Preferences ⇨ Quit System Preferences.

Controlling access to shared files

Sometimes you may need to set different permissions for individual files you place within shared folders. For example, you may want to allow both John and Anna to read the same document, allow Anna to change the document, but prevent John from changing it.

Genius

You can set individual permissions for a file as described here, but normally it's easier and more efficient to set permissions for a folder and then put the appropriate files in it. If you need to create several different sets of permissions, create a different folder for each.

Here's how to change permissions for a file or folder:

1. **Open a Finder window, Control+click or right-click the file or folder, and then click Get Info.** The Info window for the file or folder opens.

2. **If the Sharing & Permissions area at the bottom is collapsed, click the disclosure triangle to expand it.**

3. **If the padlock icon is closed, click it and type your username and password in the Authenticate dialog, and then click OK.**

4. **If the user or group doesn't appear in the Name column, click the Add (+) button to open the Select a new user or group dialog.** Click the user or group, and then click the Select button to add the user or group to the list in the Info window.

5. **Click the user or group in the Name column, and then choose the permission in the Privilege column.** To continue the example, choose John's account, and then choose Read only (see Figure 4.12).

6. **If you're changing permissions for a folder rather than a file, you can click the Action button (the gear icon at the bottom of the window) and choose Apply to enclosed items.** In the dialog that Mac OS X displays warning you that you cannot undo the change you're making, click OK if you're sure you want to proceed.

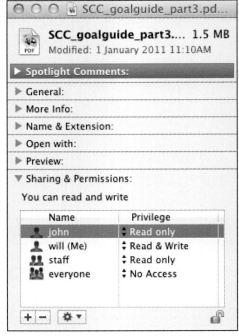

4.12 You can change permissions for an individual file or folder using the Info window.

7. **Click the padlock icon to lock the permissions again.**

8. **Close the Info window.**

Note

If you decide against the permission changes you've made, click the Action button (the gear icon) and choose Revert Changes.

Sending and receiving files with a Guest user

Putting files in your account's Public folder is often convenient for sharing. If several users need to work on files and make them available to others, it's usually easier to use the Guest user feature to send and receive files in shared folders.

Here's how to make sure the Guest user is set up to use shared folders:

1. **Choose Apple menu ⇨ System Preferences.** The System Preferences window opens.

2. **In the System section, click the Users & Groups icon to open Users & Groups preferences.**

3. **Look at Guest User in the accounts list.** If it says Sharing only, you're set; quit System Preferences now. Otherwise, follow the remaining steps.

4. **If the padlock icon is closed, unlock it.** Click the button, type your username and password in the Authenticate dialog, and then click OK.

5. **Click Guest User in the accounts list.** The Guest User settings appear.

6. **Select the Allow guests to connect to shared folders check box.** This setting turns on sharing.

7. **Make sure the Allow guests to log in to this computer check box is cleared unless you have a guest user visiting.** It's not safe to allow guest login when you don't actually have guests.

8. **Click the padlock icon to close the lock.**

9. **Quit System Preferences.** Press ⌘+Q.

When Sharing is on for the Guest user, you can make a folder's contents available to guests by setting the appropriate permission for Everyone. For example, set the Read permission to allow guests to copy the files in the folder.

Transferring files quickly to nearby Macs with AirDrop

Mac OS X Lion includes a new feature — called AirDrop — for transferring files quickly and easily to other Macs via Wi-Fi.

Genius

Your iMac doesn't need to be connected to a wireless network to use AirDrop. When you fire up AirDrop, the Macs establish a peer-to-peer network connection rather than sending the files through an infrastructure network. This means that you can use AirDrop to share files with people casually — for example, in a coffee shop, airport, or dorm. AirDrop encrypts the files in transit, and uses a firewall to make sure others can't access your Mac across the wireless connection.

As long as you have your iMac's Wi-Fi turned on, Lion can automatically sniff out other Macs in the area that also have Wi-Fi on and AirDrop running. The AirDrop category then appears at the top of the sidebar in the Finder, showing the names and contact photos of the users. To transfer a file using AirDrop, follow these steps:

1. **Open a Finder window.** For example, click the Finder icon on the Dock.

2. **In the Sidebar, click the AirDrop icon.** AirDrop detects the Macs around you that are running AirDrop and displays an icon for each (see Figure 4.13). The icon shows the user's picture, as set in the Users & Groups preferences.

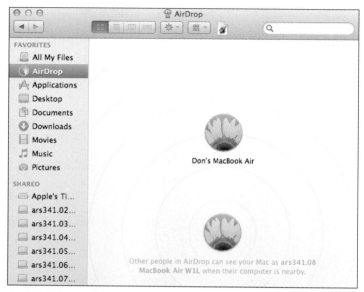

4.13 Click the AirDrop icon in the Sidebar to display the Macs around you that are also running AirDrop.

3. **Drag the file you want to send onto the user's name in the AirDrop pane.** Mac OS X displays a confirmation dialog (see Figure 4.14).

4. **Click the Send button.** When the user accepts the file, Mac OS X starts transferring it.

Genius

If the AirDrop category doesn't appear in the Finder, AirDrop is either turned off or your iMac can't use it. Click the desktop to activate the Finder, then choose Finder ⇨ Preferences to open the Finder Preferences window. Click the Sidebar tab. If AirDrop appears in the Favorites list, select its check box to make AirDrop appear in Finder windows. If AirDrop's not listed, your iMac doesn't support it.

When someone sends you a file via AirDrop, the Finder displays a message box (see Figure 4.15) alerting you to the incoming file and asking what you want to do with it. Click the appropriate button:

- **Save.** Click this button to save the file to the folder you choose.
- **Save & Open.** Click this button to save the file and automatically open it in a suitable application so that you can see what the file contains.
- **Decline.** Click this button to refuse the file.

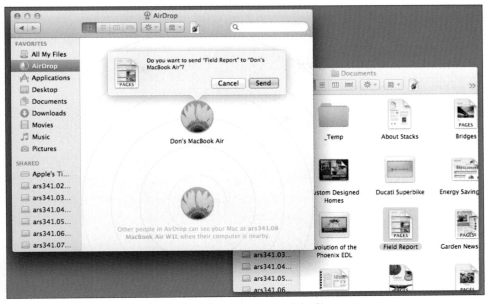

4.14 Click the Send button in the confirmation dialog to send the file.

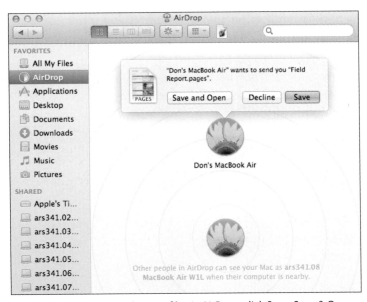

4.15 When someone sends you a file via AirDrop, click Save, Save & Open, or Decline.

Sharing Internet access

Mac OS X's Internet Sharing feature lets you easily share an Internet connection connected directly to your iMac. For longer-term Internet sharing, you may decide to invest in a hardware router, which takes the strain of sharing off your Mac and helps improve network performance.

Using Mac OS X's Internet Sharing

If your Internet connection connects directly to your iMac rather than to a switch or hub, you can share it easily by using Mac OS X's built-in Internet Sharing feature.

First, decide how to share the connection. For example, if your iMac is connected to the Internet connection via Ethernet, you could share the connection via AirPort to your other Macs. But if the computers all have FireWire and are located close together (say, in the same room), you can even share the Internet connection by connecting the computers via FireWire cables. Or you could choose to share both via AirPort and FireWire.

Connect the computers if you chose a wired means of sharing, and then set up the sharing in Mac OS X:

1. **Choose Apple menu ⇨ System Preferences.** The System Preferences window opens.

2. **In the Internet & Wireless section, click the Sharing icon to open Sharing preferences.**

3. **In the list box on the left, click Internet Sharing to display its options (see Figure 4.16).** Don't select the check box just yet — simply click the Internet Sharing item in the Service column.

4. **In the Share your connection from pop-up menu, choose the Internet connection you want to share.** In Figure 4.16, the Internet connection is connected via Ethernet.

5. **In the To computers using box, select the check box for each connection type you want to use.** Normally, your choices are Ethernet, FireWire, and Wi-Fi.

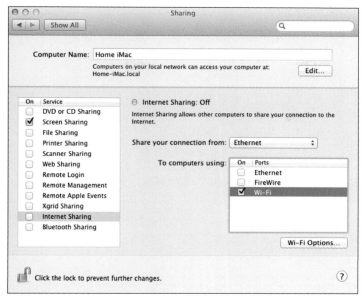

4.16 Internet Sharing lets you quickly share your iMac's Internet connection with other Macs and PCs on the network.

6. **If you selected the Wi-Fi check box, click Wi-Fi Options to open the Configure an internet-sharing network dialog (see Figure 4.17).** To set up the wireless network, follow these steps:

- **Type the name for the network in the Network Name box.**

- **In the Security pop-up menu, choose 128-bit WEP.**

- **Type a 13-character password in the Password box and the Confirm Password box.**

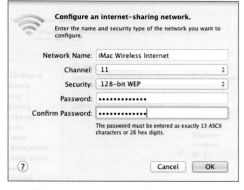

4.17 When you use Internet Sharing via Wi-Fi, set up a wireless network in the Configure an internet-sharing network dialog.

- **Click OK.** The Configure an internet-sharing network dialog closes, returning you to Sharing preferences.

Caution

Never use 40-bit WEP for your Internet sharing. This encryption doesn't give enough protection for even temporary networks. ·

7. **Select the Internet Sharing option from the list box on the left.** Mac OS X displays a confirmation message warning you that turning on Internet Sharing may disrupt the network.

8. **Click Start to start Internet Connection sharing.**

The other Macs can now access your Internet connection depending on which means of sharing you chose:

- **Ethernet.** Mac OS X automatically establishes a network connection.

- **Wi-Fi.** You connect to the wireless network you just created using the connection techniques discussed in this chapter.

- **FireWire.** Mac OS X automatically establishes a network connection.

Speeding up Internet Sharing with a hardware router

Mac OS X's Internet Sharing feature works pretty well, and it's great for situations when you can't share an Internet connection via the network using a router or switch — for example, when you're stuck in a dorm or hotel room with a single Ethernet connection. But for sharing an Internet connection permanently on a home network, you'll get better performance by using a hardware router or switch. You also will be able to put your iMac to sleep, or turn it off, without cutting off the Internet connection for the other computers on the network.

When choosing a hardware router, look for the following features:

- **Gigabit Ethernet speeds.** Fast Ethernet is still quick enough for transferring files these days, but you will probably want to transfer even more data in the future, so Gigabit Ethernet is the better choice when buying new equipment.

- **One Ethernet port for each computer or device you will connect.** You will probably want to connect all your Macs, PCs, printers, and your DSL or cable router (unless the router includes DSL or cable functionality). You may also want to connect a network-attached storage device.

- **USB ports for sharing networked drives and printers.**

- **A wireless access point built in.**

If you need all these features, you may find that an Apple AirPort is your best choice.

Connect the router to its power supply, and connect each of the PCs and devices with an Ethernet cable. You will then need to decide whether the router or your DSL or cable router will handle DHCP for the network.

Sharing hardware

If your hardware router can share items such as networked drives and printers, this is usually your easiest way of sharing these devices. But if your hardware router doesn't support sharing, you can use other means of sharing, such as Mac OS X's built-in features for sharing printers or network storage devices. You can also share scanners and cameras on the network.

Sharing a printer

Here's how to share a printer you've set up on your iMac:

1. **Choose Apple menu ⇨ System Preferences.** The System Preferences window opens.

2. **In the Internet & Wireless section, click the Sharing icon to open Sharing preferences.**

3. **In the left list box, select the Printer Sharing check box.** Mac OS X turns Printer Sharing on.

4. **Select the check box for the printer you want to share.** The Users list box shows the list of users who are permitted to use the printer. By default, the Everyone group receives the Can Print permission, so every user is allowed to print.

5. **To restrict printing, set the No Access permission for the Everyone group, and then add the individual users or groups you will allow to print.** To add a user or group, click the Add (+) button, click the user or group in the resulting dialog, and then click the Select button.

6. **Quit System Preferences.** Choose System Preferences ⇨ Quit System Preferences.

To connect to a shared printer, follow these steps:

1. **Choose Apple menu ⇨ System Preferences.** The System Preferences window opens.

2. **In the Hardware section, click the Print & Scan icon to open Print & Scan preferences.**

3. **Click the Add (+) button to open the Add Printer window.**

Note If clicking the Add (+) button produces a pop-up menu, see if the printer you want to add appears on that menu. If it does, click it. If not, click Add Other Printer or Scanner to open the Add Printer window.

4. **On the Default tab, click the printer in the Printer Name list (see Figure 4.18).** The printer appears as Bonjour Shared in the Kind column (Bonjour is Apple's *zero-configuration* networking technology).

5. **Change the name and location information for the printer to something more helpful, if you want.**

6. **If necessary, select the driver in the Print Using pop-up menu.**

7. **Click Add.** Mac OS X adds the printer to the Print & Scan preferences.

8. **Quit System Preferences.** Press ⌘+Q.

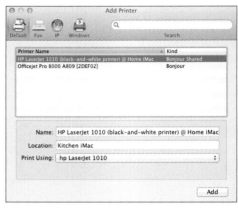

4.18 Shared printers appear as Bonjour Shared in the Add Printer window.

Installing network storage

You can add storage to your network in two ways:

● **Connect a USB drive to a hardware router or wireless access point such as an AirPort Extreme.** Use the tools that come with the router or access point to share the drive on the network. For example, when you connect a USB hard drive to an AirPort Extreme, the access point automatically makes the drive available to all computers on the network. (Windows PCs require Bonjour for Windows to access the drive.)

● **Connect a network-attached storage device to your network switch.** A network-attached storage device is basically an external hard drive with a brain or a simple server. Most network-attached storage devices use a web-based configuration tool that lets you configure them from any operating system and any browser (for example, Safari). You can then connect to the device by activating the Finder and choosing Go ⇨ Connect to Server.

Sharing scanners

To share a scanner on your network, use Scanner Sharing like this.

1. **Choose Apple menu ⇨ System Preferences.** The System Preferences window opens.

2. **In the Internet & Wireless section, click the Sharing icon to open Sharing preferences (see Figure 4.19).**

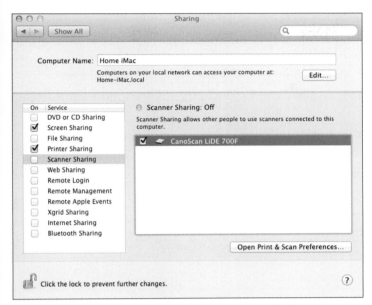

4.19 In the Scanner Sharing pane, select the check box for the scanner you want to share on the network.

3. **In the left list box, select the Scanner Sharing check box.** Mac OS X turns Scanner Sharing on.

4. **Select the check box for the scanner you want to share.**

5. **Quit System Preferences.** Press ⌘+Q.

You can now connect to the scanner from another Mac using the Print & Scan preferences. Use the same technique as is used for connecting to a shared printer (described earlier in this chapter).

Sharing music and video

iTunes lets you share your songs and videos with other users of iTunes on Windows as well as on the Mac. You can share items either via Home Sharing, which enables you to copy items from one computer to another, or by choosing to share items so that others can play them but not copy them, create playlists of them, or burn them to CD.

Using Home Sharing

Home Sharing gives you an easy way to transfer songs between different computers. As its name suggests, Home Sharing is designed for use within the home rather than in larger settings (such as a dorm). You must use the same Apple ID for each of the computers on which you use Home Sharing.

149

Turning on Home Sharing

First, turn on Home Sharing on each Mac or PC that will participate. Here's what to do:

1. **In iTunes, expand the Shared category in the Source list by holding the mouse pointer over it and then clicking the word Show that appears.**

Note
To use Home Sharing, you need an Apple ID, which you get when you set up iTunes Store account. If you don't have one, you can set one up easily enough by clicking the Need an Apple ID? link on the Home Sharing screen.

2. **Under the Shared category heading, click the Home Sharing item to display the Home Sharing screen (see Figure 4.20).**

4.20 Start by using your Apple ID to turn on Home Sharing.

3. **Type your Apple ID in the iTunes Account text box.** If iTunes has entered an account name already; make sure it's right.

4. **Type your password in the Password text box.**

5. **Click Create Home Share.** iTunes checks your details with the iTunes Store and then turns on Home Sharing.

6. **Click Done.** iTunes then removes the Home Sharing item from the Shared category.

After you turn on Home Sharing on each computer, you can click one of the entries in the Shared list to see all the songs that another computer is sharing. Figure 4.21 shows an example. From here, you can do the following:

● **Play songs or other items.** To play an item, double-click it, and then use the play controls as usual.

4.21 Choose a shared library within the Shared category in the Source list to view the library's contents.

● **View a category of items.** Within the shared library, click the category you want to see. For example, click the Movies category to see only the movies the shared library contains.

● **View items that aren't in your library.** Open the Show pop-up menu and choose Items not in my library instead of All items. You'll then see a list of only the items you may want to transfer.

● **Search for songs or items.** With the shared library or part of it selected, click in the Search box, and then search as usual.

● **Import items.** Select the items you want to import from the shared library to your iTunes library, and then click Import. iTunes hauls in the items hand over fist.

Note

If you decide you want to stop using Home Sharing, choose Advanced ⇨ Stop Home Sharing. (And if you then want to turn it back on again, choose Advanced ⇨ Turn On Home Sharing.)

- **Automatically transfer new purchases.** Click Settings near the lower-right corner of the Home Settings screen to display the Home Sharing Settings dialog (see Figure 4.22).

Sharing playlists

As well as using Home Sharing to share your iTunes library with your other Macs and PCs, you can use iTunes' standard sharing features to share either your whole music library or one or more playlists you've created. In standard sharing, other people can play the items you're sharing, but they can't copy them to their computers.

4.22 In the Home Sharing Settings dialog, choose which types of items you purchase from the iTunes Store you want to transfer automatically to another library.

Here's how to tell iTunes to share some — or all — of your songs and to show you which songs other people on your network are sharing:

1. **Choose iTunes ⇨ Preferences.** The iTunes Preferences dialog appears.

2. **Click the Sharing button to display Sharing preferences (see Figure 4.23).**

3. **If you want to share songs from your iMac, select the Share my library on my local network check box.** Choose which songs to share and whether to use a password:

   - **Select the Share entire library option if you want to share all your songs.** Otherwise, select the Share selected playlists option, and select the check box for each playlist you want to share. Sharing carefully chosen playlists is often more effective than sharing your whole library.

   - **Select the Require password check box if you want to password-protect your library.** Type the password in the text box. If you're sharing in a home with only a few computers, you may not need to use a password. If your iMac is on a bigger network, you may need to restrict access to only those who know the password.

4. **Click the General button to display the General preferences.** In the Library Name text box, type the name under which you want the shared library to appear on the network.

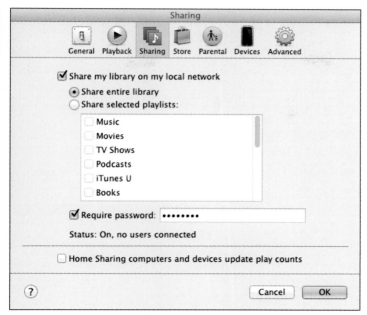

Sharing

| General | Playback | Sharing | Store | Parental | Devices | Advanced |

☑ Share my library on my local network
　⦿ Share entire library
　◯ Share selected playlists:

　　☐ Music
　　☐ Movies
　　☐ TV Shows
　　☐ Podcasts
　　☐ iTunes U
　　☐ Books

☑ Require password: ••••••••

Status: On, no users connected

☐ Home Sharing computers and devices update play counts

(?)　　　　　　　　　　　　　Cancel　　OK

4.23 iTunes' Sharing preferences let you turn on both sharing of your own library and looking for others' shared libraries.

5. **Click OK to close the dialog and apply the sharing.** If iTunes displays a reminder that "Sharing music is for personal use only," select the Do Not Show This Message Again option, and then click OK.

Genius

Once you've chosen to share some playlists, you can quickly share others you create. Simply Control+click or right-click the playlist you want to share, and then click Share (placing a check mark next to Share). To stop sharing a playlist, Control+click or right-click it, and then click Share again (removing the check mark).

Libraries that other iTunes users on your network are sharing appear in the Shared category in the Source list in iTunes. If the Shared category is collapsed, move the mouse pointer over it, and then click the word Show that appears.

Click the shared library you want. If iTunes displays the Shared Library Password dialog, type the password, select the Remember Password check box if you want iTunes to store the password, and then click OK.

Avoiding iTunes' Restrictions for Sharing Music

One reason you may want to use a password on your shared music is that iTunes lets you share with only five other computers per day. On any but the smallest network, this can be limiting. (The sixth person who tries to connect sees a message saying that the library "accepts only five different users each day." This restriction is for copyright reasons.)

If you find iTunes' five-users-per-day restriction too much of a bind, consider setting up a music server for sharing the music. By storing the music files on the server and adding them to iTunes from there, each person in the household can enjoy the songs without having to use iTunes' own sharing.

After iTunes displays the library's contents (see Figure 4.24), you can browse through them and play the songs you want to hear. If you want to open a shared library in a separate window rather than in the main iTunes window, double-click it.

4.24 You can use the same techniques to browse a shared music library as your own library.

When you finish using a shared library, disconnect from it by clicking the Eject button next to its name in the Source list.

154

Transmitting music with AirPlay

In the AirPort Express, Apple produced an ingenious solution to the problem of having several computers that can play music, but only one set of speakers to play the music through. You simply plug the speakers into the AirPort Express, and send the music across the network to the AirPort to play it. Apple calls this feature AirPlay.

After you set up the AirPort Express as described in this chapter and connect your speakers to the combined analog and optical input, you can transmit music to it across the wireless network. In iTunes, simply choose the AirPort from the Speakers pop-up menu that appears on the right side of the iTunes status bar when an AirPort is available. Choose Computer in the Speakers pop-up menu when you want to switch back.

Note To play iTunes music through your iMac as well as AirPort Express speakers, choose Multiple Speakers from the Speakers pop-up menu. In the Remote Speakers dialog that appears, select the check box for each set of speakers you want to use, and then click Close.

If you have connected your AirPort Express to an Ethernet network, you need to enable AirPlay before you can play music this way. Here's what to do:

1. **Click Finder on the Dock, choose Go ⇨ Utilities, and then double-click AirPort Utility.** AirPort Utility opens.

2. **Click AirPort Express in the list box, and then click Manual Setup.** The configuration screen appears.

3. **Click the Music button in the toolbar.**

4. **Select the Enable AirPlay check box.**

5. **If you want to protect the speakers with a password, type the password in the iTunes Speaker Password box and the Verify Password box.**

6. **Click Update.** AirPort Utility updates the AirPort Express's configuration.

7. **Quit AirPort Utility.** Press ⌘+Q.

Genius If you want to send audio to the AirPort Express from a source other than iTunes, look at Airfoil from Rogue Amoeba (www.rogueamoeba.com/airfoil/mac). This is great if you want to listen to web music sites such as Pandora (www.pandora.com) or services such as Spotify (www.spotify.com).

Viewing Mac content on Apple TV

After you connect your Apple TV to your TV, configure it, and connect it to your network either via its built-in Wi-Fi card or via an Ethernet cable, you need to pair the Apple TV with iTunes before you can view content from your Mac on Apple TV.

Here's how to pair the Apple TV with iTunes:

1. **Launch iTunes on your iMac.**
2. **In the Source list, expand the Devices list if it's collapsed, and click Apple TV.**
3. **When prompted for the passcode, type the five digits that appear on the TV screen.**

After pairing, you can browse the music, TV shows, movies, and so on in your iTunes library directly from the Apple TV. Similarly, you can browse the photos in your iPhoto library, and play back slide shows with music.

Note   You can make your Apple TV work with any remote control by holding down Menu and Previous/Rewind on that remote for 6 seconds. If the status light on the Apple TV flashes amber, the remote you're trying to use isn't paired with the Apple TV. When you're using a paired remote, the status light flashes white.

Creating an Ad Hoc Network

Mac OS X makes it easy to set up an ad hoc (temporary) network quickly so that you can share files, devices, or your Internet connection. You can set up a temporary network using Wi-Fi, FireWire, or Ethernet.

After you make the connection, you can share Internet access or devices, as discussed in this chapter. For example, by turning on Internet Sharing on one of the Macs and selecting the appropriate check box (Wi-Fi, Ethernet, or FireWire) in the To Computers Using list, you can allow the other Mac to access the Internet via the first Mac's Internet connection. You can also share devices with Windows computers by using Bonjour for Windows.

Using Wi-Fi

Wi-Fi is often the easiest choice for an ad hoc network, because you can get good performance without needing to string cables among the computers.

To set up an ad hoc network using Wi-Fi, first create the network on one Mac like this:

1. **Open the Wi-Fi menulet, and click Create Network.** The Create a computer-to-computer network dialog appears (see Figure 4.25).

2. **Type the network name in the Name box.**

3. **Choose 128-bit WEP in the Security pop-up menu.** 40-bit WEP is too weak to offer enough protection.

4. **Type a 13-character password in the Password box and the Confirm Password box.** You can type 26 hexadecimal digits (0 to 9, A to F) instead, but a regular password is much easier to remember.

5. **Click Create.** Mac OS X creates the network and closes the dialog.

Create a computer-to-computer network.
Enter the name and security type of the network you want to create.

Network Name: Home Wireless
Channel: 11
Security: 128-bit WEP
Password: ••••••••••••
Confirm Password: ••••••••••••

The password must be entered as exactly 13 ASCII characters or 26 hex digits.

Cancel   Create

4.25 It takes only a minute to set up an ad hoc wireless network using your iMac.

Genius

On the Create a computer-to-computer network dialog, leave the Channel set to Automatic (11) at first. If you find that computers have difficulty connecting to the network, it may be because the airwaves are full. In this case, try setting up the network again using a different channel, and see if connections improve.

Next, connect your iMac (and your other Macs) to the wireless network using the techniques discussed in this chapter. When Mac OS X prompts you for the WEP password (see Figure 4.26), type it, and click OK.

To disconnect from the wireless network, open the Wi-Fi menulet and choose the Disconnect From command.

The Wi-Fi network "Home Wireless" requires a WEP password.

Password: ••••••••••••

☐ Show password
☑ Remember this network

Cancel   Join

4.26 Other Macs can then join the ad hoc network by giving the right password.

Using FireWire

FireWire is an easy way of connecting two or more Macs that are positioned near each other — preferably in the same room.

To create a FireWire network, connect the Macs via FireWire cables. For FireWire 800 ports, use a nine-pin cable; for FireWire 400 ports, use six-pin cables rather than four-pin cables. Use a FireWire hub if necessary, and make certain that no two Macs are connected to each other twice. (This is easier to do than you might think.)

After you connect the Macs, each automatically assigns itself an IP address in the 169.254.x.x range, which is used for private networks. The Macs can then communicate through the FireWire cables, allowing you to share files, printers, and other hardware.

Using Ethernet

For a small temporary network, you can connect two computers by running a single Ethernet cable between them.

After you connect the cable, each Mac automatically assigns itself an IP address in the 169.254.x.x range, which is used for private networks. The Macs can then communicate through the network cable, allowing you to share files.

Genius

Ideally, the Ethernet cable connecting the two computers should be a crossover cable, one in which some of the wires cross from one position at one end to a different position at the other end. But most modern Macs (and some PCs) are able to detect when they are receiving a signal that should be crossed over, and to automatically redirect the input on the wires that need redirection. This allows you to network two computers by using a standard Ethernet cable without a crossover.

Note

Normally, two Macs connected via an Ethernet cable automatically use DHCP to assign themselves IP addresses. If you find the Macs cannot communicate, open Network preferences, click Ethernet in the left box, and choose Using DHCP from the Configure pop-up menu.

After you make the connection, you can then share Internet access or devices as discussed in this chapter. For example, by turning on Internet Sharing on one of the Macs and selecting the Ethernet option in the To computers using list box, you can allow the other Mac to access the Internet through the first Mac's Internet connection.

Sharing printers with Windows computers

To share printers with Windows computers on your network, you can use Bonjour Print Services for Windows.

Download Bonjour Print Services for Windows from the Apple website (http://support.apple.com/kb/DL999) and follow the installation routine. There are two decisions to make:

- **Create a shortcut.** Choose whether to create a shortcut on the Desktop for the Bonjour Printer Wizard. Usually it's best not to clutter your Desktop and instead run the wizard from the Start menu when you need it.

- **Automatically update Bonjour Printer Services and other Apple software.** Usually updating the software is a good idea, but you may prefer to apply updates manually at a time of your choosing.

After you install Bonjour for Windows, you can

- **View a list of Bonjour resources in Internet Explorer.** Click the Bonjour button on the Internet Explorer toolbar to display the Bonjour pane. Click a resource in the Bonjour pane to access it.

- **Connect to a shared printer by running the Bonjour Printer Wizard (see Figure 4.27).** To run the wizard, choose Start ⇨ All Programs ⇨ Bonjour ⇨ Bonjour Printer Wizard.

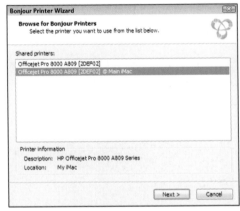

4.27 Use the Bonjour Printer Wizard to connect Windows PCs to printers your Macs are sharing.

How Can I Use My iMac as an Entertainment Center?

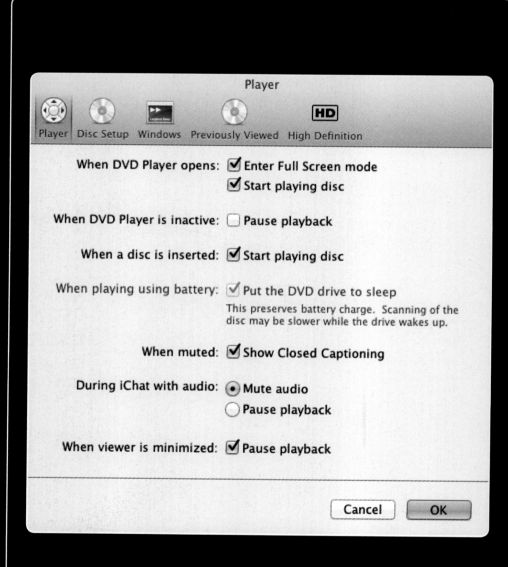

With its large, widescreen display and built-in speakers, plus the Apple Remote (if you have one), your iMac makes a great entertainment center right out of the box — but I'm betting you want to do more than that. This chapter explains how to extend your iMac to play music through external speakers or your home stereo, make the most of the DVD Player application, play video on a video projector or a television, or even watch TV right on your iMac.

Playing Music with iTunes

iTunes, your iMac's main application for playing music, is straightforward to use at its simplest but packs plenty of power, especially if you make the most of playlists, as discussed in Chapter 6.

To start with, iTunes plays music through your iMac's built-in speakers, which you may find enough when you're working at the iMac. But to enjoy your iMac as an entertainment center, you'll probably want to use external speakers to give as much deep, thundering bass and crisp, clear highs as your neighbors can tolerate. You 2nd can play music back through external speakers in either of two ways:

- **Connect the speakers to your iMac.** The most direct solution is to connect a set of amplified speakers to your iMac's audio port. All the sound output then goes through the speakers, and you can crank up the volume as far as you need.

Genius
Instead of connecting the iMac directly to amplified speakers, you can connect its output to the receiver in your home stereo so that you can play through the speakers connected to the stereo.

- **Play through AirPlay on AirPort Express.** If you have an AirPort Express wireless access point, you can connect your speakers to its audio port and play music through them from your iMac by using the AirPlay feature. See Chapter 4 for details. The advantage of this arrangement is that you can switch the iTunes output from your iMac's speakers (or speakers you've connected directly to your iMac) to the speakers connected to AirPort — for example, to play in a different room.

Genius
An AirPort Express can be a great addition to your network because you can also play music through it from an iPhone, iPad, or iPod touch.

Pairing the Apple Remote with Your iMac

If you have more than one Apple Remote or more than one Mac in the same room or area, pair your iMac with your remote so that it will only respond to that remote. To pair a device and a remote, follow these steps:

1. **Choose Apple menu ➪ System Preferences.** The System Preferences window opens.

2. **In the Personal section, click the Security & Privacy icon to display Security & Privacy preferences.**

3. **Click the General tab to display the General pane.**

4. **If the preferences are locked, click the padlock icon to unlock them and authenticate yourself.**

5. **Click the Pair button.** Mac OS X then displays a message box telling you to press the Menu and Next buttons on the remote.

6. **Press and hold down the Menu button and the Next button for about 5 seconds, until the message box disappears and an icon showing a remote and a couple of chain links appears on screen.**

7. **Quit System Preferences.** Press ⌘+Q.

To remove the pairing, click the Unpair button in the General pane of Security preferences. To prevent a Mac from responding to an Apple Remote, select the Disable remote control infrared receiver check box in the General pane.

Adding TV to Your iMac

If you want to make your iMac a total entertainment center, add TV to it by connecting a TV tuner. You can then watch TV on your iMac rather than on a TV, pausing live TV and recording shows as needed.

Apple doesn't make a TV tuner, so you'll need to buy a third-party tuner. That means the first thing to look for is Mac compatibility, as many models of TV tuner work only with Windows. You can get around this concern by buying a model sold by the Apple Store, which lists only Mac-compatible models.

When choosing a TV tuner, there are four main features to look for:

- **Analog and digital reception.** With analog signals gradually being phased out, get a tuner that provides digital reception as well.

- **USB connection.** Most current models of TV tuners connect to your iMac via USB. As long as your iMac has a USB port free, you're in business.

- **Hardware encoding.** More-expensive TV tuners include hardware encoders that do the hard work of converting the TV signal into a format your iMac can play. Less-expensive tuners require your iMac to do the encoding, which may slow it down, especially if it's working hard on other tasks for you at the time.

- **Storage.** Some TV tuners include built-in storage for recorded TV programs, which is useful if you want to be able to move the tuner (and recorded programs) from one Mac to another. Others store the TV programs on your iMac. This works well provided your iMac has plenty of free space.

Beyond these key features, some TV tuners provide automatic export of recorded programs to iTunes (from which you can synchronize them with an iPhone, iPad, or iPod), the ability to stream TV to an iPhone, iPad, or iPod touch or start a recording from one of these devices, or software for editing recorded programs (for example, to remove ads or other unwanted content).

Watching Video on Your iMac

Your iMac comes with iTunes and QuickTime Player already installed, so you can play most kinds of video files immediately:

- **iTunes.** If the video file is one you've downloaded from the iTunes Store or added to iTunes, you can play the video in iTunes by double-clicking it. To add a video file to iTunes, either click the file in a Finder window and drag it to the Library section of the iTunes source list, or choose File ⇨ Add to Library, click the file in the Add To Library dialog, and then click Choose.

Note QuickTime Player can play many video formats, but you may need to add another player for formats that QuickTime Player doesn't support. For example, download Windows Media Player from the Microsoft website (free; www.microsoft.com/mac/downloads.mspx) to play files in the widely used Windows Media Video (WMV) format. The VLC player (free, www.videolan.org) can also play a wide variety of video formats.

- **QuickTime.** If you haven't added the video file to iTunes, open a Finder window to the folder that contains the file. Control+click or right-click the file, and then choose Open With ⇨ QuickTime Player to open the file in QuickTime Player. Click the Play button to start playback.

Both iTunes and QuickTime can play either in a window or full screen:

- **iTunes.** Choose View ⇨ Full Screen, press ⌘+F, or click the button on the control bar that shows two arrows pointing in opposite directions to switch to full screen. To return to the window, click the X button that appears in the upper-left corner of the screen when you move the mouse, press either Esc or ⌘+F again, or click the button on the control bar that shows two arrows pointing toward each other.

- **QuickTime.** Choose View ⇨ Enter Full screen or press ⌘+F to switch to full screen. To return to the window, press Esc, press ⌘+F, or click the button that shows two arrows pointing toward each other.

Watching DVDs with DVD Player

DVD Player, the DVD-playing application that comes with Mac OS X, springs to life when you insert a playable DVD in your iMac's drive. DVD Player is easy to use, either with the control panel it displays when playing in a window or the control bar that you can pop up by using the mouse when playing full screen, but it also includes helpful features such as marking points of interest with bookmarks and resuming playback where you stopped playing a DVD last time. You may also need to deal with DVDs encoded for different sales regions — and if you have an Apple Remote, you'll almost certainly want to control DVD Player with it.

Note

Your iMac's DVD drive doesn't play Blu-ray DVDs, because Apple has chosen not to support Blu-ray.

Controlling whether DVD Player opens and starts automatically

If you prefer not to have DVD Player launch automatically when you insert a DVD, follow these steps:

1. **Choose Apple menu ⇨ System Preferences.** The System Preferences window opens.

2. **In the Hardware section, click the CDs & DVDs icon to open CDs & DVDs preferences (see Figure 5.1).**

5.1 In CDs & DVDs preferences, you can choose not to launch DVD Player when you insert a DVD, or to open another application instead.

3. **Open the When you insert a video DVD pop-up menu and choose Ignore instead of Open DVD Player.**

4. **Quit System Preferences.** Press ⌘+Q.

If you want DVD Player to open automatically when you insert a DVD but not start playing the DVD until you're ready, follow these steps:

1. **Open DVD Player.**

2. **Choose DVD Player ⇨ Preferences to display the Preferences dialog.**

3. **Click the Player tab to display the Player pane (shown on the opening page of this chapter).**

4. **In the When DVD Player opens area at the top, deselect the Start playing disc check box.**

5. **Click OK to close the Preferences dialog.**

Marking a point in a DVD

If you want to mark a point in a DVD so that you can easily return to it, create a bookmark like this:

1. **Choose Controls ⇨ New Bookmark or press ⌘+= to display the Bookmark dialog (see Figure 5.2).** You don't need to pause playback — DVD Player does that for you automatically.

2. **In the Bookmark text box, type a descriptive name for the bookmark.**

3. **If you want to make this bookmark your default bookmark for this DVD, select the Make Default Bookmark check box.**

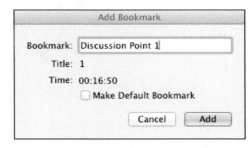

5.2 You can create a bookmark at any point in the DVD to which you want to return easily.

4. **Click Add.** DVD Player closes the dialog and resumes playback if the DVD was playing.

To return to a bookmark, choose Go ⇨ Bookmarks, and then click the bookmark on the Bookmarks submenu. To go straight to your default bookmark, choose Go ⇨ Default Bookmark. To browse bookmarks visually when DVD Player is playing full screen, move the mouse pointer to the top of the window, and then click the second icon in the upper-left corner.

Genius

If you need to play a particular DVD often, create a default bookmark at its beginning. You can use this bookmark to skip the trailers and anti-piracy notices that plague commercial DVDs.

Resuming playback on a DVD

When you insert a DVD that you've played before, DVD Player recognizes it and automatically starts playing it back from where you last stopped.

If having playback restart automatically doesn't suit you, change it. Follow these steps:

1. **Choose DVD Player ⇨ Preferences to display the Preferences dialog.**

2. **Click the Previously View tab to display the Previously Viewed pane (see Figure 5.3).**

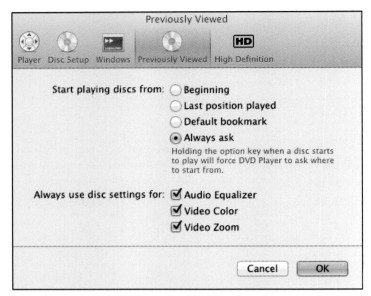

5.3 In the Previously Viewed pane in DVD Player's Preferences dialog, select the Always ask option to make DVD Player ask where you want to resume playing the disc.

3. **In the Start playing discs from area, select the appropriate option button: Beginning, Last position played, Default bookmark, or Always ask.** Selecting the Always ask option makes DVD Player display the dialog shown in Figure 5.4 when you insert a disc and gives you the most flexibility. You can click Last Time Played to pick up where you left off, click Beginning of Disc to start at the beginning of the disc as usual, Default Bookmark to start at a default bookmark you've set, or Cancel to dismiss the dialog without starting playback.

4. **Click OK to close the Preferences dialog.**

5.4 DVD Player's Last Time Played button lets you restart playback where you left off.

Dealing with DVDs from different regions

To reduce DVD piracy and discourage people from buying cheaper DVDs from other parts of the world, the DVD industry uses regional coding. Most DVDs are encoded for one of seven regions, the first six geographical and the seventh for international vehicles (such as airplanes and cruise ships).

Your iMac's DVD drive comes set to play DVDs that have your region's encoding. For example, if you live in the United States or Canada, you're in DVD region 1, so your iMac's DVD drive comes set to play region 1 DVDs. You can change the drive's region, but you can do so only five times; after that, the drive remains locked on the region you last changed to.

If you insert a DVD coded for another region, DVD Player displays the Drive Region dialog (see Figure 5.5), showing the drive's current region and the region the DVD is coded for. You can unlock the drive by clicking the padlock and authenticating yourself in the dialog that appears. After that, you can click Set Drive Region to set the drive's region to the DVD's region (or another region you choose in the Change drive region to pop-up menu).

If you click Cancel in the Drive Region dialog, DVD Player ejects the DVD.

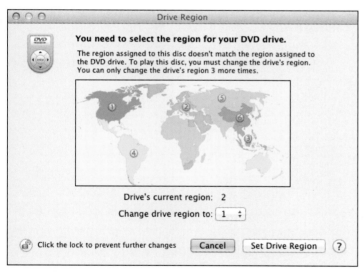

5.5 DVD Player warns you if your DVD drive is set to the wrong region for the DVD you want to play.

Genius

If you buy DVDs from another DVD region, consider getting an external DVD drive to use for that region so that you don't have to switch DVD regions on your iMac's built-in drive and run out of changes.

Controlling DVD Player with the Apple Remote

No surprises here — the Apple Remote does pretty much the same things for your iMac running DVD Player that your DVD player's remote does for it. The buttons have two sets of functions, one for when video's playing and another that kicks in when you're navigating a DVD's menu screens. Check out Table 5.1 for the full set of functions.

Table 5.1 Apple Remote Functions in DVD Player

Button	On a Menu Screen	While Playing Media
Select/Play/Pause	Select an item in a menu or list.	Play and pause audio or video.
Next/Fast-Forward		Go to the next DVD chapter. *Or* Press and hold to fast-forward.
Previous/Rewind		Go to the previous DVD chapter or the beginning of the current chapter. *Or* Press and hold to rewind.
Volume Up	Move up in a menu.	Turn Mac system volume up.
Volume Down	Move down in a menu.	Turn Mac system volume down.
Menu	Press and hold to resume playback where you left off.	Press and hold to back up to the previous menu screen.

Showing Your iMac's Output on a Video Projector

For the ultimate big-screen viewing experience, you can hook up a digital video projector to your iMac. These are great for watching sports events or movies, or for playing games. But they're less practical for everyday use, because you typically have to change the bulb every 1,000 to 2,000 hours of viewing time. Projectors start at well under $500 at this writing, and they come in two types: LCD (liquid crystal display, as usual) and DLP (Digital Light Processing).

LCD projectors, with their small sizes and low power consumption, are what started a drop in projector prices, but DLP is now more popular. DLP projectors give better image quality and are based on the same technology used in movie theaters for displaying digital films. The quality of an image projected by a theater-type projector is almost as good as that produced by an old-fashioned film projector — only without any scratches.

Eliminating Problems with Projectors

When using a projector, you can avoid most problems by being prepared and taking your time:

- **Bring every adapter you might need.** When you will use someone else's projector, arm yourself with every video adapter in sight to make sure you're covered.

- **Turn off the iMac.** Turn off your iMac while plugging in the video connector, and be sure to plug everything in firmly. Wait a minute after turning on the projector before restarting the iMac.

- **Turn off your screen saver and the Energy Saver sleep function.** Choose Apple menu ⇨ System Preferences, click the Desktop & Screen Saver icon, and then click the Screen Saver tab. Click and drag the Start screen saver slider to the Never position on the right so that the screen saver won't kick in. Click the Show All button at the top of the window, click the Energy Saver icon, and then click and drag the Computer sleep slider and the Display sleep slider all the way to the Never position. Quit System Preferences.

You connect a video projector to your iMac in the same way you connect a second monitor. Find out which type of connection the video projector uses — Mini DisplayPort or DVI connections are the best because they're digital, but many projectors use analog VGA, S-video, or composite connections — then find or buy the type of adapter needed to connect the projector to your iMac's Mini DisplayPort.

The following list shows the three types of adapter and connection you're most likely to need. You can buy these from the Apple Store (http://store.apple.com) or from computer stores either online or offline.

- **Mini DisplayPort to DVI adapter.** If you're lucky enough to have a projector with a DVI input, get this adapter.

- **Mini DisplayPort to VGA adapter.** Use this adapter to connect your iMac to a projector with an old-style VGA input.

- **Mini DisplayPort to VGA adapter and a VGA adapter cable.** For a projector that uses S-video or composite video connectors, you first need to use a Mini DisplayPort to VGA adapter, and then an adapter from VGA to S-video or composite.

After your projector is plugged in and you see a signal, set up the projector as you would set up a display:

1. **Choose Apple menu ⇨ System Preferences.** The System Preferences window opens.

2. **In the Hardware section, click the Displays icon to open Displays preferences.**

3. **Click the Arrangement tab to display the Arrangement pane.**

4. **Select the Mirror Displays check box if you want the projector to show the same picture that's on the Mac's screen.** Deselect this check box if you want the projector to display an extended desktop.

5. **In the Display preferences window that appears on the projector's screen, click the Display tab, and then choose the right resolution for the projector.** You may also need to change the refresh rate for the projector.

6. **Quit System Preferences.** Press ⌘+Q.

Showing Your iMac's Output on a Television

If you don't have a projector but you have a large-screen TV, you can show your iMac's output on the TV. This can be great for watching movies or videos with more people than can fit comfortably around your iMac's screen.

How you connect the iMac to the TV depends on what kind of TV you have and how old it is. Most cathode-ray tube TVs connect via an analog connection (such as an S-video connection, a component video connection, or a VGA connection) and produce a blurry, flickering picture, so you're usually better off using a newer, flat-panel TV — especially as a flat-panel TV is more likely to have a digital input (such as a DVI port or an HDMI port) that you can easily connect your iMac to.

For each of these options, you need to use one or more adapters to get the signal from the iMac to the TV. Here's what to shop for:

- **Mini DisplayPort to DVI adapter.** Use this type of adapter to connect your iMac to a DVI input on a TV.

- **Mini DisplayPort to HDMI adapter.** Use this adapter combination to connect your iMac to an HDMI input on a TV.

- **Mini DisplayPort to VGA adapter, and a VGA adapter cable.** For a TV that uses S-video or composite video connectors, you first need to use a Mini DisplayPort to VGA adapter, and then an adapter from VGA to S-video or composite.

After you make the connection, set up the TV using the same technique as for a projector. See the previous section for details.

What Can I Do with My Digital Images and Music?

It's easy to get started with iPhoto and iTunes, but they both include advanced features for making the most of your digital images and your music. Did you ever wonder how to create slide shows using iPhoto and iMovie? Or how to publish your photos? What about how to use them in screen savers on your Desktop or as window backgrounds? This chapter tells you all this and more, including how to access and use specialized iTunes features for playing back your music and sharing it. Even the Visualizer has some tricks up its sleeve, which you can learn about in this chapter.

Displaying and Publishing Photos

To get the most enjoyment out of your photos, you can create either instant slide shows or more complex slide shows. You can share photos with specific people via email or on your account on Facebook or Flickr. You can also display your photos on your iMac's Desktop, make screen savers and account icons from them, or even use them as backgrounds in Finder windows.

Making an instant slide show

After you transfer some photos from your digital camera to your iMac, you probably want to kick back and check them out full screen. To do so, you can use iPhoto's feature for setting up an instant slide show:

1. **Open iPhoto and select the photos you want to include in the slide show.** For example, to make a slide show of the last batch of photos you imported, click the Last Import item in the Source list.

2. **Click the Slideshow button on the toolbar across the bottom of the iPhoto window.** iPhoto displays the first slide full screen and opens the Slideshow dialog with the Themes tab selected (see Figure 6.1).

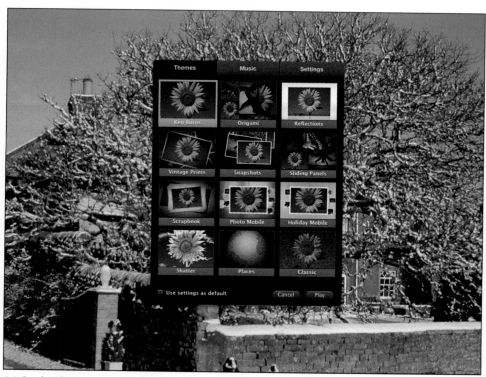

6.1 On the Themes tab of the Slideshow dialog, pick the overall theme for the slide show.

3. **Click the Classic theme or the Ken Burns theme.**

   - **Classic uses a simple transition between slides with no fancy effects.** This is the best choice if you want to concentrate purely on the photos.

   - **Ken Burns automatically applies a small pan-and-zoom effect to add visual interest.** This is good for engaging the audience's attention if your photos lack zip.

4. **Click the Music tab of the dialog (see Figure 6.2).**

6.2 On the Music tab of the Slideshow dialog, choose the music for the slide show. If you prefer silence, deselect the Play music during slideshow check box.

Genius

The ten other themes are more dramatic and intrusive than Classic and Ken Burns. For example, Scrapbook presents the photos at different angles, with some overlaid on others; Shatter uses in-your-face spinning transitions between photos; and Snapshots lays each new photo at an angle on top of the previous photo, making a stack of photos that moves slowly up the screen.

5. **Select the Play music during slideshow check box if you want music with the slideshow.** To contemplate the photos in peace, deselect this check box and skip the next step.

6. **Choose the song you want to play from the Sample Music folder, the Theme Music folder, your GarageBand compositions, or your iTunes library.** You can search by using the Search box, and preview music by clicking Play. If you've already created a playlist in iTunes for the slide show, choose iTunes Playlists, and then click the playlist.

Note

To create a custom playlist for the slide show, select the Custom Playlist for Slideshow check box. The dialog then displays a list box at the bottom. Click and drag the songs you want into this list box, and then click and drag them into your preferred order.

7. **Click the Settings tab to bring it to the front of the dialog (see Figure 6.3).**

8. **In the Play each slide for a minimum of box, choose how many seconds you want to display each slide for.** If you prefer to let the length of the music you choose dictate the timing, select the Fit slideshow to music option instead.

9. **If you want to use transitions between slides, follow these steps:**

   ● **Select the Transition check box.**

   ● **In the Transition pop-up menu, choose the transition.** None is a good choice when you're simply

6.3 On the Settings tab, choose timings, transitions, and other settings for your slide show.

reviewing your photos and don't need effects. For consistent effects, choose a transition such as Dissolve, Flip, or Twirl. If you're feeling more adventurous, choose Random to have iPhoto pick a different transition for each change of slide.

   ● **Look to see whether the four direction buttons are available (the arrows are white) or unavailable (the arrows are gray).** If two or more directions are available, click the direction you want to use for the transition.

   ● **Drag the Speed slider to set the speed of the transition.**

Note

The options available on the Settings tab change depending on which theme you have chosen on the Themes tab. The options discussed here are for the Classic theme and the Ken Burns theme.

10. **Choose other options to make the slide show run the way you want:**

   ● **If you want to include captions, select the Show Caption check box.** In the pop-up menu, choose the text: Titles, Descriptions, Titles and Descriptions, Places, or Dates.

   ● **Select the Show title slide check box if you want to have a title slide at the beginning of the show.**

- **Choose whether to shuffle the slides into a different order and whether to repeat the slide show when it reaches the end.**

- **Select the Scale photos to fill screen check box if you want to make each photo fill the screen.** Usually it's best not to do this, because scaling the photos often distorts them.

- **Select the Use settings as default check box if you want to apply the settings you choose to all slide shows in the future (unless you change them).** This check box appears on all three tabs, so you need to select or deselect it only once.

11. **Click Play.** iPhoto closes the Slideshow dialog and starts playing the slides.

12. **Use the pop-up controls at the bottom of the screen (see Figure 6.4) to control the slide show.** You can

    - **Pause the slide show and then restart it.**

    - **Move backward or forward through the photos by clicking the Previous button and the Next button.**

6.4 Use the pop-up controls at the bottom of the screen to control the slide show.

    - **Move the mouse pointer to the bottom of the window, and then click another photo on the bar that appears.**

    - **Open the Themes tab, Music tab, or Settings tab of the Slideshow dialog.**

13. **Press Esc or click anywhere outside the control bar to end the slide show.**

Creating and saving a custom slide show

Running a quick slide show, as described in the previous section, is great for quickly going through photos to see how they are. But when you want to create a slide show in which you choose the order of the photos and control exactly how long and in what way each appears, you need to take a different approach.

To create a slide show and save it for future use, follow these steps:

1. **Click the album on which you want to base the slide show, or select the photos you want to use.**

2. **Click the Create button in the lower-right corner of the iPhoto window to open the Create pop-up panel, and then click the Slideshow button.** iPhoto adds the slide show to the Slideshows category in the Source list, gives it a default name, and displays the Slideshow toolbar (see Figure 6.5).

6.5 Ready to create a slide show with custom settings.

3. **Type the name for the slide show over the default name and press Return.**

4. **Choose the theme for the slide show.** Click the Themes button, choose the theme in the Choose a Slideshow Theme dialog, and then click the Choose button.

5. **Choose the music — or lack of it — for the slide show:**

   ● **Click the Music button to display the Music dialog, which closely resembles the Music tab of the Slideshow dialog (shown earlier in this chapter).**

   ● **To use music, select the Play music during slideshow check box, and then choose the song or playlist.** If you want to create a custom playlist, select the Custom Playlist for Slideshow check box, and then assemble the playlist in the list box that opens.

   ● **Click the Choose button to close the dialog.**

6. **Choose default settings for the whole slideshow:**

   - **Click the Settings button to display the Slideshow Settings dialog (see Figure 6.6).** Make sure the All Slides tab is at the front.

   - **Set the number of seconds to display each slide for, or select the Fit slideshow to music option to have iPhoto automatically divide the length of the music by the number of slides and apply the result.**

   - **To use transitions, select the Transition check box.** Choose the transition in the pop-up menu, and pick a direction if the direction buttons are available. Drag the Speed slider to set the default speed.

6.6 Choose default settings for a slide show before you adjust the settings for individual slides.

- **Choose whether to show captions (and if so, choose which text in the pop-up menu) and a title slide.**

- **Choose whether to repeat the slide show and whether to scale the photos to fill the screen (which may distort them).**

- **In the Aspect Ratio pop-up menu, choose This Screen if you want to display the slide show on your iMac's screen.** Otherwise, choose the HDTV (16:9) format for HDTV or widescreen displays, the iPad/TV (4:3) format for an iPad or a regular-format TV, or the iPhone (3:2) format for the iPhone and iPod touch.

- **Leave the Slideshow Settings Options dialog open for the moment.**

7. **In the filmstrip at the top, drag the pictures into the order in which you want them to play.** Put the first slide on the left.

8. **Click the first picture, click the This Slide tab in the Slideshow Settings dialog (see Figure 6.7), and then choose settings for the slide:**

- **Effect.** To apply an effect to the slide, choose Black and White, Sepia, or Antique.

- **Duration.** To override the setting you've applied to the slide show as a whole, select the Play this slide for check box, and then set the number of seconds in the text box.

- **Transition.** To use a different transition between this slide and the next than the default transition you've applied to the slide show, select the Transition check box. Open the pop-up menu and choose the transition you want. To change the speed, drag the Speed slider. To change the direction, click one of the available direction buttons.

6.7 The This Slide tab of the Slideshow Settings dialog lets you apply an effect to the slide, control how long it appears, add a transition, and apply the Ken Burns effect.

- **Ken Burns.** Select this check box if you want to use the panning and zooming effect on this slide. If necessary, zoom by dragging the Size slider in the main iPhoto window, and then drag the picture to where you want its starting position to be. Move the Start/End switch on the This Slide tab of the Slideshow Settings dialog to the End position, and then drag and zoom in the main iPhoto window to set the end position.

9. **Close the Slideshow Settings dialog and click the Preview button on the toolbar to preview the effect for the slide.** If needed, reopen the dialog and change the settings.

10. **Reopen the Slideshow Settings dialog and repeat Step 10 for each of the other slides in the slide show.**

11. **Click the Play button when you're ready to view your slide show.**

iPhoto automatically saves the changes you make to your slide show, so you don't need to save them manually.

Note

Using iMovie to Make Complex Slide Shows

As you saw earlier in this chapter, iPhoto's custom slide shows give you enough control over each slide to easily make a powerful slide show.

But if you need even greater control over how the slides in the presentation appear and how they behave, you can also use iMovie to create a slide show. For complex slide shows, iMovie offers several advantages over iPhoto, of which the following are usually the most important:

- **A custom soundtrack.** Instead of using just one source of music (a song or playlist from iTunes, one of your GarageBand compositions, or whatever), you can arrange multiple background tracks in iMovie. This lets you match the slides to the music (or narration) much more exactly.

- **Sound effects for particular slides.** Apart from the soundtrack, you can add sound effects to the slide show exactly where they'll deliver maximum effect.

- **Greater control over Ken Burns effects.** If you find iPhoto's method of controlling Ken Burns effects difficult, try using iMovie instead. Not only are the controls easier to use, but also you can create a sequence of Ken Burns effects for the same photo — for example, you can pan right while zooming in on one feature in a photo, then pan to the right while holding the zoom, and finally zoom back out and pan to show the whole photo.

- **Better export options.** From iMovie, you can easily export a slide show to a variety of movie formats so that you can distribute the slide show in whichever media you need to.

Controlling iPhoto with the Apple Remote

Running a slide show using the keyboard or mouse works well when you're the only one watching, but when you're running the slide show for an audience, you'll probably want to use the Apple Remote (if you have one) so that you can conjure up the magic from a distance.

Select the photos you want, and then press the Play/Pause button to start the slide show. You can then use the Previous button and Next button to navigate from slide to slide, use the volume buttons to control the volume, or press and hold the Menu button for a couple of seconds to end the slide show.

Genius

You can also use the Apple Remote's Previous button and Next button to navigate from photo to photo in iPhoto's viewing area. The Previous button moves the focus to the photo above the current one, and the Next button moves the focus to the photo below the current one. To make this work well, zoom so that there is only one column of photos in the iPhoto viewing area.

Emailing photos from iPhoto

You can email photos from Mac OS X's Mail application by using Mail's Photo Browser (choose Window ⇨ Photo Browser), but when you're working in iPhoto, you can use iPhoto's method of starting a message and its extra features for making the message attractive.

Setting up iPhoto to use the right email account

Before you can send photos from iPhoto, you need to set up iPhoto to use the right email account. Follow these steps:

1. **Select the photo or photos you want to send.** If you simply click in an album or other collection, iPhoto assumes you want to use all the photos it contains. Often, this is too many photos to email.

2. **Click the Share button to display the Share pop-up panel, and then click Email.** iPhoto displays the Do you want to set up iPhoto to Email photos? dialog (see Figure 6.8).

3. **Click the button for the type of email account you want to set up: MobileMe, Hotmail, Yahoo! Mail, Gmail, AOL Mail, or Other.**

6.8 In the Do you want to set up iPhoto to Email photos? dialog, click your email provider, and then click the Setup button.

Genius
You can also set up iPhoto to use the right email account by choosing iPhoto ⇨ Preferences, clicking the Accounts button on the toolbar, and then working in the Accounts pane. Use this method when you need to add further accounts for sending email. For setting up the first account, it's easiest to choose Share ⇨ Email command, as described a little later in this chapter.

4. **Click the Setup button.** iPhoto displays a dialog showing the information required to set up the account. Figure 6.9 shows the Add MobileMe Account dialog.

5. **Enter the account details, and then click the Save button.** iPhoto creates a message, which you can then customize and send as discussed next.

6.9 Enter the details of the email account from which you want to send photos, and then click the Save button.

Note
The dialogs for setting up other account types are similar to the Add MobileMe Account dialog, but the Add Other Email Account dialog includes an Outgoing Email Server section. In this section, you fill in your email provider's server address, the port to use, and your user name and password. Consult the provider for this information if you don't have it.

Sending photos via email

Here's how to send photos via email from iPhoto:

1. **Select the photo or photos you want to email.** If the photos are in the same event or album, select the photos by dragging, Shift+clicking, or ⌘+clicking them. If the photos are in different events or albums, select them from the Photos library, flag them, or pull them into their own album.

2. **Click the Share button to display the Share pop-up panel, and then click Email.**
Alternatively, choose Share ⇨ Email from the menu bar. iPhoto creates a new email message containing the photos (see Figure 6.10).

6.10 You can quickly create and send an email message containing one or more photos from your iPhoto library.

3. **In the pane on the right, select the design for the email message.**

4. **In the Photo Size pop-up menu, choose the size you want to send.** Table 6.1 explains the options.

Caution

Check the file size shown in the Mail Photo dialog; some mail servers reject email messages larger than about 5MB. The threshold varies depending on what the mail server's administrator has chosen; some servers allow up to 10MB.

Genius

When the recipient needs to work with the photos you're sending, it's best to choose Actual Size in the Mail Photo dialog. The recipient can then create smaller or lower-quality versions of the photos as needed. The disadvantage to sending full-size photos is that the email message can become huge.

5. **Add any text needed to identify or explain the pictures.** Most of the message designs include placeholders for descriptive text.

6. **Address the message, type a subject and any body text needed, and then click Send.**

Table 6.1 Resolutions and Sizes for Sending Photos Via Email

Size	Resolution (May Vary)	File Size (Approx.)	Use This Option When
Optimized	Original resolution	Original file size (up to several MB)	You want the photos to look as good as possible in the email message, but the recipient will probably not use them for other purposes.
Small (Faster Downloading)	320 × 240 pixels	25KB	Low-resolution photos are enough — for example, when you expect the recipient to view the photos only in the email message.
Medium	640 × 480 pixels	60KB	The recipient needs moderate-quality photos for uses such as web pages.
Large (Higher Quality)	1280 × 960 pixels	180KB	The recipient needs good-quality photos for uses such as web pages but not full-quality photos.
Actual Size (Full Quality)	Original resolution	Original file size (up to several MB)	You want to send the photos as they are — for example, so that the recipient can edit them.

Publishing photos online from iPhoto

iPhoto gives you several easy ways to use your photos online: by posting them to a MobileMe Gallery, by posting them to Flickr, or by posting them to Facebook. To post the photos, select them in iPhoto, click the Share button on the toolbar, and then click the appropriate item on the Share pop-up menu: MobileMe Gallery, Flickr, or Facebook. The first time you give the command, iPhoto walks you through setting up your account. After that, you can publish photos in just a few clicks.

Caution

If you already have a MobileMe account, posting your photos to a MobileMe Gallery is easy, and it gives you fair control over who views them. You can make a MobileMe Gallery album available to everyone who browses your MobileMe galleries, to specific people you choose, or only to those people you give the Gallery's URL. But as Apple will end MobileMe support on June 30, 2012, and the iCloud service that replaces MobileMe doesn't offer Galleries, this is a short-time solution only.

Using color management

When you work with photos and graphics, you want to make sure that the colors you see on your iMac's screen are the same as the colors you get when you print the photos or share them with other people. Otherwise, you can spend ages adjusting a photo so that it looks just perfect on your iMac only to find that it doesn't look right — or even looks bad — on other screens.

To get colors right, you can use the options in your iMac's Color preferences to create custom color profiles and switch among them. You can also apply standardized color profiles that come with Mac OS X. If you connect an external monitor to your iMac, you can create and apply separate display profiles to it.

Creating a ColorSync profile

Here's how to create a ColorSync profile:

1. **Choose Apple menu ⇨ System Preferences.** The System Preferences window opens.

2. **In the Hardware section, click the Displays icon to open the Display preferences.**

3. **Click the Color tab (see Figure 6.11).** If the Show profiles for this display only check box is selected, the Color tab normally shows only your iMac's default display profile (called iMac) and any profiles you've created; if you deselect this check box, the Color tab also lists several standard display profiles, as in the figure.

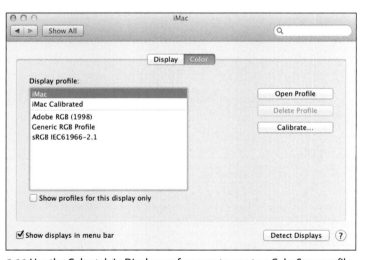

6.11 Use the Color tab in Display preferences to create a ColorSync profile for your iMac's display.

Note If you want other users to be able to use the ColorSync profile you create, log on as an Administrator user and create the color profile using that account. On the Administrator Options screen of the Display Calibrator Assistant, select the Allow other users to use this calibration check box. Otherwise, any ColorSync profile you create is for your user account only.

4. **Click Calibrate.** The Display Calibrator Assistant opens.

5. **Select the Expert Mode check box if you want to set all possible options, including the Native Gamma settings.** If you prefer to set only a subset of options, deselect the Expert Mode check box.

6. **Click Continue, and then work your way through the screens of the Display Calibrator Assistant, clicking Continue when you've chosen settings.** Figure 6.12 shows the first of the five Native Gamma screens that appear only if you selected the Expert Mode check box. The changes you make in the Display Calibrator Assistant apply to your iMac's screen as a whole, not just within the Assistant's window.

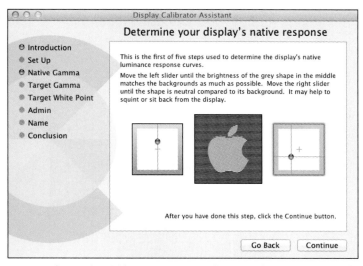

6.12 Use the Display Calibrator Assistant to fine-tune the color balance of your display.

7. **On the Give the profile a name screen of the Assistant, type a descriptive name for the new profile you've created.** This is the name that appears in the Display preferences.

8. **On the Conclusion screen of the Assistant, click Done.** The Assistant closes and adds the new profile to the Display Profile list on the Color tab of Display preferences. The Assistant automatically applies the new profile to the display on which you created it.

Note

The Display Calibrator Assistant lets you set up a custom color profile manually. Another option is to use a tool for calibrating your iMac's color profile automatically, such as the Spyder tools from Datacolor (http://spyder.datacolor.com; prices start around $89). These tools let you apply standard color profiles to your computer quickly and easily.

Switching from one ColorSync profile to another

When you need to switch from one ColorSync profile to another, open Display preferences, click the Color tab, and then click the profile you want.

You can select the Show profiles for this display only option to narrow down the Display Profile list to only the default profile that came with your iMac and custom profiles you've already created.

To see the details of a profile, click it on the Color tab, and then click Open Profile. The ColorSync Utility opens, showing the settings used for different color components. You can then choose File ⇨ Save As to save the profile to another folder as needed, or choose ColorSync Utility ⇨ Quit ColorSync Utility to quit ColorSync Utility.

Note

When you no longer need a profile, delete it. Click the profile on the Color tab of Displays preferences, click Delete Profile, and then click Delete in the Alert dialog that appears. If the Delete button is not available, most likely the profile is not one of yours, but a profile that another Administrator has created and is sharing.

Setting color-management options when printing

When you're ready to print a photo, make sure you use your preferred color profile. Here's how to do so:

1. **Follow through the printing process until you reach the Print dialog.** If the Print dialog appears at its small size, click the down-arrow button to expand it to its full size.

2. **Click the Show Details button to expand the dialog and display the extra print options.**

3. **Open the pop-up menu in the middle of the dialog and choose Color Matching.** The Color Matching options appear (see Figure 6.13).

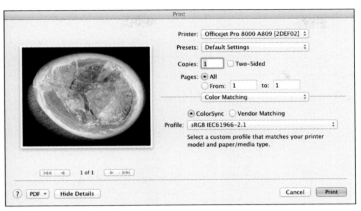

6.13 You can choose a color profile in the Print dialog to make sure the printer uses your preferred color settings.

4. **Select the ColorSync option rather than the Vendor Matching option.**

5. **Open the Profile pop-up menu, and click Other Profiles.** The Select ColorSync Profile dialog appears.

6. **Click the profile you want to use, and then click OK.** The Select ColorSync Profile dialog closes, and the profile you chose appears in the Profile pop-up menu.

7. **Choose other printing options as needed, and then click Print to print the photo.**

Note

This technique isn't specific to iPhoto — you can use your color profiles when printing from other applications as well.

Making your own account icon

Apple provides a good selection of account icons, but for that custom touch, you'll probably want to create your own account icon. You can either take a picture of yourself using your iMac's built-in iSight or carve an icon out of one of your photos from iPhoto or Photo Booth.

Here's how to create a custom account icon:

1. **Choose Apple menu ⇨ System Preferences.** The System Preferences window opens.

2. **In the System section, click the Users & Groups icon to open Users & Groups preferences.**

191

3. **Make sure your account is selected in the list box on the left.** If not, click it.

4. **Click your picture (to the left of the Change Password button), and then click Edit Picture on the pop-up panel.** The Edit Picture dialog appears, showing your current picture.

5. **To use a picture from iPhoto, open iPhoto and position its window so that you can see the Edit Picture dialog as well.**

6. **Drag the photo you want from iPhoto to the Edit Picture dialog (see Figure 6.14).**

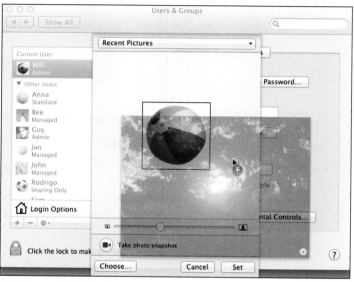

6.14 To create your own account icon, you can click and drag pictures from iPhoto or a Finder window to the Edit Picture dialog.

Note

If you want to take a picture of yourself, click the Take photo snapshot button instead and wait for the countdown to complete.

7. **Click and drag the size slider to zoom in to the part of the picture you want.**

8. **After you zoom the picture, click in the preview and drag if you want to display a different part of it.**

9. **Click Set.** The Edit Picture dialog closes, and your new icon appears in the Accounts window.

10. **Close System Preferences.** Press ⌘+Q.

Genius Instead of clicking and dragging a photo from iPhoto or Photo Booth, you can click Choose in the Edit Picture dialog. In the Open dialog that appears, click Photos in the Media category of the sidebar, choose the photo from the list of iPhoto events and albums, and then click Open. Alternatively, click and drag a picture from a Finder window to the Edit Picture dialog.

Displaying your own photos on your Desktop

Mac OS X comes with a good selection of Desktop pictures, but if you prefer to use your own pictures, you can do so easily:

1. **In iPhoto, select the picture you want to use.** If you want to use several pictures, select them.

2. **Choose Share ⇨ Set Desktop from the menu bar.**
    - **If you selected a single picture, Mac OS X makes it your Desktop wallpaper.**
    - **If you selected two or more pictures, Mac OS X makes the first of them your Desktop wallpaper, and sets Desktop & Screen Saver preferences to change the pictures automatically.** To control how frequently the pictures change, open System Preferences and alter the setting in the Change picture pop-up menu as necessary (for example, choose When logging in or Every hour instead of the default setting, Every 30 minutes).

Genius You can change the Desktop picture from System Preferences. Control+click or right-click the Desktop and choose Change Desktop Background to open the Desktop tab of Desktop & Screen Saver preferences. Click the picture source in the left column, and then click the picture you want in the right list box.

Creating and sharing screen-saver slide shows

If you use screen savers on your iMac rather than letting it go to sleep as quickly as possible to save power, you'll love the screen savers you can make using your photos.

Follow these steps to create custom screen savers using your photos from iPhoto:

1. **In iPhoto, create an album or Smart Album that contains the photos you want to use for your screen saver.** You can also use your entire library or an existing category such as Last 12 Months, Last Import, or Flagged.

2. **Choose Apple menu ⇨ System Preferences.** The System Preferences window opens.

3. **In the Personal section, click the Desktop & Screen Saver icon to open Desktop & Screen Saver preferences.** Click the Screen Saver tab unless it's already displayed.

4. **In the Screen Savers list, scroll down to the Pictures section, and then click the album or other item that contains the photos.** The first photo appears in the Preview box (see Figure 6.15).

6.15 To personalize your iMac, create screen savers using the photos from your iPhoto library.

5. **Under the Preview box, click the Display Style button for the effect you want:**

   ● **Slide show (left button).** This setting produces a conventional slide show, showing each photo for a few seconds, with optional cross-fading transitions and panning.

   ● **Collage (center button).** This setting assembles a collage by gradually spinning in each photo to add it. You can choose to include the titles and comments to help you identify photos of interest.

   ● **Mosaic (right button).** This setting gradually zooms out to a mosaic showing all the photos at a tiny size, repeated as necessary to fill the screen.

6. **Click Options.** The Options dialog opens. The options available are different for each type of screen saver. Figure 6.16 shows the three different Options dialogs.

7. **Click OK to close the Options dialog.**

8. **Click Test to test the screen saver full screen.** Press Esc or move the mouse to cancel the test when you've seen enough.

9. **Click and drag the Start screen saver slider to set the number of minutes before the screen saver starts.**

10. **Select the Show with clock option if you want to have the time readout superimposed on the screen saver.**

11. **Quit System Preferences.** Your screen saver runs after your iMac's keyboard and mouse have been inactive for the length of time you specified or if you move the mouse pointer to the hot corner you've set to activate the screen saver. (To set a hot corner, choose Apple menu ⇨ System Preferences, click the Desktop & Screen Saver icon, click the Screen Saver tab, and then click the Hot Corners button.)

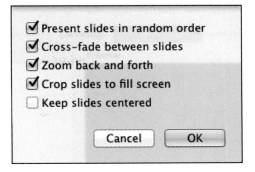

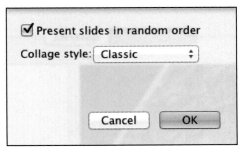

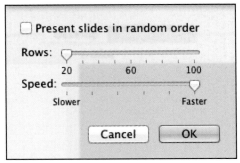

6.16 The Options dialog provides different options for Slide Show (top), Collage (middle), and Mosaic (bottom).

Note

If you've attached a second display to your iMac, you can select the Main screen only check box in Screen Saver preferences to restrict the screen saver only to the main screen. (The main screen is the screen on which the menu bar and Dock appear.) Otherwise, the screen saver plays on both displays.

Genius

If you want to see your screen-saver slide show in its full glory, open the Energy Saver preferences and deselect the Automatically reduce brightness before display goes to sleep check box. Otherwise, the slide show may appear at reduced brightness.

Using photos as window backgrounds

When you've taken a great photo, you may want to make it part of the Mac OS X interface so that you see it frequently. You can do so by making it the background to Finder windows you open showing a folder in Icon view.

Note Using photos as the background for your most useful Finder windows makes it much easier to pick out the window you need when you have several Finder windows open. The window's icon in the Dock shows the photo as well.

Here's how to set a photo as a window background:

1. **Open iPhoto and find the photo you want to use.**

2. **Open a Finder window to the folder to which you want to apply the photo.**

3. **Choose View ⇨ Show View Options.** The View Options window opens.

4. **Switch to Icon view if the folder is in any other view.** Click the Icons button on the toolbar or press ⌘+1.

5. **Select the Always open in icon view check box.** The background doesn't appear in List view, Columns view, or Cover Flow view, so make the Finder display the folder in Icon view.

6. **In the Arrange By pop-up menu, choose None.** If you select any other arrangement, you can't apply a background picture.

7. **In the Background area, click the Picture option button.**

8. **In iPhoto, click the photo and drag it to the Drag image here placeholder.** The photo appears as the background in the Finder window.

9. **Close the View Options window.** Click the Close button or choose View ⇨ Hide View Options.

Note If the picture is not in iPhoto, open a Finder window from which you can click and drag the picture to the View Options window.

Genius When you set a photo as a window background, the Finder displays whichever portion of the photo fits in the window without resizing it. If you find you're seeing only the upper-left corner of the photo, go back to iPhoto, select the photo, and choose File ⇨ Export to make iPhoto export a version the right size for your Finder windows.

Playing and Sharing Music — Legally

If you're looking to get more out of your music, explore the features iTunes offers. You can tell iTunes to pick out playlists that match criteria you set, and then update them automatically. You can burn songs to disc so that you can listen to them on an audio CD player or an MP3 CD player, or simply back them up to CD or DVD. You can adjust the Visualizer to your liking — and then control it from the keyboard. And you can listen to Internet radio stations using iTunes, even if they don't appear in iTunes' own listings.

Controlling iTunes with the Apple Remote

Playing songs with the iTunes interface is easy, but you can also use the Apple Remote (if you have one). This works much as you'd probably expect:

- **If iTunes isn't running, press the Remote's Play/Pause button to launch iTunes.**
- **Press the Play/Pause button to start or pause playback.**
- **Press the Next button to skip to the next song.**
- **Press the Previous button once to go back to the start of the current song.** Press again to go to the previous song.
- **Press the volume buttons to adjust the volume.**

Creating unchanging playlists and self-updating playlists

Sometimes you want to create playlists that contain only the songs you choose, in exactly the order you prefer them. For example, you might burn such a playlist to a CD so you can enjoy it in the car, or post it as an iMix playlist to the iTunes Store so that others can enjoy your taste in music. (You can find a discussion of iMix playlists later in this chapter.) At times like this, you need to create an unchanging playlist.

Creating an unchanging playlist

Here's the easiest way to create an unchanging playlist:

1. **Select the songs you want.** Click a song to select it; Shift+click to select all the songs from the currently selected song to the song you click; or ⌘+click to add individual songs to the selection.

2. **Click in the selection and drag the songs to the open space at the bottom of the Source list.** iTunes creates a new playlist and puts an edit box around the name.

3. **Type the name you want to give the playlist.**

4. **Click and drag the songs into your preferred order.**

Alternatively, choose File ⇨ New Playlist, name the playlist, and then click and drag songs to it.

Creating a self-updating playlist

Other times, it's more fun to have iTunes create playlists for you — playlists that update themselves with new songs. You tell iTunes what kind of songs you want, and how many, and it chooses them for you. iTunes calls these Smart Playlists.

Genius You can edit any Smart Playlist by Control+clicking it and choosing Edit Smart Playlist, so you can easily peek at the criteria for iTunes' built-in Smart Playlists to see how they work.

Here's how to create a Smart Playlist:

1. **Option+click the Create Playlist button (the + button) in the lower-left corner of the iTunes window to open the Smart Playlist dialog (see Figure 6.17).** Alternatively, press ⌘+Option+N or choose File ⇨ New Smart Playlist. The Smart Playlist dialog starts with just one line of controls, but you can set up a dozen or more conditions if needed.

6.17 The Smart Playlist dialog lets you set one or more criteria for choosing songs.

2. **Set up the first condition using the controls on the top line.**

- **The first pop-up menu contains about 40 fields of tag information and other information iTunes stores about each song, from Album and Artist all the way through Composer and Plays to Time (length) and Year.**

- **The second pop-up menu contains options suitable for the field you set, such as contains, does not contain, is, is not, starts with, and ends with.**

- **The text field lets you type text to specify the comparison or details.** For example, to create a Smart Playlist of various kinds of rock music, choose Genre in the first pop-up menu and contains in the second pop-up menu, and type Rock in the text box.

3. **Add other conditions as needed.** Click the Add (+) button to add another line of controls, and then set up your second condition. For example, to get songs from before 2005, choose Year Is Less Than 2005. As soon as you set up two conditions, iTunes replaces the Match the following rule option in the Smart Playlist dialog with the Match all/any of the following rules option.

4. **Choose all or any from the Match pop-up menu.**

   - **If you choose all.** This makes each condition depend on the one before it. For example, the first condition in Figure 6.18 restricts the playlist to songs in the Rock genre. From those songs, the second condition chooses only the ones from 2004 or earlier. And from those, the third condition takes only the songs rated in the four-star to five-star range.

6.18 Choosing all in the Match pop-up menu applies each of the conditions you've created in sequence.

   - **If you choose any.** This applies each condition separately. For example, the first condition in Figure 6.19 chooses songs that have Bruce Springsteen as the sole artist. The second condition chooses songs where the artist's name includes Tom Petty. So the playlist will contain songs by Bruce Springsteen, Tom Petty, and Tom Petty and The Heartbreakers, assuming the library contains songs by all three.

6.19 Choosing any in the Match pop-up menu treats the conditions separately.

5. **Choose whether to restrict your playlist to a certain length or number of songs.** If you want to create a limited playlist, select the Limit to check box. Choose the type of limit in the pop-up menu. Your choices are items, minutes, hours, MB, or GB. Type the number in the text box before it: for example, 2 hours. Choose the selection method in the selected by pop-up menu on the right — for example, random, least recently played, or most recently added.

6. **Select the Match only checked items option if you want to exclude songs whose check boxes you've deselected.** If you deselect a check box when you decide you don't like a song that's playing, you probably want to select this check box.

7. **Select the Live updating check box if you want iTunes to keep updating the Smart Playlist.** Automatic updating is one of the most compelling features of Smart Playlists, so selecting this check box is usually a good idea. Other times, though, you may want to draw together a Smart Playlist and not update it.

8. **Click OK to create the Smart Playlist.** iTunes adds the playlist to the Source list and displays an edit box around its name.

9. **Type the name for the Smart Playlist, and press Return to apply the name.**

Genius

Use the Smart Playlist dialog's Limit to option to create playlists suitable for the devices you have. For example, I use Limit to 700MB when creating Smart Playlists for my 1GB iPod shuffle, which contains about 200MB of data as well. Try using Limit to 70 minutes for creating a playlist to burn to audio CD, or Limit to 20 items for a workout playlist.

The moment you see which songs iTunes has selected for the Smart Playlist, you may realize that your Smart criteria need improving. If so, Control+click or right-click the Smart Playlist's name in the Source list and choose Edit Smart Playlist to open the Smart Playlist dialog again so that you can tweak the criteria.

To create a more complex Smart Playlist, you can nest rules, creating nested rules that apply only within a particular rule. After you've set up your main rules, click the ellipsis button (the … button) at the right end of the rule under which you want to create nested rules.

Take a look at the Smart Playlist shown in Figure 6.20. Here's how it breaks down:

- **At the top, the overarching command is "Match all of the following rules."**

- **The first top-level rule specifies "Last Played is in the last 12 months."** In other words, the song has been played within the last year.

- **Under this top-level rule is an "any of the following rules" condition that uses two nested rules: The song must match either "Plays is in the range 0 to 4" or "Skips is greater than 1."**

- **The second top-level rule specifies "Genre contains Alternative," so any matching song must be in one of the Alternative categories (for example, plain Alternative, or Alternative & Punk).**

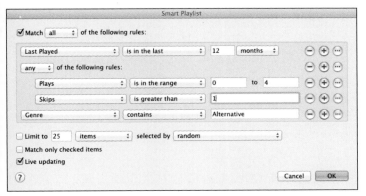

6.20 You can create nested rules to specify more complex criteria for your Smart Playlists.

Genius

You can nest rules up to five levels deep — but you may find that more than a couple of levels of nesting becomes confusing. Still, it's great to have the power to do this in case you need it one day.

Burning CDs with iTunes

If you want to play your iTunes songs on a CD player or share them with a friend, you can burn them to CD. You can also use either CD or DVD to back up your songs.

To burn songs to CD, you must add them to a playlist. This can be either a regular playlist or a Smart Playlist.

iTunes lets you create three different types of CD:

- **Audio CDs.** These play in any CD player or computer, just like any regular music CD you might buy. Most audio CDs can contain 74 minutes or 80 minutes of music.

- **MP3 CDs.** These play only in a computer's CD drive or in a CD player or DVD player that can play MP3 files (which most cannot). An MP3 CD can contain from around 4 hours of music (at top quality) to around 50 hours (at minimal quality).

- **Data CDs.** These work only in computers. You can use data CDs for backup or to transfer files from one computer to another.

Note iTunes limits you to burning any given playlist seven times at this writing. But you can then create another playlist — containing the same songs if necessary — and then burn that seven times.

Note If your iMac has a SuperDrive or other burner, you can burn data DVDs as well as data CDs, which is great for backup. You can't burn audio DVDs or MP3 DVDs.

Here's how to burn a CD:

1. **In the Source list, Control+click or right-click the playlist you want to burn, and then click Burn Playlist to Disc on the context menu.** You can also click the playlist and choose File ➪ Burn Playlist to Disc from the menu bar. iTunes displays the Burn Settings dialog (see Figure 6.21).

6.21 In the Burn Settings dialog, tell iTunes which kind of CD you want to create — for example, an Audio CD.

2. **In the Preferred Speed pop-up menu, choose the speed at which to burn the CD.** Normally, it's best to use the Maximum Possible setting unless you find this produces CDs with errors — in which case, reduce the speed.

3. **In the Disc Format area, select the option for the type of CD: Audio CD, MP3 CD, or Data CD or DVD.** If you choose Audio CD, choose options under it.

   - **Gap Between Songs.** Choose None, or the number of seconds from 1 second to 5 seconds. Having a gap is useful if you plan to rip the CD on another audio program. Try 2 seconds to start with.

   - **Use Sound Check.** Select this option if you want to use the Sound Check feature to normalize the volume of the songs. Normalizing the volume helps avoid having some songs much louder than others but may squash the dynamic range of the songs too much. Experiment with Sound Check and see if it suits your music.

   - **Include CD Text.** Select this option if you want to include CD text information on the CD. This is useful if you have a CD player that supports CD text and can show you the name of the artist and song currently playing.

4. **Click Burn.** iTunes prompts you to insert a blank disc.

5. **Insert the disc in your iMac's optical drive.** iTunes burns the disc and gives it the same name as the playlist.

6. **Eject the disc, label it, and then test it.**

Publishing your playlists to the iTunes Store

If you want to find a wide audience for a playlist, you can publish it to the iTunes Store. Anyone who visits the iTunes Store can find your playlist and listen to it.

Here's how to publish a playlist to the iTunes store:

1. **In the Source list, click the playlist you want to publish.**

2. **Choose Store ⇨ Publish Playlist.** iTunes displays the Sign in to publish your Playlist dialog (unless you've already signed in to the iTunes Store).

Note   When you publish a playlist to the iTunes Store, iTunes includes only the songs that are available in the iTunes Store. Similarly, when you share a playlist with a friend by Control+clicking or right-clicking the playlist and choosing Export, iTunes includes only the songs that are in the iTunes library into which your friend imports the playlist. You're sharing only the list and order of songs, not the song files themselves.

3. **Sign in with your Apple ID or AOL screen name and password, just like when you're buying from the iTunes Store, and then click Continue.** iTunes checks to see which songs in your playlist are available in the iTunes Store, and then displays the Create a Playlist on iTunes screen (see Figure 6.22).

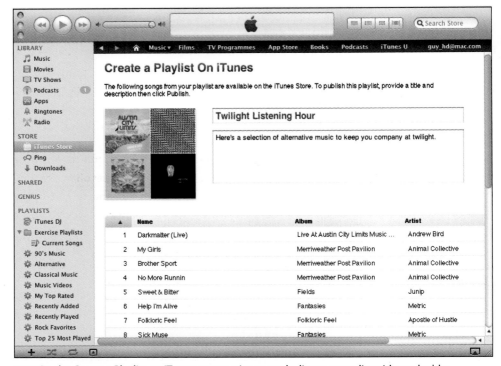

6.22 On the Create a Playlist on iTunes screen, give your playlist an appealing title, and add a description that will help draw the audience to it.

4. **Look through the songs that remain on the playlist.** iTunes removes any that are not available in the iTunes Store. (If none of your songs is available, iTunes displays a message box telling you so, but doesn't display the iMixes screen.) iTunes may also substitute a different version of a song if the version you used isn't available. If your playlist needs adjusting, click Cancel, go back to iTunes to fix the playlist with other songs that may be available, and start again from Step 1 of this list.

5. **Drag the songs into your preferred order.** Even if your playlist was in the right order, you may need to rearrange the songs after iTunes has removed ones that aren't available.

6. **Change the title for the playlist if you want (iTunes suggests the playlist's title, but you may need to improve on it), and type a description.**

7. **Click Publish.** iTunes adds the iMix to the iTunes Store list and displays the Thanks for submitting your iMix screen. Click Done.

Getting the visualizations you want

Being able to have iTunes accompany the music you're enjoying with dramatic, ever-changing visualizations can be wonderful, especially when you're kicking back. But what's even better is that you can control the visualizations so that iTunes conjures up the types you prefer and skips those that aren't appealing.

Choosing which Visualizer to use

To increase your enjoyment of your songs, iTunes includes several different Visualizers. To turn the Visualizer on, press ⌘+T or choose View ➪ Show Visualizer. To turn the Visualizer off, either press ⌘+T again or choose View ➪ Hide Visualizer. You can switch from one to another by choosing View ➪ Visualizer and then choosing the Visualizer you want from the submenu: iTunes Visualizer, iTunes Classic Visualizer, Lathe, Jelly, or Stix.

Each of the iTunes Visualizers is special in its own way, and you'll want to spend time with them to find out which of them best suits your music and what you like to watch as it plays.

Choosing whether to run the Visualizer full screen from the start

If you haven't already told iTunes whether to run the Visualizer full screen from the start, do so first:

1. **Choose iTunes ➪ Preferences to open the Preferences window, and then click Advanced to display the Advanced pane.**

2. **Select the Display visualizer full screen check box if you want full-screen visualizations the moment you turn the Visualizer on.** (If you prefer to start visualizations at a small size instead, you can choose View ➪ Full Screen or press ⌘+F when you want to switch to full screen.)

3. **Click OK to close the Preferences window.**

Using advanced Visualizer tricks with the Classic Visualizer

If you use the iTunes Classic Visualizer, you can control its behavior directly by pressing keystrokes. This is a great way of getting visualizations that you enjoy watching. The Visualizer uses a combination of three elements to produce its mesmerizing effects: behaviors, color schemes, and color themes. Table 6.2 shows you the keystrokes you can press to control these elements and the Visualizer's other features.

Table 6.2 Keystrokes for Controlling the iTunes Classic Visualizer

Keystroke	Effect
W	Switch to the next behavior.
Q	Return to the previous behavior.
A	Switch to the next color scheme.
S	Return to the previous color scheme.
Z	Switch to the next color theme.
X	Return to the previous color theme.
Shift+0 to Shift+9	Save the current Visualizer configuration (saving up to ten configurations).
0 to 9	Switch to the specified saved configuration.
R	Change to another visualization at random.
D	Reset the Visualizer to its default settings.
F	Toggle the display of the frame rate on or off.
T	Toggle frame rate capping at 30 frames per second on or off.
I	Toggle the display of song information on or off.

Fixing songs that won't play

iTunes comes equipped to play files in five major audio formats:

- **AAC (Advanced Audio Coding).** Apple's preferred format for iTunes, the iPod, and the iPhone.

- **MP3 (MPEG-1 Audio Layer 3).** A very widely used format.

- **Apple Lossless Encoding.** Provides full-quality audio at the cost of large file sizes.

- **WAV.** An uncompressed format used on Windows, Mac, and other operating systems.

- **AIFF.** An uncompressed format used mostly on the Mac.

Normally, all these file types play just fine on iTunes, iPhones, iPads, and iPods, but you can run into problems with AAC files.

Dealing with problems playing AAC files

If an AAC file won't play, in most cases the problem is that it's a protected file from the iTunes Store that will play only on authorized Macs and PCs. If you've hit your quota of five authorized computers, you won't be able to play the song on another computer.

Genius

The iTunes Store used to sell protected AAC files to discourage piracy. It now sells AAC files without protection.

iTunes should warn you that the AAC file is protected and give you the chance to authorize your iMac to play the song. If iTunes doesn't warn you, you can check whether the song is protected as follows:

1. **In iTunes, Control+click the file and choose Get Info to open the Info dialog for the song.**

2. **Click the Summary button if any other pane is displayed.**

3. **See if the Kind readout says Protected AAC Audio File.** If the song isn't protected, look at the Encoded With readout to see whether iTunes or another encoder made the file.

4. **Click OK to close the Info dialog.**

If the song is protected, you may need to choose Store ⇨ Deauthorize This Computer to deauthorize one of the computers that's currently authorized to play songs you've purchased before you can authorize your iMac to play the song.

If the song isn't protected, the problem is most likely that the song was encoded using a program other than iTunes. In this case, if iTunes can't play the song, it's genuinely incompatible with iTunes because it uses a different AAC format. You will need to convert the file to another format before iTunes can read it.

If you have the application that created the AAC file, open the file, and then export it to another format, such as MP3 or AIFF, and then import it into iTunes. If you received the AAC file from someone else, ask that person to provide it in another format such as MP3 (or AIFF if transferring a larger file is not a problem).

Dealing with file formats that iTunes can't play

If you have audio files in formats that iTunes can't play, you will need either to convert them to one of the formats iTunes supports or add software to iTunes that enables it to play the files.

207

The three audio formats you're most likely to have trouble with are

- **WMA (Windows Media Audio).** This is the format used by Microsoft's Windows Media Player (usually installed with Windows) and music stores such as Napster (before 2009). WMA files can be protected with digital rights management (DRM).

- **Ogg Vorbis.** This is a free encoder for compressed audio, roughly comparable to MP3 in quality and file size.

- **FLAC (Free Lossless Audio Codec).** This is a free encoder with full audio quality, roughly comparable to Apple Lossless Encoding in quality and file size.

WMA is widely used, whereas Ogg Vorbis and FLAC are not yet widely used.

Here are the two best approaches for adding unprotected WMA files to iTunes:

- **If you have a PC with iTunes available, drag the WMA files from a Windows Explorer window to the library in the iTunes window.** iTunes automatically converts the WMA files to the audio format set in the Importing preferences. Copy the resulting files to your Mac, and then import them into your iTunes library.

- **If you don't have a PC with iTunes available, use a tool such as EasyWMA (www.easywma.com; $10; demo available) to convert the files to AAC or MP3 on the Mac.** Import the converted files into your library.

To add protected WMA files to iTunes, you must burn them to CD from Windows Media Player on Windows, and then rip the CD using iTunes. Doing this works, but it contravenes the user agreements of most stores that sell protected WMA files.

To add FLAC files to iTunes, use an application such as xACT (freeware; http://download.cnet.com and other sites) to decode the FLAC files to AIFF or WAV. Then import those files into iTunes, and convert them to your preferred format.

Dealing with "lost" CDs

If you have inserted a CD in your iMac's optical drive, and the CD doesn't appear on the Desktop, in the Finder, or in iTunes, you won't be able to eject it normally. Instead, try these remedies:

1. **Open Disk Utility.** Click the Desktop, choose Go ➪ Utilities, and double-click Disk Utility. If the CD appears in the list pane, click it, and then click the Eject button.

2. **If that doesn't work, close all your applications and restart your iMac.** When your iMac plays its system startup chime, either click the mouse button and hold it down for the rest of the boot process or press and hold down the Eject key. This may make your iMac eject the CD.

3. **Failing the mouse button trick, restart your iMac again.** Line up your fingers over the keys ⌘+Option+O+F. When your iMac plays its system startup chime, press these keys to enter Open Firmware mode. At the prompt, type **eject CD** and press Return. Restart your iMac by typing **mac-boot** and pressing Return.

Adding your favorite Internet radio stations

When you've had enough of your own songs for the time being, you can listen to Internet radio through iTunes.

Note If the Radio item doesn't appear in the Source list, choose iTunes ⇨ Preferences to open the Preferences window, click the General button, and then select the Radio check box. If a message box opens telling you that you cannot select radio because the parental controls are blocked, click the Parental button, open the lock icon and authenticate yourself, and then deselect the Radio check box in the Disable area.

Here's how to listen to one of the radio stations in iTunes' listings:

1. **Click Radio in the Source list.** The list of radio stations appears.

2. **Expand the category of radio you're interested in to see the stations.** Click the disclosure triangle to expand or collapse a category.

3. **Sort the stations so that you can find what you want.** You can sort the stations by Stream or by Comments by clicking the column heading; click again to reverse the sort order.

Genius To get good-quality radio, you'll probably want to see the bit rates at which the stations are broadcasting. Control+click or right-click the Comments heading to display the context menu, and then click Bit Rate to display the Bit Rate column to the left of the Comments column. You can then sort by the Bit Rate column. 128 Kbps is the minimum for good audio quality.

4. **Double-click the station you want to start playing.** Click the Stop button when you want to stop the radio playing.

If the station you want to hear doesn't appear in iTunes' listing, open it like this:

1. **Find the URL for the radio stream.** For example, go to the station's website, find the URL, and copy it.

2. **Choose Advanced ⇨ Open Stream to display the Open Stream dialog.**

3. **Type or paste the URL, and then click OK.**

How Can I Use My iMac to Keep in Touch?

Your iMac comes equipped with three powerful applications for keeping in touch online: the Mail application for communicating via email; iChat for chatting via text, audio, or video; and FaceTime for making video calls to Mac, iPhone, iPad, and iPod touch users. FaceTime is mostly straightforward to use, but while it's easy to get started with Mail and iChat, each application contains many advanced features that you'll want to dip into in order to get the most from it. For example, if you've wondered how to set up multiple email accounts in Mail, create Smart Mailboxes, and process mail automatically with rules, look at the first third of this chapter. If you want to enhance your iChat chats with video effects, record them for posterity, or display movies in them, read the second third. And if you want to use Apple's FaceTime technology to hold video chats, read the final third of the chapter.

Getting the Most from Email

To get the most from email, you'll probably need to set up multiple email accounts, process your incoming messages automatically, and quickly locate the messages you need. You may also need to deal with spam, respond to messages automatically, or access your email via the web.

Setting up multiple email accounts

The first time you run Mail, it takes you through the process of setting up an email account — probably your main account. But after that, you can add as many other email accounts as you need. You can then either manage all your email in a single Inbox or view a single account's Inbox at a time.

In Mac OS X Lion, the recommended way to manage your communications accounts is by using the Mail, Contacts & Calendars preferences. Here, you can set up an account for use with not just Mail but also Address Book, iCal, and iChat. You can also add email accounts directly in Mail.

Adding an account using Mail, Contacts & Calendars preferences

Here's how to add an account using Mail, Contacts & Calendars preferences:

1. **Choose Apple ⇨ System Preferences to open the System Preferences window.**

2. **In the Internet & Wireless section, click Mail, Contacts & Calendars.** The Mail, Contacts & Calendars preferences open (see Figure 7.1).

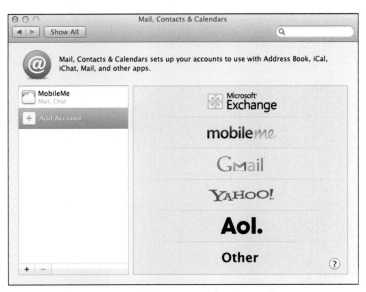

7.1 Click Add Account in Mail, Contacts & Calendars preferences to start adding a new account.

3. **Click Add Account in the left column.** The list of account types appears: Microsoft Exchange, MobileMe, Gmail, Yahoo!, AOL, and Other.

4. **Click the account type you want to add.** A dialog opens showing the information required for that account type. Figure 7.2 shows the Gmail dialog, which is a common choice.

5. **In the Full Name field, type your name the way you want it to appear on messages you send.**

6. **Enter the email address and password.**

7. **Click Set Up.** Mac OS X verifies the account, and then displays a dialog containing options. The options depend on the account type. Figure 7.3 shows the options for a Gmail account: Mail & Notes, Calendars, and Chat.

8. **Deselect the check box for any feature you don't want to use.** For example, if you don't want to use this account for chat, deselect the Chat check box.

7.2 Enter the name, email address, and password for the account in the dialog that opens.

7.3 Once Mac OS X has verified the account, choose which features to use, and then click Add Account.

Note If you want to change the name Mac OS X displays for the account, click the account in Mail, Contacts & Calendars preferences, and then click Details. In the dialog that opens, type the name in the Description text box, and then click OK.

9. **Click Add Account.** Mac OS X sets up the account for the features you chose. The account then appears in Mail, Contacts & Calendars preferences (see Figure 7.4). Here, you can turn features on by selecting their check boxes or off by deselecting their check boxes.

10. **Quit System Preferences.** Press ⌘+Q.

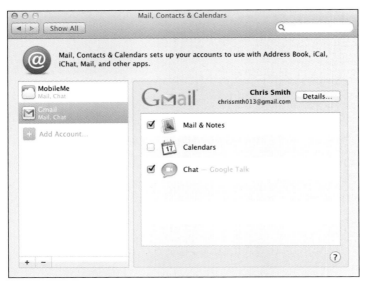

7.4 The Account appears in Mail, Contacts & Calendars preferences.

Adding an email account in Mail

Here's how to add another email account to Mail:

1. **Choose File ⇨ Add Account.** The Add Account assistant opens (see Figure 7.5).

2. **In the Full Name box, type your name as you want it to appear in messages you send.**

3. **Type your email address in the Email Address box.** If the domain name indicates an account type that Mail can set up automatically, the Add Account assistant displays the Create button in place of the Continue button. For example, the .me domain name indicates a MobileMe account or an iCloud account, and the .gmail domain name indicates a Gmail account. Mail can set up these account types automatically.

4. **Type your password in the Password box.**

5. **If the Create button appears, click it, and then go to Step 17.** Otherwise, click the Continue button, and then follow the remaining steps in this list. The Incoming Mail Server dialog opens (see Figure 7.6).

7.5 To add an email account from within Mail, you use the Add Account assistant.

7.6 Set up the details of the Incoming Mail Server here.

Note

You can also start adding a new account from the Accounts pane in Mail preferences. Choose Mail ▷ Preferences to open the Mail Preferences window, and then click Accounts on the toolbar. In the lower-left corner of the Accounts pane, click Add (+) to launch the Add Account assistant.

6. **Choose the account type, and then fill in the account details.**

   • In the Account Type pop-up menu, choose POP, IMAP, Exchange, or Exchange IMAP.

   • The Description text is for your benefit, so type a name that will help you distinguish this account from your others.

   • For the Incoming Mail Server, User Name, and Password, type (or paste) the details given to you by the mail provider.

7. **Click Continue.** The Incoming Mail Security dialog opens (see Figure 7.7).

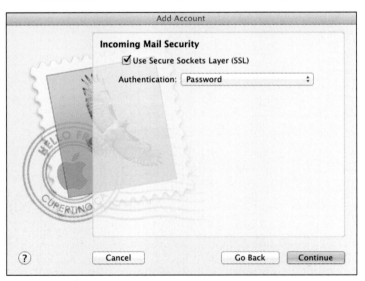

7.7 In the Incoming Mail Security dialog, specify the type of authentication and choose whether to use Secure Sockets Layer.

8. **If your email provider requires you to use Secure Sockets Layer (SSL) for incoming mail, select the Use Secure Sockets Layer (SSL) check box.**

9. **In the Authentication pop-up menu, choose the type of authentication.** Password is the most widely used option, with External (TLS client Certificate), Kerberos Version 5 (GSSAPI), NTLM, and MD5 Challenge-Response mostly used in corporations and organizations.

10. **Click Continue.** The Outgoing Mail Server dialog appears (see Figure 7.8).

7.8 Specify the Outgoing Mail Server here, and choose whether to use authentication.

Genius

The Outgoing Mail Server settings appear straightforward, but you can set Mail to send outgoing mail using a different mail provider if necessary. For example, some free email accounts let you send email only through their web-based interfaces even though you can receive incoming messages freely using an email application such as Mail. In this case, you need to use a different outgoing mail server for that email account — for example, the server for your main email account. Similarly, some ISPs block mail on the standard port to prevent misuse. In this case, you will need to set a different outgoing port for the mail.

11. **Type a description for the server, and choose which server to use.** You can either type the server name in the Outgoing Mail Server box or choose an existing server from the pop-up menu.

12. **If your server requires authentication, select the Use Authentication check box and type the username and password.**

13. **Click Continue.** The Outgoing Mail Security dialog appears. This dialog has the same controls as the Incoming Mail Security dialog.

14. **If your email provider requires SSL for sending mail, select the Use Secure Sockets Layer (SSL) check box.**

15. **In the Authentication pop-up menu, choose the type of authentication.** As with incoming mail, Password is the most widely used means of authentication. Choose None if the outgoing mail server does not require authentication.

16. **Click Continue.** The Account Summary dialog appears.

17. **Deselect the check boxes for any features you don't want to use.**

18. **Verify the details, and then click Create.** If you don't want Mail to put the new account online immediately, deselect the Take account online check box before clicking Create. Mail adds the account to the left pane. The account also appears in the Accounts list in Accounts preferences.

19. **If you want to rename the account, follow these steps:**

    1. **Choose Mail ⇨ Preferences.** The Mail Preferences window opens.

    2. **Click Accounts in the toolbar to display the Accounts pane.**

    3. **Click the account in the Accounts list on the left.**

    4. **Type the new name in the Description box.**

    5. **Click Close to close the preferences window.**

Saving and opening attachments

Email is a great way to transfer files quickly because they simply arrive as attachments in your Inbox without your needing to fetch them the way you do with FTP. You can then either view them quickly from Mail or save them to folders.

Before you save an attachment, use Quick Look to see what it is. Knowing this should help you decide whether to save the attachment at all (rather than delete it immediately) and choose the folder in which to save it.

To view an attachment using Quick Look, open the message in the Message Viewer window (the main Mail window), and then click the Quick Look button. If the message has multiple attachments, you can move forward or backward through them or set them to play as a slide show, even if they're different file types.

You can save an attachment in any of these ways:

- **Click and drag the attachment icon to your Desktop or a Finder window.**

- **Save all attachments to your default folder.** Click the Save button on the Attachments line in the message window.

- **Save all attachments to a folder you choose.** Click the Save pop-up button, and then choose Save All from the pop-up menu. In the dialog that appears, click the folder, and then click Save.

- **Save one attachment to a folder you choose.** Click and hold down the Save button on the Attachments line for a second, and then click the attachment's name in the pop-up menu. In the dialog that appears, click the folder, and then click Save.

After you save an attachment, remove it from the email message before filing the message. Removing attachments helps keep down the size of your mailbox, which otherwise can grow rapidly. To remove an attachment, choose Message ⇨ Remove Attachments.

Note

To set the default folder in which Mail saves attachments, choose Mail ⇨ Preferences, click General, and choose the folder in the Downloads folder pop-up menu.

Genius

You can also remove attachments from messages in any mailbox — so if you need to file the message with attachments at first, you can get rid of them when you no longer need them. But by removing the attachments as soon as you've saved the files, you eliminate the risk of your forgetting to remove them later.

You can open an attachment by clicking its link in the message window or by opening Quick Look for the attachment and then clicking the Open With button in the upper-right corner of the Quick Look window.

The problem with opening an attachment like this is Mail protects the original file that came with the message. So if you save changes to an attachment you've opened directly from an email message, you create another copy of the file. For example, if you receive an attachment called Letter. docx, and you open it and edit it directly from the message and then save it, Word saves the attachment as Letter-1.docx. Open it again from the message, and you get the original document. Save it again, and you get Letter-2.docx.

This is a recipe for confusion, so usually it's best to save the attachment to a folder before opening it. After you save the attachment, open it either by double-clicking it in a Finder window or by using the Open command from the application in which you want to open the file.

Genius

If you want to save an attachment on the server but not on your iMac (for example, because you're running out of space), choose Mail ➪ Preferences, click Accounts, click the account you want to use, and then click the Advanced tab. Open the Keep copies of messages for offline viewing pop-up menu and choose All messages, but omit attachments. Close the preferences window.

Sorting messages automatically with rules

Email overload is a sad fact of modern life, and opening your Inbox to find a tsunami of messages all clamoring for your attention is daunting. But Mail provides a great tool for dealing with this problem: Rules.

Understanding what you can do with rules

Mail lets you create rules for sorting your messages. You can set up rules that use a wide variety of criteria, including these:

- Who the message is from, who it is to, who is on the Cc list, and what the subject is.
- Whether the message is addressed to you by your full name or not.
- Whether the sender is in your Address Book or your Previous Recipients list, or is a member of a particular group in your Address Book.
- Whether the message contains particular words.
- What the message's priority is.
- Whether the message includes an attachment.
- Whether the message is a mail message, a note, or an RSS article. RSS (discussed later in this chapter) is a way for websites to publish new stories quickly.

When a message matches a rule, you can apply one or more of a healthy range of actions, including these:

- Move or copy the message to a mailbox.
- Change the message's background color (to pick it out).
- Play a sound, or bounce the Mail icon in the Dock, to alert you to the message.
- Reply to the message, forward it, redirect it, or simply delete it.
- Run an AppleScript on the message to take a more complex action that you define.

Genius

Mail starts you off with one rule, which is called News From Apple and is automatically applied unless you turn it off. If the message comes from any of a long list of email addresses associated with Apple, the rule sets the background color for the message in the message list in the Message Viewer to light blue. This is why messages from Apple, Apple Developer Connection, MobileMe, and so on, appear highlighted in the message list.

Creating a rule

Here's how to create a rule:

1. **Choose Mail ⇨ Preferences.** The preferences window opens.

2. **Click Rules to display Rules preferences (see Figure 7.9).** Here you'll find all the rules that have been defined so far in Mail — perhaps only the News From Apple rule.

3. **Click Add Rule to start creating a new rule.**

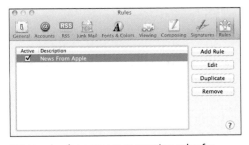

7.9 Here's where you start creating rules for processing email messages automatically.

4. **Type a descriptive name for the rule in the Description box.** This example uses the name Select Priority Messages. Figure 7.10 shows the rule under construction with two conditions added.

7.10 Creating a rule that matches either of two conditions.

5. **Use the first line of controls to set up the first condition for the rule.** For example, choose Sender is member of Group in the first pop-up menu and Business Contacts in the second pop-up menu to make the rule apply to contacts who appear in the Business Contacts group in Address Book.

6. **Add another condition if needed by clicking the Add (+) button on the first line, and then specify the condition.** For example, choose Sender is member of Group in the first pop-up menu and Los Angeles clients in the second pop-up menu to make the rule apply to contacts in the Los Angeles clients group as well.

7. **After you set up multiple conditions, choose any or all as appropriate in the If any/ all of the following conditions are met pop-up menu.**

   - **Any.** Choose any when each condition stands on its own: for example, when you want to identify messages whose sender is either a member of the Business Contacts group or the Los Angeles clients group.

   - **All.** Choose all when each subsequent condition restricts the previous conditions: for example, when you want to identify messages whose sender is in your Address Book and whose priority is High.

8. **Add further conditions as needed.**

9. **In the Perform the following actions area, set the action or actions for the rule to take.** Continuing the example, you might move your high-priority messages to a special folder called Priority Messages.

Genius

If your email provider adds X-SPAM ratings to messages, you may want to add a header so that you can sort by these ratings. To do so, choose Edit Header List in the first pop-up menu to open the Message Headers window. Click the Add a Header button (the + button), type the name you want to give the header, and then click OK.

10. **Add the Stop evaluating rules action after your main action.** Adding this action prevents Mail from applying further rules to the message and perhaps doing something with it that you hadn't intended.

11. **Click OK.** Mail closes the dialog and asks whether you want to apply your rules to messages in selected mailboxes (see Figure 7.11).

Do you want to apply your rules to messages in selected mailboxes?

Applying rules to the selected mailboxes may change their contents. Active rules will always be applied to new messages.

Don't Apply   Apply

12. **Click Apply if you want to apply the rule to the messages.** Otherwise, click Don't Apply.

7.11 Choose whether to apply your new rule to your existing messages.

13. **Create more rules as needed.** Leave Rules preferences open so you can get your rules into order, as described next.

Getting your rules in order

After you create two or more rules, use the list in Rules preferences to drag the rules into the order in which you want Mail to apply them.

If you create many complex rules, choosing the right order for rules can take some work. This is especially true if you don't use the Stop evaluating rules action at the end of some of the rules, because after matching such a rule, Mail continues to apply the next rule in the list to the message until it runs into a matching rule that does use the Stop evaluating rules action.

To stop using a particular rule, deselect its check box in the Active column.

Creating Smart Mailboxes

One of Mail's greatest features is the capability to create Smart Mailboxes — mailboxes that automatically gather all the email messages that meet the criteria you specify. Even if you file your messages consistently, Smart Mailboxes can help, especially for messages that fit into two or more categories.

Here's how to create a Smart Mailbox:

1. **Choose Mailbox ⇨ New Smart Mailbox.** The Smart Mailbox dialog appears.

2. **Type the name for the Smart Mailbox.** Make it descriptive, as you'll probably want to create various Smart Mailboxes.

3. **On the Contains line, choose all in the pop-up menu if you want each message in the Smart Mailbox to match all your criteria.** If you want it to match any of the criteria, choose any.

4. **Set up the conditions for the Smart Mailbox using the techniques discussed in the previous section.** Figure 7.12 shows an example of a Smart Mailbox that pulls together messages related to a project.

7.12 Create Smart Mailboxes that automatically draw together the messages you want to view as a group.

5. **Select the Include messages from Trash option if you want to include messages you have deleted.**

6. **Select the Include messages from Sent option if you want to include messages you've sent but not yet filed.** You'll often need to select this check box to get all relevant messages into the Smart Mailbox.

7. **Click OK.** Mail creates the Smart Mailbox and adds it to the Smart Mailboxes category in the sidebar. (If this is your first Smart Mailbox, the Smart Mailboxes category appears for the first time.)

You can now click the Smart Mailbox you've created to display its contents. If you find you need to change its criteria, Control+click or right-click the Smart Mailbox and choose Edit Smart Mailbox.

Dealing with spam

Few things are more dispiriting than finding your Inbox stuffed with spam, or junk mail. Luckily, Mac OS X includes junk mail filtering to help you cut down on the amount of spam you receive. Here's how to make sure junk mail filtering is turned on and configured for your needs:

1. **Choose Mail ⇨ Preferences.** The preferences window opens.

2. **Click Junk Mail to display Junk Mail preferences (see Figure 7.13).**

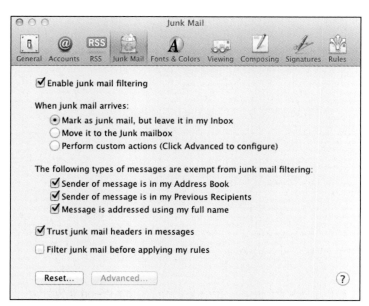

7.13 It's a good idea to configure Mail's Junk Mail preferences to cut down on junk mail as much as possible.

3. **Make sure the Enable junk mail filtering check box is selected.** This check box is normally selected by default. If you deselect it, all the other controls in the Junk Mail preferences become unavailable.

4. **In the When junk mail arrives area, select the option you want:**

   - **Mark as junk mail, but leave it in my Inbox.** This option is usually the best choice while you're training the junk mail filters, as you get to see all your incoming mail but receive a warning about the messages that Mail thinks are junk. You can then check that a message actually is junk and delete it if it is.

   - **Move it to the Junk mailbox.** Select this option if you're confident that Mail's junk mail filtering is pretty accurate. Having Mail move the junk messages to the Junk folder can slim down your Inbox dramatically, but you will need to check that the filter isn't catching nonjunk messages as well. Otherwise, a valuable message may end up languishing in the Junk folder.

   - **Perform custom actions.** Select this option if you want to customize junk mail filtering. Click Advanced and use the dialog that appears (see Figure 7.14) to set up rules for handling junk mail. These rules work just like those explained in the previous section.

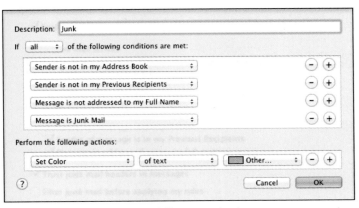

7.14 You can adjust the junk mail filter to catch other messages or to take other actions with them.

5. **In the section called The following types of messages are exempt from junk mail filtering, select the check box for each exemption you want to use.** Normally, all three exemptions are useful.

6. **Select the Trust junk mail headers in messages check box if you want Mail to accept your ISP's or email provider's claim about a message being junk mail.** If your ISP or provider is overly aggressive in labeling messages as junk, deselect this check box.

7. **Select the Filter junk mail before applying my rules check box if you want to apply junk mail filtering before running your own rules.** Normally, it's best to run your own rules first, as these allow you to pick out valuable messages that Mail might otherwise label as junk.

When you finish choosing junk mail filtering options, close the preferences window.

Subscribing to RSS feeds

RSS is an abbreviation for Really Simple Syndication, a way for websites that change often to publish a list of the changes so that anybody interested can quickly see the changes. This list of changes is called an *RSS feed*, a *news feed*, or simply a *feed*.

RSS feeds are a great way of having websites send information on changes and updates out to you so that you don't have to visit the sites to find out whether they've changed.

Bookmarking an RSS feed

The best way to find RSS feeds is by browsing in Safari. When you find a page that has an RSS feed, which is identified by a blue icon with the letters RSS appearing at the right end of the Address box, click the icon to switch to RSS view. If clicking the icon displays a pop-up menu of different news feeds, as in Figure 7.15, choose the one you want.

7.15 In Safari, choose the type of RSS feed you want to use.

Safari switches the web page to the RSS view. You can then create a bookmark for the web page by choosing Bookmarks ⇨ Add Bookmark (or pressing ⌘+D) and specifying a bookmark name and location in the dialog that opens (see Figure 7.16).

To create a bookmark in Safari, select the Safari check box, and then choose the location in the pop-up menu — for example, on the Bookmarks Bar or in the News folder. To create a bookmark in Mail, select the Mail check box. Click Add when you've made your choice.

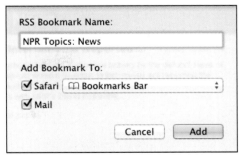

7.16 Safari lets you create bookmarks in Safari, in Mail, or in both.

Subscribing to an RSS feed

If you've already bookmarked RSS feeds in Safari without adding them to Mail, you can import your RSS feeds from Safari into Mail. Follow these steps:

1. **In Mail, choose File ⇨ Add RSS Feeds.** The dialog shown in Figure 7.17 appears.

2. **Select the Browse feeds in Safari bookmarks option.**

3. **In the Collections box, select the collection of RSS feeds.** For example, select All RSS Feeds to view all RSS feeds.

4. **Select the check box for each feed you want to add.**

5. **Select the Show in Inbox check box if you want to display the feeds in your Inbox rather than just in the RSS category.** Depending on how you use Mail, showing the feeds in the RSS category is usually easiest.

6. **Click Add.** Mail closes the dialog and adds the RSS feeds.

7.17 You can import RSS feeds from Safari into Mail and add them to the Inbox if you want.

Reading RSS feeds in Mail

To read your RSS feeds in Mail, show the RSS category in the Source list on the left, and then click the RSS feed you want. Mail displays the list of messages for that feed (see Figure 7.18), and you can double-click a message to display it in a separate window. Most messages end with a Read more link that you can click to see the full story.

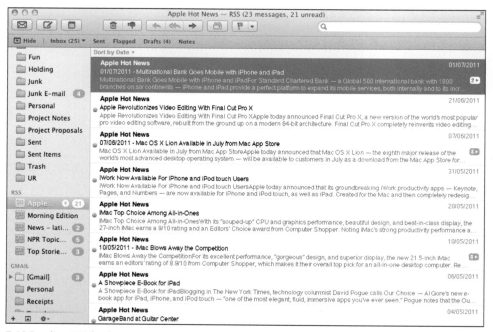

7.18 Reading RSS feeds in Mail.

After you click an RSS feed in the Mail sidebar, you can click the gray up arrow that appears in its name to move the feed up to the Inbox. Click the gray down arrow to move an RSS feed back down from the Inbox to the RSS category.

Genius

If you have many RSS feeds, create separate folders in the RSS category so that you can sort the RSS feeds into groups. Click the RSS category, and then choose Mailbox ⇨ New Mailbox. In the New Mailbox dialog, make sure RSS is selected in the Location pop-up menu. Type a name for the folder, and click OK. You can then drag the appropriate RSS feeds into the folder.

Configuring your RSS preferences

Mail's RSS preferences (see Figure 7.19) let you choose your default RSS reader (Safari, Mail, or another application), how frequently to check for updates (every 30 minutes, every hour, or every day), and whether to remove articles automatically after a specific period of time (for example, one day or one week) or manually.

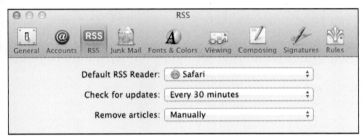

7.19 Choose your default RSS reader, how frequently to look for updates, and whether to remove articles manually or automatically.

Setting up forwarding and autoresponders

You can use rules in Mail to automatically forward messages or respond to them. These are your options:

- **Forwarding.** Forwarding is great when you need to manage multiple email addresses.

- **Autoresponder.** An autoresponder lets you tell people that you're out of the office. Or if you set up an email address that's unique to the rule, you can automatically supply information on a particular topic. For example, you may set up an email address for providing information about your company or services via an autoresponder.

To automatically forward a message, create a rule that uses the Forward Message action to forward the message to the appropriate address. If you want to add text indicating that the message has been forwarded, click the Message button that appears when you select Forward Message, and then type the text in the Reply Message dialog (see Figure 7.20).

7.20 When you create a rule to forward a message or respond automatically, use the Reply Message dialog to specify the text to send.

Caution For both forwarding and an autoresponder, your Mac must be powered on and connected to the Internet, and Mail must be running. If either of these is inconvenient, look into forwarding or autoresponding options that your email provider offers.

To set up an autoresponder, create a rule that uses the Reply To Message action (see Figure 7.21). Click the Reply message text button to open the Reply Message dialog, type the text, and then click OK.

7.21 Setting up an autoresponder in Mail.

Caution Be careful with autoresponders. First, you usually won't want to apply the new rule to the messages in selected mailboxes. Second, if you create an autoresponder to tell people you're out of the office, turn it off as soon as you come back by deselecting its check box in the Rules preferences. Third, be aware that the autoresponder will include the full message text plus any attachments. If you want to avoid returning the full text and attachments, you need to use an AppleScript such as the one you can download from About.com (http://email.about.com/od/macosxmailtips/qt/et022106.htm).

Creating custom stationery templates

Mail's stationery templates (which you can apply by clicking the Show Stationery button in a new message window) let you give your messages predefined looks. But what you'll probably want to do is create stationery templates of your own that contain precisely the text or graphics that you need to create effective messages in moments.

Here's how to create a custom stationery template:

1. **Start a new message.** Press ⌘+N.
2. **Add the text, graphics, and formatting that the template needs.**
3. **Choose File ⇨ Save as Stationery to open the Save as Stationery dialog.**
4. **Type the name for the stationery, and then click Save.**

You can then apply the stationery template from the Custom category at the bottom of the Stationery picker.

Genius

To make your custom stationery templates more accessible, click and drag them to the Favorites category at the top of the Stationery picker.

Accessing email on the web

You can't easily carry your iMac with you wherever you go, but you should be able to access your email from pretty much any computer that has an Internet connection. Here are ways to do just that:

- **MobileMe or iCloud email.** If you have a MobileMe or iCloud email account, you can easily access your email via the Mail feature at the MobileMe website (www.me.com) or the iCloud website (www.icloud.com).

- **Other ISPs and email providers.** Many other ISPs and email providers offer web mail interfaces. For some, you must set up a password other than your main mail password for added protection in case someone intercepts your web password.

- **Web email services.** If your ISP or email provider doesn't offer a web mail interface, you can forward your messages to a web email account (for example, a Gmail account or a Hotmail account).

Chatting with Friends and Colleagues Using iChat

If you want to keep in touch with your friends in real time, iChat is the application to use. Basic chat is easy to use, but you'll probably also want to create custom status messages, chat in groups rather than one-on-one, add video effects, and record your chats.

Setting up status messages

iChat's status readout (just below your username, near the top of the iChat Buddy List window) lets you quickly choose from around a dozen canned options:

- **Available and Away options.** These range from Available or Reading email to Away, Out to lunch, or In a meeting.

- **Custom Available and Custom Away options.** Select one of these options to modify your current status message. Type the text you want in the status box that appears, and then press Enter.

- **Current iTunes Song.** Select this option to display the artist and song you're currently playing. Your buddies can click the gray arrow button to launch iTunes and display the song in the iTunes Store.

- **Invisible.** Select this option to remain online but hide so that others can't see your status.

- **Offline.** Select this option to go offline.

To add custom messages to the status pop-up menu, click the Status button, choose Edit Status Menu, and then work in the dialog that appears (see Figure 7.22). Select the Remember check box if you want iChat to store your custom messages, and choose All, Last 5, Last 10, or Last 20 in the pop-up menu as needed. Click OK when you finish customizing the menu.

7.22 You can customize iChat's status menu with descriptions you prefer.

Chatting on a local network

iChat has Bonjour networking built in, so you can use iChat to chat over a local area network without your chat going over the Internet. This means that you avoid not only overloading your Internet connection with audio and video signals but also that your chat can take place at higher speeds (because your local network is almost certainly faster than your Internet connection). This is great when you're chatting via video or sharing your screen.

To connect to a Bonjour contact, click the disclosure triangle to expand the Bonjour section of the iChat Buddies window. You can then click a contact (see Figure 7.23) and click the appropriate button at the bottom of the Bonjour List window to start a chat — you can choose from Text Chat, Audio Chat, or Video Chat, and you can also opt for screen sharing. The icon to the right of the buddy's name indicates whether he or she is available for video chat (a video camera icon appears) or audio chat (a phone icon appears).

You can share your screen or request to see another contact's screen by clicking the Screen Sharing button and then choosing Share My Screen with Buddy or Ask to Share Buddy's Screen (where Buddy is your buddy's name) from the pop-up menu.

7.23 From the Bonjour List window, you can quickly start either a chat or screen sharing.

Genius

You may need to configure iChat's Bonjour preferences. To do so, choose iChat ⇨ Preferences, click Accounts to display Accounts preferences, and then click Bonjour in the Accounts box on the left. The Enable Bonjour instant messaging check box controls whether Bonjour is on. You can also choose whether to publish your email and instant-messaging addresses, whether to send text as you type (rather than when you press Return), and whether to block others from seeing that you're idle.

The picture on the opening pages of this chapter shows screen sharing. Click the miniature My Computer window to switch back to viewing your Mac's Desktop with the remote computer in a small window. Click the small window to switch to the remote computer again. To end the screen-sharing session, click the Screen Sharing button in the iChat Buddies window and choose End Screen-Sharing from the pop-up menu.

Starting a group chat

Chatting one-on-one is often the best way to communicate, but iChat also lets you chat with up to nine other people in an audio chat and up to three other people in a video chat.

To start a group chat, simply select all the buddies in the iChat Buddy List window by clicking the first name and ⌘+clicking each of the other names, and then click the appropriate button at the bottom of the window. iChat invites each of the buddies to the chat. Those who accept the invitation join the chat.

Note

To see a breakdown of which iChat features your Mac can run, choose Video⇨Connection Doctor, and then choose Capabilities in the Show pop-up menu. Most of the capabilities are straightforward: 1-on-1 video chat, Host multiperson video, Share my screen, and so on. The Video effects item and Backdrop effects item are for Photo Booth video effects (discussed in a moment).

Starting a one-way audio or video chat

If someone with whom you want to chat doesn't have a microphone or web cam, you can invite him to a one-way audio chat or video chat rather than a two-way chat. A one-way chat tends to feel weird, especially for the person on the receiving end of the broadcast, but it can be effective in a pinch. The person on the receiving end can open a text chat window to respond to the broadcaster.

Using Photo Booth video effects in chat

To enliven your video chats, you can use the same video effects in iChat as in Photo Booth. Click the Effects button at the bottom of the Video Chat window, and select the effect from the panel (see Figure 7.24).

Recording a video or audio chat

Communicating via audio or video in iChat is great, but what's even better is being able to record the chats so that you can play them back later.

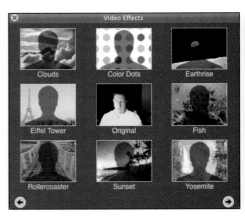

7.24 You can add video effects to your video chats in iChat.

After you establish a video chat or audio chat, choose Video ⇨ Record Chat. iChat prompts the other participant for permission to record the chat. If he or she clicks the Allow button, iChat starts recording and displays a red lamp button in the upper-right corner of the video window to remind you that recording is on.

Choose Video ⇨ Stop Recording to stop the recording. When you close the chat window, iChat automatically saves the chat in your ~/Documents/iChats/ folder under a name such as Audio Chat with Ron.m4a or Video Chat with Claire.mov.

iChat then automatically adds the recording to iTunes. To play back a chat, select the iChat Chats category in the Source list, and then double-click the chat you want to play.

Transferring files via iChat

You can also use iChat to transfer files to your buddies. iChat lets you transfer only a single file at a time, but the process could hardly be easier:

- **Transfer a file in an existing chat.** With the focus in the Chat window, choose Buddies ⇨ Send File, select the file in the dialog that appears, and click Send. Your buddy can choose whether to accept the file.

- **Start a new chat to transfer a file.** Click the buddy in the AIM Buddy List window or the Bonjour List window, choose Buddies ⇨ Send File, select the file in the dialog that appears, and then click Send. iChat starts a text chat with the buddy and prompts him or her to accept the file.

Displaying images, movies, or documents via video chat

After you establish a video chat, you can use it to display images, movies, or even documents to your buddy or buddies:

- **Images.** To share images from iPhoto, launch iPhoto if it's not already running, then (in iChat) choose File ⇨ Share iPhoto With iChat Theater. In the iPhoto dialog that appears, click the album or event you want to share, and then click Share. Your buddy then sees a slide show of the album or event, as do you.

- **Movies.** To share a movie via iChat Theater, choose File ⇨ Share a File With iChat Theater. In the Share with iChat Theater dialog that appears, select the movie, and then click Share.

● **Documents.** You can share most kinds of documents by choosing File ⇨ Share a File With iChat Theater, but for files such as word-processing documents or spreadsheets, the resolution on your buddy's computer is probably too low for him to read the file's contents. It's better to invite the buddy to Screen Sharing, where you can control the size at which the document displays to make it more readable.

To stop sharing an item, choose File ⇨ Stop Sharing With iChat Theater.

Note

When someone's sharing a file with you via video chat, choose Video ⇨ Hide Local Video to get your own video window out of the way.

Making Video Calls with FaceTime

As you saw in the previous section, you can use iChat to make video calls to one or more other computer users. But your iMac has an even easier way of making video calls: FaceTime.

FaceTime is Apple's application for making video calls. At this writing, FaceTime works with all Macs running Mac OS X 10.6.6 or later, the iPhone 4, the iPad 2, and the fourth-generation iPod touch and later models. Your iMac has a built-in video camera and microphone, so it is ready to use FaceTime right out of the box.

Note

FaceTime contacts an iPhone by its phone number. For Macs, the iPad, and the iPod touch, FaceTime uses an email address.

Setting up FaceTime

Before you can use FaceTime, set it up on your iMac using your Apple ID. If you don't already have an Apple ID, you can create one during the setup process.

Here's how to set up FaceTime:

1. **Launch FaceTime by clicking its icon on the Dock or by clicking the Launchpad icon and then clicking FaceTime on the Launchpad screen.** You'll see the FaceTime window (see Figure 7.25).

7.25 Type your Apple ID and password in the Enter Apple ID pane in FaceTime, and then click Sign In. If you don't have an Apple ID, click Create New Account.

2. **Type your Apple ID in the user name box and your password in the password box, and then click Sign In.** FaceTime prompts you to specify the email address at which people will call you. FaceTime suggests the primary email address for the Apple ID you're using.

Note If you don't have an Apple ID, click Create New Account in the Enter Apple ID pane. In the New Account pane that opens, type your details, click Next, and follow through the procedure of setting up the account.

3. **Type a different address if necessary, and then click Next.** FaceTime verifies your account details, and then displays the Contacts pane (see Figure 7.26).

Make and receive calls with FaceTime

To make a call with FaceTime, click the contact in the Contacts pane, and then click the phone number or email address to use. FaceTime places the call, and if your contact accepts it, displays your contact's video feed and starts playing audio.

Similarly, when a contact calls you, the FaceTime window opens and shows the contact's name or phone number, together with an Accept button and a Decline button. Click the Accept button if you want to accept the call. You'll then see and hear your contact.

7.26 From the Contacts pane, you can call any contact who uses FaceTime. Use the Favorites tab at the bottom to keep a list of people you call frequently. Use the Recents tab to see whom you've called, and who's called you, recently.

Genius

You don't need to keep FaceTime running to receive calls. Even when the application is not open, FaceTime listens for incoming calls. When it detects a call, it opens the FaceTime window automatically. If you want FaceTime to stop listening for calls, Control+click or right-click the FaceTime icon on the Dock, and then click Turn FaceTime Off; you'll then need to click Turn FaceTime On before you can use FaceTime again.

To control the call, move the mouse pointer over the FaceTime window so that the control bar appears (see Figure 7.27).

You can then click the Mute button to mute the call, click the Full Screen button (the button with the two diagonal arrows pointing apart) to expand FaceTime to full screen, or click the End button to end the call.

7.27 Move the mouse pointer over the FaceTime window to produce the control bar, which contains controls for muting the call, ending the call, and expanding the window to full screen.

How Can I Use My iMac to Get Organized?

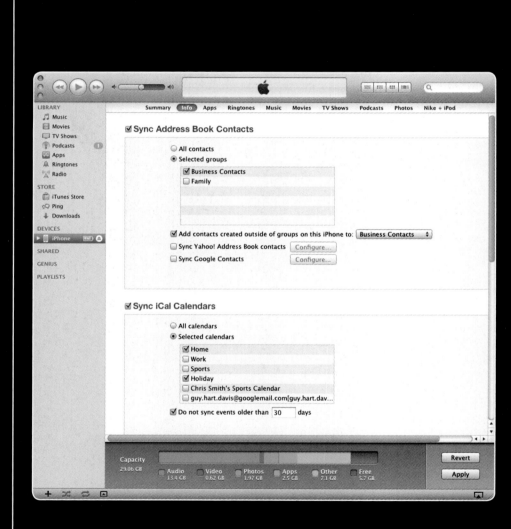

Whether you've decided that it's finally time to get organized or you've been a calendar-and-contacts fanatic for years, you'll find that iCal and Address Book are a powerful combination. This chapter shows you how to make the most of iCal and Address Book and their integration with your iMac's other applications, such as Mail. You also learn how to synchronize your calendar events and contacts with an iPhone, iPad, or iPod so that you can take them with you wherever you go.

Scheduling Your Life

To help you track your events, commitments, and tasks, your iMac includes the powerful iCal calendar application. iCal is linked to other applications that come with your Mac, most notably Address Book and Mail, so you can get more done in less time — provided you learn iCal's ways and tricks.

Syncing calendars among multiple Macs

If you use two or more Macs, you'll probably need to synchronize your calendar data among them. The easiest way to do so is to sign up for Apple's iCloud service and then select the Calendars check box in the iCloud pane in Mail, Contacts & Calendars preferences (see Figure 8.1).

Note If you have a MobileMe account, open the Sync pane in MobileMe preferences. Select the Calendars check box. MobileMe is the current service at this writing, but Apple is phasing it out and introducing iCloud in its place. On June 30, 2012, Apple will shut down MobileMe, and the transition to iCloud will be complete.

8.1 If you have an iCloud account, you can use it to sync all kinds of data, including your calendars, to any Mac logged in to that account.

If you don't have a MobileMe account, and iCloud doesn't suit you, you can use Google Calendar to sync iCal calendars by copying your information to calendars on Google Calendar and then publishing that data so that iCal can drop it back into the calendars on your other Macs or PCs.

In most cases, the best application for this is Spanning Sync ($25/year, $65/lifetime; www. spanningsync.com). This application and service combo takes care of all the messy details of making your iCal calendars sync with your Google calendars, and vice versa.

If you only want to sync your calendars on your local network, try BusySync ($40; www.busymac. com), which allows multiple users to share and edit iCal calendars on a local area network (LAN). BusySync can also sync with Google Calendar, but you can use it just on your LAN if that's what you need. You can make changes to a calendar whether or not you're connected to the network; when you reconnect, BusySync checks all your calendars and updates them if necessary.

Publishing calendars with and without MobileMe or iCloud

When you need to let other people see your calendar but not edit it, publish the calendar on iCloud, MobileMe, or another service, such as the free iCal Exchange (www.icalx.com) or a calendar service that your company or organization runs.

Here's how to publish a calendar:

1. **In iCal, click the Calendars button to display the Calendars pop-up panel.**

2. **In the Calendars pop-up panel, Control+click or right-click the calendar, and then choose Publish from the shortcut menu.** The Publish calendar dialog opens (see Figure 8.2).

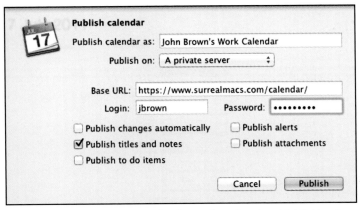

8.2 To publish a calendar on a calendar service other than MobileMe, choose A private server in the Publish on pop-up menu in the Publish calendar dialog.

3. **In the Publish calendar as text box, type the name you want to give the calendar online.** You'll often need to use a more descriptive name — for example, one that includes your name — for the published calendar than you use in iCal.

4. **In the Publish on pop-up menu, choose where to publish the calendar:**

   - **MobileMe.** Choose MobileMe to publish the calendar on MobileMe. iCal uses your existing credentials, so you don't need to type them here.

   - **A private server.** Choose A private server to publish the calendar on iCal Exchange or a private server, such as your company's server. Type the server's address in the Base URL text box, your username in the Login text box, and your password in the Password text box.

5. **Choose publishing options.** If you have a constant Internet connection, select the Publish changes automatically check box so that you don't need to update the published calendar manually whenever you make a change.

6. **Click Publish.** iCal publishes the calendar. If you're using a private server, iCal displays a dialog giving the URL. If you're using MobileMe to publish your calendar, you'll also see a button that can take you directly to that calendar's page on the web.

Caution

Be sure you don't select the Publish alarms option unless you really want anyone who's subscribed to your calendar to get a reminder every time you're supposed to take an action.

Accessing your calendar online

The easiest way to access your calendar when you're away from home or the office is to use MobileMe or iCloud. Once you've chosen to sync your calendar with MobileMe or iCloud, you can not only view your calendar as a web page on MobileMe or iCloud but also edit it there and have the changes appear back on the Macs that you're synchronizing with MobileMe or iCloud.

Note

You can access your calendars on MobileMe or iCloud in two ways. First, you can go directly to the MobileMe website (www.me.com) or the iCloud website (www.icloud.com), log in, and then click the Calendar button on the toolbar. Second, you can get a direct link from iCal like this: Click the Calendars button to display the Calendars pop-up panel, then Control+click or right-click the calendar's name and choose Send Publish Email. In the email message that iCal creates, click the calendar's URL to open it in Safari, and then bookmark it. Close the email message without sending it.

To view your calendar online without MobileMe or iCloud, follow these steps:

1. **Set up a Google account if you don't have one.** Go to www.google.com, click the Sign In link, and follow through the procedure for creating an account. This account is free.

2. **Sign up for an iCal Exchange account.** Go to www.icalx.com and create an account. This account is also free.

3. **Launch iCal and publish the calendar as described in the previous section.** Follow these steps:

   1. **In the Publish on pop-up menu, choose A private server, and then type the details of your iCal Exchange account.**

   2. **Choose which publishing options you want.** For example, publish changes automatically, but don't publish alarms or attachments.

   3. **Click Publish.** When iCal displays the Calendar Published dialog, click Send Mail to create a message containing the address.

   4. **In the message, select the calendar's URL, and then copy it.**

4. **Sign in to your Google Calendar account (http://calendar.google.com) and add the calendar like this:**

   1. **Click the Add link, and then choose Add by URL from the pop-up menu to display the Add by URL dialog.**

   2. **Paste in the URL you copied.**

   3. **Make sure the Make the calendar publicly accessible? check box is unselected unless you want to air your calendar in public.**

   4. **Click Add Calendar.** Google Calendar pulls in your calendar from iCal Exchange.

After adding your calendar to Google Calendar like this, you can view your calendar appointments at any time by going to http://calendar.google.com and logging in.

Using invitations in iCal

To let people know about the events you want them to attend, send them event invitations and reminders from iCal. Each invitation email includes a special attachment that adds the event to the recipient's calendar when he or she double-clicks it.

Before you invite people to an event, make sure you have a card in Address Book that you've marked as your My Card. Follow these steps:

1. **Click the Address Book icon on the Dock to open Address Book.**

2. **If you have an existing card, make sure it contains the information you want.** If not, click the Add (+) button, and then type your information.

3. **Choose Card ➪ Make This My Card.**

4. **Quit Address Book.** Press ⌘+Q.

With your card in place, you can invite people to an event like this:

1. **In iCal, double-click the event you want to invite people to.** Then click Edit to open the event for editing.

2. **Click Add Invitees next to the invitees field and type the email address for the person you want to invite (see Figure 8.3).** Or, if the person's info is in your Address Book, just type the person's name.

3. **To add another invitee, press Return, and then type another person's name or email address.** To remove someone from the attendees list, click the arrow next to that person's name and choose Remove Invitee.

4. **When you finish adding invitees, click Send.** As your attendees respond to your invitation, you'll see their status in the Notifications box. The symbol next to each attendee's name indicates that person's status: an arrow for no reply, a check mark for an acceptance, an "x" for regrets, and a question mark for a maybe.

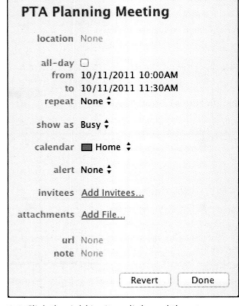

8.3 Click the Add Invitees link, and then type each invitee for the event in the invitees field.

Note

Don't forget to click Send again if you modify the event, so that your attendees receive a notification of the changes.

When someone invites you to an event, you'll receive an email. What's usually most convenient is to have iCal automatically get the invitations from Mail so that it can tell you about them.

You can set that up like this:

1. **Open iCal if it's not already running.**

2. **Choose iCal ⇨ Preferences (or press ⌘+, [comma]) to open the Preferences window.**

3. **Click the Advanced button on the toolbar to display the Advanced pane.**

4. **Select the Automatically retrieve CalDAV invitations from Mail check box.**

5. **Click the Close (x) button to close the Preferences window.**

If you choose not to use this automatic retrieval, you'll need to open the email and double-click the attachment (its filename should end in .ics) to tell iCal about the invitation.

Whichever way iCal receives the invitation, iCal adds it to your Notifications box in the lower-left corner of the iCal window. If the Notifications box isn't visible, click the Notifications button (the envelope icon) to display your invitations. In the list, click the invitation to which you want to reply, and then click Maybe, Decline, or Accept (see Figure 8.4).

When the event is in your calendar, you can open it just like any other event, but you can change only a couple of aspects. You can add an alarm to remind you of the event, and you can change your reply by choosing a new status from the pop-up menu and then clicking Reply again.

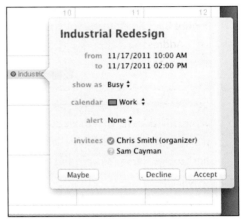

8.4 Use the buttons in the Notifications box to respond instantly to an invitation.

Genius

To make the most of iCal, use the Note field in an event to track any information you need to keep associated with the event. You can add whatever information you need — notes on things you'll need to take to the meeting, questions you need to ask at the meeting, flight details, driving directions, or anything else. Spotlight indexes iCal, so you can locate the data instantly by searching.

Adding iCal events from Mail

If you receive an invitation in a regular email message rather than in an attached iCal invitation, you can add the event to iCal from Mail by holding your mouse over the date. Mail displays a pop-up menu with two choices:

- **Create New iCal Event.** Click this item to create a new event for the date and time specified.

- **Show This Date in iCal.** Click this item to open iCal to the day so that you can see what's already on your schedule.

Tracking Contacts

To work effectively with your contacts, put them all into your Address Book. You can then

- Access contact info from within iCal, iChat, and Mail.

- Create groups to organize your contacts.

- Print contact lists the way you need them.

- Search for Address Book data using Spotlight.

Genius

To automatically add Safari bookmarks for any URLs you enter in the Address Book, start Safari and choose Safari ⇨ Preferences. Click the Bookmarks button on the toolbar, and then select the Include Address Book check box. Safari stores your Address Book bookmarks in a new folder called Address Book at the left end of the Bookmarks bar.

Setting up Smart Groups in Address Book

If you regularly send mail or call specific groups of people, use Address Book's feature for creating Smart Groups. Address Book can filter your contacts and make a group for you that contains everyone who lives in a particular city or state, everyone who's having a birthday this month, or everyone who works at a specific company. Address Book automatically updates Smart Groups with new contacts that fit the criteria you specify.

Here's how to create a Smart Group:

1. **In Address Book, click the All Contacts card to display the All Contacts page.**

2. **Hold down Option while you click the Add (+) button in the lower-left corner.** Alternatively, choose File ⇨ New Smart Group. Address Book displays the Smart Group dialog.

3. **Type a name for the group, and then specify search criteria.** Use the pop-up menus to set the criteria on which you want the group to be based; click + to add another criterion (see Figure 8.5).

4. **Click OK.**

To edit a Smart Group, Control+click or right-click the group's name and choose Edit Smart Group from the contextual menu. You can rename a Smart Group by clicking its name in the Group column, clicking again, and then typing the new name.

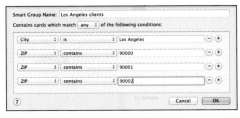

8.5 Create a Smart Group in Address Book to pull together contacts who meet the criteria you specify.

Genius Criteria for a Smart Group can include any part of a contact's address, a phone number, an email address, or IM screen name. You can also use the Notes field to insert any keyword that makes sense to you, and then create a Smart Group that looks for that keyword in the Notes field.

Trading contact info with vCards

A vCard is a small text file (with the .vcf file extension) containing contact data for one or more people. You can attach a vCard to an outgoing email to share your contact information. And when you receive a vCard attached to a message, you can click and drag it straight into the Address Book window to add a contact record for that person.

You can create a vCard for one or more contacts by clicking the contact in Address Book and dragging it to the desktop or a Finder window. If you select multiple contacts before dragging, you get a single vCard file containing the data for all those contacts.

Caution Some applications (including Microsoft's Entourage and Outlook) can't handle multicontact vCard files. If you want to create individual vCard files for multiple people, press Option and hold it down as you click and drag the contacts out of the Address Book window. This produces a single file per contact, each named after that contact. You can drag a whole slew of these individual files into Entourage or Outlook at the same time, so there's no real time lost.

You can create a vCard file for yourself by clicking and dragging, but it's best to sort out your card's details beforehand. Follow these steps:

1. **In Address Book, make sure you have a contact record.** Choose Card ⇨ Go To My Card to display the card that Address Book currently holds for you. If this command is unavailable, create a card with your information, and then choose Card ⇨ Make This My Card to tell Address Book that this is your card.

2. **Make the card private to you like this:**

   1. **Choose Address Book ➪ Preferences to open the Preferences window.**

   2. **Click the vCard button on the toolbar to display the vCard pane.**

   3. **Select the Enable private me card check box.**

   4. **Click the Close button (the red button) to close the Preferences window.**

3. **Tell Address Book which fields to include in your vCard:**

   1. **With your card still selected, click Edit to turn on editing.** Address Book displays a check box next to each field.

   2. **Clear the check box for each field you want to keep out of the vCard.**

   3. **Click Done to turn off editing.**

You can now export the vCard, either by clicking and dragging or by choosing File ➪ Export ➪ Export vCard.

Accessing and sharing your Address Book online

If you have a MobileMe account or iCloud account, you can both check your Address Book online and share your iMac's Address Book info with any other MobileMe members or iCloud members you specify.

Note Before you can share your Address Book online, you must sign in to MobileMe or iCloud if you have not already done so. Choose Apple menu ➪ System Preferences to open the System Preferences window, and then click the MobileMe icon or iCloud icon in the Internet & Wireless section. In the preferences pane that opens, type your user name and password, and then click Sign In.

To share your Address Book online, follow these steps:

1. **Choose Address Book ➪ Preferences to open the Preferences window.**

2. **Click the Accounts button on the toolbar to display the Accounts pane.**

3. **Click the Sharing tab to display the Sharing pane.**

4. **Select the Share your address book check box.**

5. **Type the names of any other MobileMe members or iCloud members who should have access to your contact info.**

6. **Click Send Invitation to send these people an email telling them how to access the information.**

Removing duplicate contacts

If you have many contacts, it's easy to get duplicate contacts in Address Book. Here's how to get rid of them:

1. **Open Address Book.**

2. **Choose Card⇨ Look for Duplicates.** Address Book sifts through your contacts and displays a dialog (see Figure 8.6) telling you how many duplicates it has found.

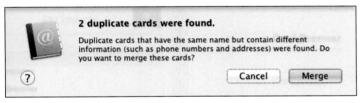

2 duplicate cards were found.

Duplicate cards that have the same name but contain different information (such as phone numbers and addresses) were found. Do you want to merge these cards?

Cancel   Merge

8.6 Merging cards combines all the information from each card into a single card for each person.

3. **Click Merge.**

Genius

You can also merge contacts manually if necessary. Click the first contact, ⌘+click each other record for the same person, and then choose Card⇨ Merge Selected Cards.

Printing contacts

Keeping your contacts on your Mac and your iPhone, iPad, or iPod is great most of the time, but sometimes you may need to print your contacts so that you can use them. Address Book offers four styles of printout so you can get just what you want.

Here's how to print contacts from Address Book:

1. **In Address Book, select the contacts or groups you want.** As usual, click an item to select it, or ⌘+click to add another item to your current selection.

2. **Choose File⇨ Print to open the Print dialog.** You can also press ⌘+P, the Mac-standard shortcut for Print.

3. **Open the Style pop-up menu in the middle of the dialog, and then choose the printout style you want:**

- **Mailing labels.** Use these when addressing envelopes that can't fit through your printer or when there are too many of them to bother putting them through. You can choose a label size from a menu of common Avery sizes or define a custom label size. Choose which addresses to print (for example, home addresses or work addresses), the printing order (by name or by postal code), and a font and point size for the text. You can also choose whether to include the company name and the country name. If you include the country name, you can choose to include it only for countries other than your country.

- **Envelopes.** First, specify an envelope size from the built-in list or define a custom size; then choose the font and point size and whether to include your return address (you can't choose a different one).

- **Lists.** Select a paper size, choose which fields to include in the list (Phone, Email, Address, and so on), and choose a font size (Regular or Large). You can't change the font or type a specific point size.

- **Pocket Address Book.** This style is good if you prefer to have a paper address book. You choose either compact or indexed layout (with letter tabs on the side of each page), and then set the paper size. Specify the fields to include and pick a font to use; a condensed font such as Arial Narrow usually works well.

4. **Click Print to print the data.**

Syncing Your Calendar and Contacts with an iPhone, iPad, or iPod

If you have an iPhone, iPad, or iPod touch, you can synchronize your calendar appointments and contacts with it easily. You can then carry the information with you and edit it as needed on the go.

Here's how to synchronize your calendar and contacts with an iPhone, iPad, or iPod touch:

1. **Connect your iPhone, iPad, or iPod touch to your iMac as usual with the Dock Connector cable.** If iTunes isn't already running, Mac OS X launches it.

2. **In the Devices section of the Source list in iTunes, click the iPhone, iPad, or iPod touch.** The device's control screens appear.

Note
You can also synchronize contacts and calendars with the iPod classic and the iPod nano. For these iPods, you'll find the controls in the Contacts pane rather than in the Info pane.

3. **In the tab bar at the top, click the Info tab to display the Info pane.** The illustration on the opening page of this chapter shows the Info pane for an iPhone.

4. **Select the Sync Address Book Contacts check box, and then choose which contacts to synchronize:**

   - **Select the All contacts option if you want to synchronize all contacts in your Address Book.** Otherwise, select the Selected groups option, and then select the check box for each group you want to synchronize.

   - **To tell Address Book where to store contacts you create on the device but don't assign to a group, select the Add contacts created outside of groups on this iPhone/iPad/iPod to check box, and then choose the group in the pop-up menu.**

   - **If you have a Yahoo!** Address Book, select the Sync Yahoo! Address Book contacts check box. Click Configure, and then follow through the procedure for providing your Yahoo! ID and choosing the contacts.

   - **If you have a Google Contacts list, select the Sync Google Contacts check box.** Click Configure, and then follow through the dialogs for typing your Google ID and password.

5. **Select the Sync iCal Calendars check box, and then choose which calendars to synchronize:**

   - **Select the All calendars option if you want to synchronize all your calendars.** This is often the best option, as it puts all your events in the palm of your hand.

   - **Otherwise, select the Selected calendars option, and then select the check box for each calendar you want to include.**

   - **If you want to keep down the amount of data you need to synchronize, select the Do not sync events older than *N* days check box, and then type the number of days in the text box.** The default number is 30, which provides you with a decent amount of recent history.

6. **Click Apply.** iTunes synchronizes the contacts and calendars you specified with the iPhone, iPad, or iPod touch.

How Can I Telecommute Efficiently on My iMac?

Today's relentless rise in gasoline prices, counterbalanced only by the march of ever-faster Internet connections, makes telecommuting more economical and practical than ever. And if you can get more done in your bathrobe than in business casual in the office, telecommuting should be an easy sell to your boss as well. Your iMac offers several ways to connect to your office computer, plus various options for collaborating with your colleagues across the Internet. Your iMac also gives you powerful tools that can do your work for you — effortlessly, automatically, and repeatedly. These tools include Automator, Folder Actions, and scripts and macros.

Working in More than One Place

Your iMac offers several ways of working in multiple places at the same time. If you have a Mac in the office, you can simply access it over the Internet and work on it much as if you were physically there.

Accessing your Mac over the Internet

Ideally, you'd be able to reach out from your iMac, take control of your office Mac, and simply work on it.

Provided your office Mac and your iMac both run Lion (Mac OS X 10.7), Snow Leopard (Mac OS X 10.6), or Leopard (Mac OS X 10.5) rather than an earlier version, you can do just that by using either Back to My Mac or Screen Sharing. To access your office Mac from a computer running a different operating system, you can use Virtual Network Computing (VNC) to control your office Mac's screen.

If neither Back to My Mac nor Screen Sharing is an option, you can access files on your office Mac by using File Sharing. And if you're happy working in Terminal, you can connect via Secure Shell (SSH) to transfer files or take actions.

Controlling your Mac via Back to My Mac

If you have a MobileMe membership or an iCloud account and your office Mac runs Lion, Snow Leopard, or Leopard, try Back to My Mac first for remote access. Back to My Mac uses the MobileMe service or iCloud service to track the address of each of the Macs and establish communication between them, which helps avoid problems with firewalls.

Turn on Back to My Mac on your office Mac and your iMac like this:

1. **Choose Apple menu ⇨ System Preferences.** The System Preferences window opens.

2. **In the Internet & Wireless section, click the Mail, Contacts & Calendars icon to display Mail, Contacts & Calendars preferences.**

3. **Click your iCloud account to display the iCloud pane (see Figure 9.1).** If you have multiple iCloud accounts, click the primary one. The primary account is the one that doesn't say "This is not your primary iCloud account" at the top.

4. **Scroll down to the Back to My Mac item, and then select its check box.**

5. **Click Show All to display the full set of system preferences.**

6. **In the Internet & Wireless section, click Sharing to display Sharing preferences.** Select the check box for each type of sharing you want to use — for example, Screen Sharing (discussed in more detail later in this chapter) and File Sharing (discussed in Chapter 4).

7. **Choose System Preferences ⇨ Quit System Preferences.** System Preferences closes.

9.1 Launch the Back to My Mac feature from the iCloud pane in Mail, Contacts & Calendars.

After you turn on Back to My Mac on each Mac, connect like this:

1. **Open a Finder window.**

2. **In the sidebar, expand the Shared category if it's collapsed.**

3. **Click the Mac to which you want to connect.** The Finder displays connection options.

4. **Click Share Screen if you want to share the screen.** This is usually the easiest way to work on a remote Mac. Otherwise, click the shared folder that you want to use.

5. **When your iMac connects, the Screen Sharing window showing your office Mac appears (see Figure 9.2).**

You can work in the Screen Sharing window much as if you were working directly on the office Mac. These are the main differences:

- ⊙ **Screen updating.** The screen updates more slowly, depending on the speed of the Internet connection. If updating is uncomfortably slow, try choosing View ⇨ Adaptive Quality instead of View ⇨ Full Quality.

9.2 Your office's Mac's screen appears in a Screen Sharing window after you connect using Back to My Mac or Screen Sharing itself. Here, the remote Mac is called Work iMac.

- ⊙ **Resizing the screen.** You can shrink the office Mac's screen to fit in the Screen Sharing window by clicking the Fit Screen in Window button at the left end of the toolbar. (If the toolbar isn't displayed, choose View ⇨ Show Toolbar to display it.) Usually, though, lowering the resolution until the screen fits in the window gives a more workable effect — but you will need to restore the screen resolution afterward. If you want to view the office Mac's screen at full size, choose View ⇨ Turn Scaling Off. If the office Mac's screen is too big to fit in the Screen Sharing window, you will need to scroll to reach its extremities.

- **Transferring Clipboard data.** The other two buttons on the toolbar let you retrieve the contents of the office Mac's Clipboard (to paste on your iMac) or transfer your iMac's Clipboard contents to the office PC (to paste there).

- **When you finish working on your office Mac, you can simply log out and choose Screen Sharing ⇨ Quit Screen Sharing.** If you don't need to access the office Mac before you go into the office again, shut it down before quitting Screen Sharing.

Note The preferences for the Screen Sharing application (choose Screen Sharing ⇨ Preferences) let you choose whether to start with screen scaling and adaptive quality turned on. You can also choose whether to encrypt only passwords and keystrokes or to encrypt all network data (which is more secure but slower).

Avoiding Unpleasant Surprises with Screen Sharing

Screen Sharing can be a great way to work remotely, but it has a couple of twists you need to know about.

First, if the Mac you connect to via Screen Sharing uses Fast User Switching and you leave yourself logged in, you can connect to your session in the background even while someone else is logged in and actually using the Mac in the foreground. When this happens, you're both using the Mac at the same time.

This can be an efficient way of using the Mac's powerful processor, but it can also be confusing. The person actually at the Mac receives no notice of your presence unless you take an action she can see, such as ejecting a CD or printing a document on an attached printer. Similarly, you can see from the Fast User Switching menu that the other user is logged in, but not that she's using the Mac.

If you want to find out whether someone is actually using the Mac when you connect remotely via Screen Sharing, launch FaceTime. If FaceTime says that no camera is available, you're working in a background session, and someone else is working in the foreground. If you're working in the foreground, FaceTime finds the camera and displays whatever it's pointing at — your desk chair stacked with incoming paperwork, perhaps.

When your user session is logged on in the foreground, your actions appear on the Mac's screen as normal while you work via Screen Sharing, so anybody near your Mac can see what you're doing. You won't know this person is watching unless she tries to wrest control of the apparently possessed Mac from you — so you may want to run FaceTime to see whether anyone's looking at your Mac.

Troubleshooting Back to My Mac

At this writing, Back to My Mac is an impressive feature, but it doesn't work consistently across all connections. If you have trouble making Back to My Mac work, check the following:

- **You've connected your network router directly to your cable or DSL router.** If your cable or DSL router includes the network router, you're all set.

- **Your router supports Universal Plug and Play (UPnP) or Network Address Translation Port Mapping Protocol (NAT-PMP).** UPnP is widely used in cable and DSL modems, while NAT-PMP is an Apple protocol.

- **You've turned on UPnP or NAT-PMP on the router.** For example, to turn on NAT-PMP in an AirPort Express or AirPort Extreme, launch AirPort Utility (see Chapter 4), click Manual Setup, click the Internet button in the toolbar, click the NAT tab, and then select the Enable NAT Port Mapping Protocol check box. Click Update to apply the change.

- **If your router doesn't support UPnP or NAT-PMP, you have a public, routable IP address.** This is an IP address that is "visible" from the Internet rather than being hidden behind a router.

- **If you're using a third-party firewall, you've configured it to allow UDP connections to port 4500.** Mac OS X's built-in firewall automatically allows these connections.

- **You've turned on Back to My Mac on each Mac.**

- **Both the Macs are running the same version of Mac OS X with all the latest updates applied.** This isn't an absolute requirement, but it can help when you're having trouble getting Back to My Mac to work.

Controlling your Mac using Screen Sharing or VNC

If you don't have a MobileMe account or iCloud account or can't use these services in your office, you can use Screen Sharing or VNC instead to control your office Mac from your iMac. VNC is a networking technology that provides screen sharing and remote control on most major operating systems (including Windows, Unix, and Linux).

First, set up Screen Sharing on your office Mac. Follow these steps:

1. **Choose Apple menu ⇨ System Preferences.** The Screen Sharing window opens.

2. **In the Internet & Wireless section, click the Sharing icon to open Sharing preferences.**

3. **If the padlock icon is closed, click it and type your username and password.** Then click OK.

4. **In the left list box, click Screen Sharing — just click the item in the Service list rather than selecting its check box.** Mac OS X displays the Screen Sharing controls (see Figure 9.3).

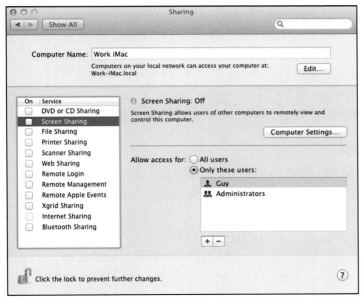

9.3 Set up Screen Sharing on your office Mac so that you can control it from home.

5. **If necessary, change the name in the Computer Name box.** If your network adminis-trator has assigned an impenetrable corporate name, you might change it to a name you can recognize more easily.

6. **If you will need to control the Mac via VNC rather than Screen Sharing, click Computer Settings.** In the dialog shown in Figure 9.4, select the VNC viewers may control screen with password check box, type the password, and then click OK. You'll then need to type your user account password to confirm the setting. You then return to Sharing preferences.

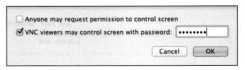

9.4 If you will use VNC to control the Mac remotely, set the password in this dialog.

7. **In the Allow access for area, choose who may access the Mac via Screen Sharing.** Normally, it's best to select the Only these users option and line up the users in the list box. You may find your name already appears there, so you don't need to add it. For security, add other users only when it becomes necessary. To add a user, click the Add (+) button, click the user's name in the dialog that opens, and then click the Select button.

8. **In the list on the left, select the Screen Sharing check box to turn on Screen Sharing.**

9. **Choose System Preferences ⇨ Quit System Preferences to quit System Preferences.**

That was the easy bit. The next part is a little trickier:

1. **If your office Mac is located behind a firewall, turn on port forwarding and configure it to route the Screen Sharing request to your Mac.** Most office networks use firewalls for security. If you don't administer the office network, ask the administrator to set up the port forwarding.

2. **Find out your office Mac's IP address.** Open the Network preferences, click your main network connection (for example, Ethernet), and look at the IP Address readout. To make sure the IP address doesn't change, configure the Mac to use a static IP address rather than a dynamic IP address. Again, you may need to ask the administrator to do this.

3. **On your iMac (your home Mac), add Screen Sharing to the Applications folder.** Click the desktop to activate the Finder, choose Go ⇨ Go to Folder, type **/System/Library/CoreServices**, and then click Go. In the CoreServices folder that opens in a Finder window, click and drag the Screen Sharing application to your Applications folder (or to the Dock, if you prefer) so that you can run Screen Sharing easily.

When you finish your preparations, you can connect your iMac (your home Mac) via Screen Sharing across the Internet like this:

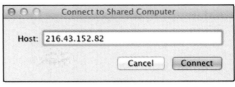

1. **Launch Screen Sharing from Launchpad or the Dock.** Screen Sharing displays the Connect to Shared Computer dialog (see Figure 9.5).

9.5 The Connect to Shared Computer dialog lets you connect to another Mac across the Internet via Screen Sharing.

2. **Type your office Mac's IP address in the Host box, and click Connect.** Screen Sharing prompts you for your name and password.

3. **Type your username and password, and select the Remember this password in my keychain check box if you want to store the password.**

4. **Click Connect.** Screen Sharing connects to your office Mac and displays its screen in a window.

You can now work on your office Mac as described in the previous section.

If your Mac doesn't have Lion, Snow Leopard, or Leopard, or if you need to connect from a PC, you can connect via VNC instead of Screen Sharing. To do so, install a VNC client (see the following list), type your Mac's IP address, and connect.

Here are free VNC clients for the leading three operating systems:

- **Mac OS X.** Chicken of the VNC (http://sourceforge.net/projects/cotvnc).

- **Windows.** VNC Free Edition (http://realvnc.com/products/free/4.1/index.html).

- **Linux.** Most distributions of Linux include a VNC client (or several), so look on your box before downloading a client. If not, try VNC Free Edition (http://realvnc.com/products/free/4.1/index.html).

Genius

You can also connect to your Mac via VNC from an iPad, iPhone, or iPod touch. You can find a wide variety of VNC apps in the Utilities area of the App Store. Even the lite versions work pretty well, though some of them struggle to deal with firewalls.

Connecting via File Sharing

If you need to copy files to or from your office Mac rather than control it remotely, you can connect via File Sharing instead of Screen Sharing. As with Screen Sharing, you need to know your office Mac's IP address or have configured port forwarding on the router to be able to reach the office Mac across the Internet.

Here's how to connect via File Sharing:

1. **Click the Finder button on the Dock, and then choose Go ⇨ Connect to Server.** The Connect to Server dialog appears (see Figure 9.6).

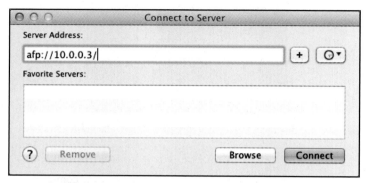

9.6 Use the Connect to Server dialog to connect to your office Mac via File Sharing.

2. **Type your office Mac's address in the Server Address box.** Click the Add (+) button if you want to add the address to the Favorite Servers list so that you can choose it more easily next time.

3. **Click Connect, and type your name and password for your office Mac when prompted.** As usual, select the Remember this password in my keychain check box if you want to save the password for future use. Mac OS X prompts you to select the volumes you want to mount (see Figure 9.7).

9.7 Choose the office Mac's volumes you want to use via File Sharing.

4. **Select each volume you want to use.** Shift+click to select a range of volumes, or ⌘+click to add a volume to those you've already selected.

Note

You can type the afp:// term before the hostname or IP address in the Connect to Server dialog to specify a connection via Apple Filing Protocol (AFP) — for example, afp://10.0.0.21. But if you omit this term, Mac OS X adds it for you automatically.

5. **Click OK.** A Finder window opens showing your office Mac in the Shared section of the sidebar, and the volumes you chose appear on your iMac's Desktop. You can then manage files as usual — for example, you can copy files from your office Mac to your iMac.

6. **When you finish using File Sharing, click the Eject button next to your office Mac in the sidebar to close the connection.**

Note

See Chapter 4 for instructions on setting up File Sharing.

Connecting via Secure Shell

When you can't connect to your office Mac via Back to My Mac, Screen Sharing, or File Sharing, you can fall back on Secure Shell (SSH) and Remote Login. This means working from the command line in a Terminal window, so you don't have the comfort of the Mac OS X graphical interface and you need to know at least a few Unix commands.

Genius

You can connect to your office Mac via Secure Shell from any computer — it doesn't have to be a Mac.

First, turn on Remote Login on your office Mac. Follow these steps:

1. **Choose Apple menu ⇨ System Preferences.** The System Preferences window opens.

2. **In the Internet & Wireless section, click the Sharing icon to open Sharing preferences.**

3. **If the padlock icon is closed, click it, type your username and password, and then click OK.**

4. **In the list on the left, click the Remote Login item (don't select the check box yet).** The Remote Login options appear.

5. **In the Allow access for area, choose who may access the Mac via Remote Login.** The default setting is the All users option, but it's best to select the Only these users option. Click the Add (+) button, click your user in the dialog that opens, and then click Select.

6. **In the list on the left, select the Remote Login check box.**

7. **Look at the login information given under the Remote Login: On indicator.** This tells you the login name and IP address to use for SSH; for example, *ssh jbrown@216.42.81.167*.

8. **Choose System Preferences ⇨ Quit System Preferences to quit System Preferences.**

Controlling Your Work PC Remotely

If you have a PC at work and a fast Internet connection both at work and home, you can use Microsoft's Remote Desktop Connection application to work on your office PC using your iMac.

You can download Remote Desktop Connection for free from the Mactopia area of the Microsoft website (www.microsoft.com/mac/remote-desktop-client).

When you use Remote Desktop Connection, you log in remotely to your PC, so anyone at your PC sees only the login screen, not what you're doing. You can set the size of the Windows Desktop to the size you need without affecting your PC's screen. And you can run Remote Desktop Connection either in a window or full screen.

You can now log in from your iMac as follows:

1. **Click the Finder button on the Dock, choose Go ⇨ Utilities, and then double-click Terminal.** A Terminal window opens.

2. **At the command prompt, type** ssh **and the login name and IP address for your office Mac, and press Return.** If you have a different username on your office Mac than on your iMac, type **ssh -l** and your username, and then the login name and IP address for the office Mac.

3. **Type your password when prompted.** You then see a prompt for your office Mac, and you can run commands on it. For example, you can use the scp command to securely copy files from one Mac to the other.

4. **Type** exit **and press Return when you're ready to end the session.**

5. **Choose Terminal ⇨ Quit Terminal.**

Connecting to your company's network

If your company won't let you connect directly to your office Mac from home, it may let you connect to the company network instead via a virtual private network (VPN) connection. A VPN uses encryption to create a secure "tunnel" across the Internet from your iMac to the company's VPN server.

Ask the network administrator for the VPN details:

● **Server address or name.** This can be either an IP address or a computer name.

● **Your login name and password.** This may be your regular login for the work network or a separate remote-access account. The administrator may require you to use a certificate rather than a password to authenticate yourself.

● **Encryption type.** This can be Layer 2 Tunneling Protocol (L2TP) over IPSec, Point-to-Point Tunneling Protocol (PPTP), or Cisco IPSec. L2TP is more secure than PPTP. Cisco IPSec is the most secure encryption type but requires Cisco hardware.

Armed with those details, set up the VPN connection on your iMac like this:

1. **Choose Apple menu ⇨ System Preferences.** The System Preferences window opens.

2. **In the Internet & Wireless section, click the Network icon to open Network preferences.**

3. **Click the Add (+) button below the service list.** The dialog shown in Figure 9.8 appears.

4. **Choose VPN in the Interface pop-up menu.**

5. **Choose the encryption type — L2TP over IPSec, PPTP, or Cisco IPSec — in the VPN Type pop-up menu.**

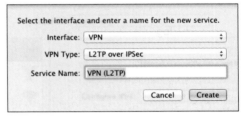

9.8 The first step in setting up a VPN is to create the network entry.

6. **Type a name for the VPN connection in the Service Name box.** This name is for your benefit, so you can make it descriptive — but keep it short so it fits in the list of network interfaces.

7. **Click Create.** The dialog closes, and the VPN connection appears in the list of network interfaces.

8. **Click the VPN item you just created to display its configuration options (see Figure 9.9).**

9. **Type the VPN server's IP address in the Server Address text box.**

10. **Type your account name in the Account Name text box.**

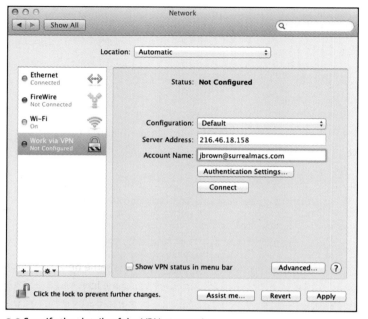

9.9 Specify the details of the VPN connection.

11. Click Authentication Settings to open the Authentication dialog (see Figure 9.10).

12. Choose your means of authentication. For example, select the Password option and type the password, or choose a certificate type, click Select, and pick the certificate file. If your network's administrator has told you to use machine authentication, enter the details in the Machine Authentication area.

9.10 Type your password or choose another means of authentication in this dialog.

13. Click OK to close the Authentication dialog.

14. Select the Show VPN status in menu bar check box. This puts a VPN menulet at the right end of the menu bar.

15. Click Apply to finish creating the VPN connection.

While you have the VPN pane open in Network preferences, you can connect to the VPN connection by clicking Connect. This is useful when you need to test the VPN connection after setting it up, but what you'll probably want to do for regular use is click the VPN menulet on the menu bar and then choose the Connect command with the VPN's name. The menulet also has a Network Preferences item that you can use to jump directly to the VPN pane in Network Preferences when you need to change settings.

After you connect to the VPN, you can access folders and resources on the network, but at much slower speeds than if you were connected directly.

To close the VPN connection, open the VPN menulet at the right end of the menu bar and click Disconnect.

Moving files with portable drives

When you need to transfer files between two computers that aren't on the same network, a portable drive is often the handiest choice. USB key drives or thumb drives come in ever-larger sizes; at this writing, 256GB drives are available at sky-high prices, but the higher-capacity drives on the horizon should bring costs down soon. If you need to move larger files than will fit on an affordable USB key drive, use a USB external drive.

To move files with a portable drive, simply copy the files from your Mac to the portable drive, eject it and take it to the other computer, and then copy the files across.

Another option is to transfer the files by using a storage site on the Internet, uploading the files from one computer and downloading them to the other. If you have a MobileMe account, your iDisk currently provides an easy way to transfer up to 20GB of files, either using your private folders or your Public folder; but Apple is closing MobileMe on June 30, 2012, and iDisk is one of the features that the iCloud Service (which is replacing MobileMe) does not provide. If you don't have a MobileMe account, you'll find plenty of other storage sites to use. Many offer a small amount of free storage to entice you to pay for an upgrade.

Genius

If you have an iPhone, iPad, or iPod, you can use it to transfer files. For an iPod other than the iPod touch, in iTunes, click the iPod in the Devices category in the Source list, click the Summary tab, select the Enable disk use option, and then click Apply. The iPod then appears as a drive in the Finder, and you can copy files to it as you would to any other drive. For the iPhone, iPad, or iPod touch, you need a third-party utility such as DiskAid from DigiDNA (www.digidna.net/diskaid) to enable disk use.

Collaborating with colleagues using iChat Theater

Reaching out to grab control of your office Mac over the Internet via Back to My Mac or Screen Sharing allows you to communicate directly with your colleagues via your office email system. But sometimes you need to go a step further and actually maintain a presence in your office — while you're not physically there.

You can do this by using the iChat Theater feature built into iChat. Your colleagues must also be running iChat.

iChat Theater enables you to give Keynote presentations, display documents, or show QuickTime movies on a remote Mac. You can also share a web page or run iPhoto slide shows, though the latter tends to be used more in home settings than business settings.

Genius

You can use iChat Theater either in an existing video chat window or to start a new video chat. If you have trouble starting iChat Theater with a file, try establishing a video chat first and verify that the connection is working satisfactorily before starting iChat Theater.

To use iChat Theater, launch iChat as usual by clicking the iChat icon in the Dock. You can then share a file like this:

1. **Choose File ⇨ Share a File with iChat Theater.** The Share with iChat Theater dialog appears.

2. **Select the file and click Share.** iChat Theater displays a message telling you to invite a buddy to a video chat (see Figure 9.11).

3. **Choose your buddy in the AIM buddy list window or in the Bonjour List window, and then click the Start a Video Chat button at the bottom of the window.** When your buddy accepts the invitation, iChat starts playing the file you chose.

9.11 To use iChat Theater, choose the file you want to show. You can then select the iChat buddy with whom you want to share the file.

4. **When the file stops playing — or after you stop it manually — you can move on to other forms of communication via iChat or simply close the window.** You can also choose File ⇨ Stop Sharing with iChat Theater to turn off the sharing.

To share a web page via iChat Theater, choose File ⇨ Share a webpage with iChat Theater. Type the URL in the Share with iChat Theater dialog (see Figure 9.12) that opens, and then click Share.

If you want to share your iPhoto library, or an event or album, choose File ⇨ Share iPhoto with iChat Theater. The iPhoto dialog appears (see Figure 9.13). Choose the library, event, or album, and click Share.

9.12 Sharing a web page with iChat Theater can be a good way of discussing a website.

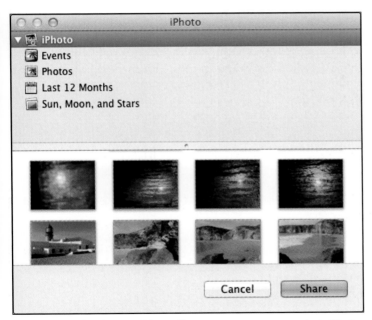

9.13 You can also share an iPhoto album or event — or your whole iPhoto library — via iChat Theater.

Connecting to Windows servers

Even if you stick with Mac OS X on your iMac, you may well need to connect to Windows servers from time to time to access files.

Here's how to connect to a Windows server:

1. **Click the Finder button on the Dock, and then choose Go ⇨ Connect to Server.** The Connect to Server dialog appears.

2. **Type the server's name or IP address in the Server Address box, putting smb:// before it to specify the Server Message Block (SMB) file-sharing protocol.** Figure 9.14 shows an example.

3. **When the server prompts you for your username and password (see Figure 9.15), select the Registered User option, and type your credentials.** Select the Remember this password in my keychain check box if you want Mac OS X to store the password, as is usually convenient.

4. **Click Connect.** Mac OS X exchanges your credentials with the server and then displays the available volumes (see Figure 9.16).

5. **Select the volumes (the shared folders) you want to use.** Click one volume to select it. Shift+click to select a range of volumes, or ⌘+click to add a volume to those you've already selected.

6. **Click OK.** Mac OS X connects to the volumes and displays a Finder window showing the contents of each.

9.14 Connecting to a server by using the Connect to Server dialog.

9.15 Type your username and password to get full access to the shared folders.

9.16 Choose the volumes (shared folders) you want to be able to access.

When you finish working with a Windows server, disconnect from it by clicking the Eject button next to its listing in the Shared category of the sidebar in a Finder window.

Making Your iMac Do Your Work for You

No matter how much you love your work, chances are you'd like to get it done more quickly so that you can pack more fun into your schedule. A great solution is to make your iMac do as much of your work as possible for you.

As you'd imagine, the tasks you can delegate to your iMac are repetitive and mechanical ones rather than one-off or creative tasks. You can use Mac OS X's Automator application to run repetitive tasks for you, add Folder Actions to key folders to process files automatically, and write or record scripts and macros that perform exactly the tasks you need. Your iMac can then handle these tasks smoothly, silently, and until the cows come home.

Automating repetitive tasks with Automator

Automator enables you to string together prebuilt actions into sequences called workflows that you can save and then run just like any other Mac program. You don't have to learn a programming language; all the programming is done via drag and drop.

With Automator, you can spend a few minutes setting up a workflow, and then take a coffee break while your iMac does the grunt work for you. In this section, I'll run you through two easy examples of creating workflows. I'll then show you how to record your own actions in Automator so that you can play them back.

Renaming files automatically

Sooner or later, you'll probably find that you need to rename a large number of files. It's a boring and repetitive job — and it's exactly the kind of work Automator was designed to take care of for you.

Here's how to create a workflow for renaming files automatically:

1. **Click the Launchpad icon on the Dock, and then click Automator on the Launchpad screen.** Automator displays the Choose a template for your workflow dialog (see Figure 9.17).

2. **Click the Application item and then click Choose to create a new workflow that you will save as an application.**

3. **In the first pane, under Library, click Files & Folders.** This category contains all kinds of actions you can perform on files in the Finder, from duplicating documents to connecting to servers. Automator displays the list of available actions in the second pane.

Choose a type for your document:

Workflow	Application	Service	Print Plugin

Folder Action	iCal Alarm	Image Capture Plugin

Workflow

Workflows can be run from within Automator.

Open an Existing Document...   Close   Choose

9.17 In the Choose a template for your document dialog, pick the type of Automator item you want to create, and then click Choose.

4. **In the second pane, click Get Folder Contents and drag it to the third pane.** This first action in your workflow determines which objects the workflow will act on. If the folders you'll be working on have folders within them that also contain files to rename, select the Repeat for each subfolder found check box.

Note

If an action has a downward-pointing triangle that overlaps a semicircular tab sticking out from the top of the next action, this indicates that these actions work together. If they don't connect visually in this way, they don't work as a sequence.

5. **In the second pane, click Rename Finder Items (scroll down if necessary) and drag it to the third pane under the first action.** Automator displays a warning pointing out that this action will change the names of the Finder items passed to it, and asks you if you want to add a Copy Finder Items action to copy the files before it renames them so that you'll have a backup. Click the Add button if you want to add the Copy Finder Items action; click the Don't Add button if you want to skip it.

Note

When you drag the Rename Finder Items action to the third pane, the action appears under the name Add Date or Time, because the first item in the first pop-up menu is the Add Date or Time item. When you choose another item in this pop-up menu, Automator changes the name displayed for the action.

6. **Using the pop-up menus in the Rename Finder Items action, choose how you want your files renamed.** If you need to use more than one type of renaming (such as Add Text and Change Case), add the Rename Finder Items action again (see Figure 9.18).

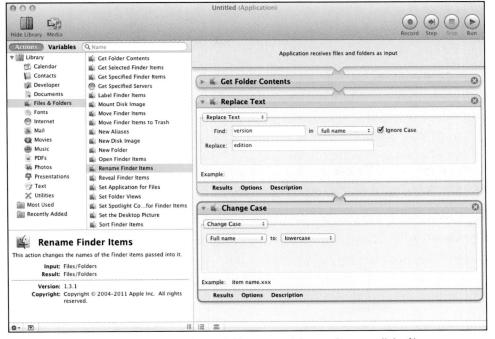

9.18 This workflow first replaces a word in each filename and then makes sure all the filenames are lowercase.

7. **Choose File ⇨ Save to display the Save As dialog.** Make sure that Application is selected in the File Format pop-up menu, then type a name, choose a location, and click Save. Because you will run the application by clicking and dragging folders to it, you may want to place it on your Desktop.

8. **Quit Automator.** Press ⌘+Q.

To run the application, click and drag a folder onto it.

Emailing a web page

RSS feeds and email notifications enable you to have the latest content from your favorite web pages delivered straight to you, so you don't have to go out looking for it. For websites that don't offer feeds or notifications, you can use Automator to have Safari open a web page at scheduled intervals, attach its text to a Mail message, and send it to you so that you can read it wherever you happen to be.

Here's how to create a workflow that emails a web page to you:

1. **Click the Launchpad icon on the Dock, and then click Automator on the Launchpad screen.** Automator displays the Choose a template for your workflow dialog.

2. **Click the iCal Alarm icon, and then click Choose to create a new workflow that you will save as an iCal alarm.**

3. **In the first pane, under Library, click Internet.** Most of the actions in this category use Safari.

4. **From the Internet category, click and drag the Get Specified URLs action into the workflow pane.** Fill in the URL of the web page you want to mail, and give it a name if you want to add it to your bookmarks.

Genius

The easiest way to get the right URL into the Get Specified URLs action is to open the web page in Safari, and then click the Current Safari Page button in Automator.

5. **From the Internet category, click and drag the Get Text from webpage action into the workflow.** This action copies all the text from the specified web page. It has no options to set.

6. **Click the Text category in the first pane, and then click and drag the New Text File action into the workflow.** Give the new text file a name in the Save as text box and choose a location for it from the Where pop-up menu. Select the Replace existing files check box to make each new version of the file overwrite the existing version.

7. **Click the Mail category in the first pane, and then click and drag the New Mail Message action into the workflow.** Fill out the To, Cc, Bcc, and Subject fields, then add a message, if you want, and choose which email account Mail to use to send the message.

8. **From the Mail category, click and drag the Send Outgoing Messages action into the workflow.** It has no options to set. Figure 9.19 shows the workflow with all its actions in place, with some of them collapsed to their names.

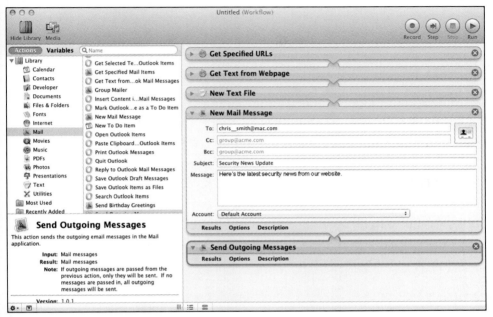

9.19 With the addition of the Send Outgoing Messages action, the workflow is complete.

9. **Choose File ⇨ Save to display the Save As dialog.** Type the name in the Save iCal Alarm as text box, and then click Save. Automator opens iCal for you and creates an event for the alarm. The alarm uses the Open File action for the file you just saved, the current date, and the current time.

10. **In iCal, change the settings for the event as needed.** For example, change the time for the event, or set it to repeat every other day.

When the appointed time comes, iCal runs the action for you, sending a message to the email address you specified.

Recording your actions for playback

Automator's library of premade actions covers a lot of different areas but has only a few commands for each. If the actions you need to build a workflow don't exist in the Library, you can create them by having Automator record a series of steps you perform.

Before you start recording, decide what your iMac should be doing when this action is played. For example, you might have earlier steps in the workflow start up certain programs, so those programs should be already running when you start recording. Once you're set up, start Automator from the Applications folder and click Workflow followed by Choose to create a new workflow. Add preexisting actions if necessary, and then click Record to create a Watch Me Do action. Figure 9.20 shows Automator recording what I'm doing.

Perform the steps that you want to record. Don't rush — you want to make sure that you don't do anything extraneous and that Automator has a chance to catch everything you do. When you're done, click the Stop button in the Automator Recording window. Now you can drag the slider to adjust the playback speed. In most cases, you'll want this action to go as quickly as possible, so you'll drag the slider all the way to the right. Complete your workflow by adding any other steps that are needed, and then save it.

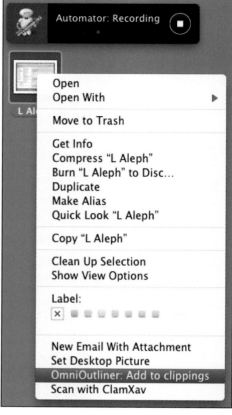

9.20 Automator also lets you turn on recording and record custom steps into the Watch Me Do action.

Note

Before you can record in Automator, you need to turn on access for assistive devices. If this feature is not turned on, Automator prompts you to enable it when you click the Record button. Click the Open Universal Access button in the dialog that Automator displays, and then select the Enable access for assistive devices check box in Universal Access preferences. Then quit System Preferences (press ⌘+Q) and return to Automator.

Attaching automated actions to folders

Folder actions are another way to make your iMac do some of the grunt work so you can spend your own valuable time on more creative endeavors. A folder action is a script that you attach to a folder; when the right trigger takes place, such as files being added to a folder, the script activates. Mac OS X includes some scripts that you can attach to folders, and you can write your own scripts in AppleScript Editor (discussed briefly later in this chapter) to perform other actions.

You can use folder actions to do things like convert all the images you drop into a particular folder to JPEG format, move documents to more appropriate locations based on their file types, or notify you whenever new files are dropped into your Public folder.

Here's how to set up Mac OS X to use folder actions:

1. **Open a Finder window to the folder that contains the folder to which you want to attach the folder action.**

2. **Control+click or right-click the folder and choose Folder Actions Setup from the shortcut menu.** Mac OS X launches the Folder Actions Setup util-ity, which displays the Choose a Script to Attach dialog (see Figure 9.21).

Choose a Script to Attach:

add – new item alert.scpt
add – new item alert.scpt~orig
add_open_new_items.scpt
close – close sub-folders.scpt
close_reopen this window.scpt
convert – PostScript to PDF.scpt
convert – PostScript to PDF.scpt~orig
Image – Add Icon.scpt
Image – Duplicate as JPEG.scpt
Image – Duplicate as PNG.scpt
Image – Duplicate as TIFF.scpt
Image – Flip Horizontal.scpt
Image – Flip Vertical.scpt
Image – Info to Comment.scpt
Image – Rotate Left.scpt

Cancel   Attach

9.21 In the Choose a Script to Attach dialog, choose the script to use for a folder action.

3. **Click the script you want to attach, and then click Attach.** The Choose a Script to Attach dialog closes, and you can see the Folder Actions Setup window with the script in place (see Figure 9.22).

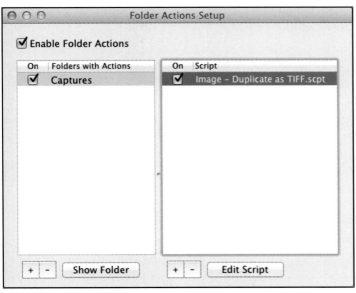

9.22 In the Folder Actions Setup window, select the Enable Folder Actions check box to turn on folder actions for your iMac.

4. **Select the Enable Folder Actions check box to tell your iMac to start using folder actions.**

5. **Quit Folder Actions Setup.** Press ⌘+Q.

Note

From the Folder Actions Setup window, you can set up further folder actions by clicking the left Add (+) button, choosing the folder in the dialog that opens, and then choosing the script in the Choose a Script to Attach dialog. You can add further scripts to a folder by clicking the folder in the left list box, clicking the right Add (+) button, and then selecting the script.

Genius

If you have a folder in which other people leave important files for you, apply the "add – new item alert" script to it. For example, apply this script to your ~/Public/Drop Box folder to receive an alert when anyone lobs a file into it for you.

Creating scripts and macros

Automator is great for performing repetitive actions using the building blocks that Mac OS X provides (plus custom actions you record), and folder actions are a handy way of setting scripts to run for a particular folder. But if you need to take the automation of your work to the next level, you will probably want to look into programming with AppleScript and creating macros for major applications that support them.

Creating scripts with AppleScript Editor

Mac OS X includes a powerful programming language named AppleScript that enables you to automate just about any action you can perform interactively with your iMac and many that you can perform only programmatically.

To work with scripts, you use AppleScript Editor (see Figure 9.23), which you'll find in the Utilities folder (click the Desktop, and then choose Go ➪ Utilities).

AppleScript is a big topic, so plan to take some time to start using it. AppleScript Editor includes the following built-in reference materials:

- **Help on using the AppleScript Editor.** From AppleScript Editor, press ⌘+? or choose Help ➪ AppleScript Editor Help.

- **Help on getting started with AppleScript.** From AppleScript Editor, choose Help ➪ AppleScript Help.

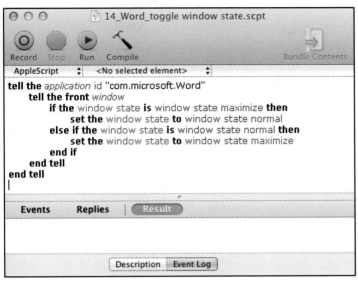

```
tell the application id "com.microsoft.Word"
    tell the front window
        if the window state is window state maximize then
            set the window state to window state normal
        else if the window state is window state normal then
            set the window state to window state maximize
        end if
    end tell
end tell
```

9.23 AppleScript Editor is Mac OS X's built-in tool for programming in AppleScript.

- **In-depth help on the AppleScript Language.** From AppleScript Editor, choose Help ⇨ Show AppleScript Language Guide. Mac OS X opens a browser window to the AppleScript Language Guide on the Apple website.

- **Sample scripts in the /Library/Scripts folder.** From AppleScript Editor, choose Help ⇨ Open Example Scripts Folder to open a Finder window showing this folder.

Creating macros to automate tasks within applications

Some applications include built-in macro languages that you can use to automate them instead of cranking up the full power of AppleScript. A macro language is normally restricted to working inside an application. For example, if you create a macro to perform actions in Microsoft Word, Word must be running in order for you to run the macro.

Here are a couple of examples of such applications:

- **Microsoft Office.** Microsoft Office 2011 includes the Visual Basic for Applications (VBA) macro language, in which you can either write macros or (in the main applications, such as Word and Excel) record them. You can then play back the macros to perform tasks automatically.

- **OpenOffice.org.** The free OpenOffice.org application suite includes the OpenOffice.org Basic programming language, in which you can write and record macros.

What Are the Best Applications for My iMac?

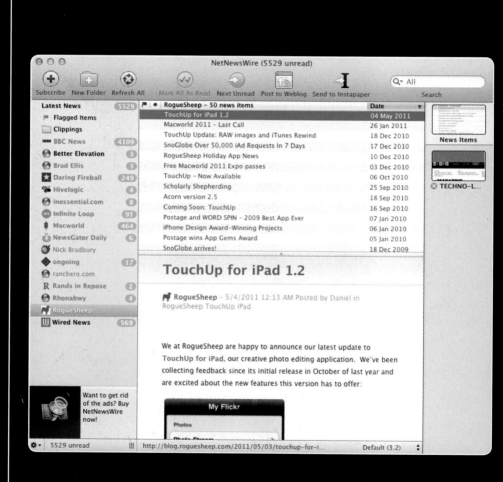

To get pretty much anything done on your iMac, you use applications, from web browsers to word processors, from an email client to a DVD player. Your iMac comes with an impressive selection of applications right out of the box, and you'll want to explore these applications fully to see how well they meet your needs. But to get the very most out of your iMac, and to finish each task as easily and quickly as possible, you'll almost certainly need to add other applications. This chapter points you in the direction of some of the best applications for web browsing, email, chat, and creating office documents.

Finding the Best Web Browser for Your Needs

Safari, the web browser Apple provides with Mac OS X, is fast, stable, and easy to use, so you'll probably want to use it for most of your web browsing. But if you use the web extensively, you may want one or more other browsers sometimes, for two reasons:

- **Displaying nonstandard sites.** Sometimes Safari runs into a site that it can't display correctly. This is usually because the site's designer hasn't stuck to web standards, but you may find that another browser can display the site with no problem.

- **You need extra features.** Safari doesn't offer some of the special features that other browsers provide, such as Opera's built-in email client.

You can install as many web browsers on your iMac as you want. You have to set one browser as the default — the browser that opens when you click a web link in an email message or in another application — but you can always switch to another browser to access a different site. For example, if you find that your online banking site doesn't work properly with Safari, you can use another browser (such as Firefox) when you need to visit that site.

General-purpose web browsers

If you're looking for a general-purpose browser as an alternative to Safari, try these five. They're all free, and each offers a different take on web browsing:

- **Firefox.** The second most widely used web browser after Microsoft's Internet Explorer, Firefox (www.mozilla.com/firefox) is built on the Mozilla Application Suite and is available for Mac OS X, Windows, Linux, and other operating systems. It's designed for simplicity, security, and extensibility, and you can add hundreds of extensions to perform different tasks, such as ones for blocking website scripts or enabling you to use Google Docs offline. Out of the box, Firefox features web browsing and display of RSS feeds.

- **Camino.** Also based on Mozilla, Camino (www.caminobrowser.org) is a Mac OS X–only browser that features a Mac look and style. Camino concentrates on being a web browser (see Figure 10.1) rather than providing features such as an email client. But Camino has some great features, such as its whitelist for pop-up blocking so that you can block pop-up ads without blocking the pop-up windows created by, say, your bank's website.

- **Opera.** A Norwegian product (www.opera.com), Opera actually consists of an entire suite of applications: web browsing, email, Usenet, RSS, BitTorrent, and chat access. Though it can be slow to start up, Opera is speedy once it's running and has been the fastest web browser around at times in the past.

10.1 Camino is an elegant and easy-to-use browser with no extraneous features.

- **Google Chrome.** Google's web browser, Chrome (www.google.com/chrome), provides a fast browsing experience in a streamlined interface. Google Chrome runs each tab as a separate process, making it more stable than most other browsers. If a problem occurs on a web page, you can usually close just the tab that web page is on rather than having to quit the whole application.

Genius

Browser manufacturers love to use speed to persuade you to use their browsers, but these days, most browsers are fast enough for minor improvements to make little difference. While having your browser display web pages quickly is helpful, chances are that you'll find other features — such as ease of navigation, bookmarks, and the ability to browse your history easily — more important in the long run.

- **OmniWeb.** Like the Mac itself, the Omni Group (www.omnigroup.com) tends to collect rabid fans. If you like its products, for the most part, you really like them. OmniWeb was the first web browser released for Mac OS X, and it's strong on power-user features such as per-site preferences, tab thumbnails (see Figure 10.2), and creating separate workspaces. OmniWeb displays web pages and RSS feeds.

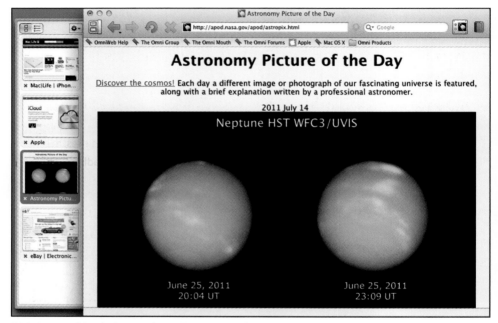

10.2 OmniWeb's tab drawer, shown here at the left side of the window, enables you to see exactly what page is displayed in each tab without having to switch.

Better browsers for reading RSS feeds

If you visit the same websites regularly, use RSS (Really Simple Syndication) to keep up with the latest news, gossip, or chatter effortlessly. With RSS, you don't need to go check each website — instead, it comes straight to you automatically. Many sites use RSS to send out regular updates that can contain anything from a list of headlines to their full content. You get the news you want, delivered straight to your browser.

As discussed in Chapter 7, Safari and Mail can display RSS feeds. Here's a quick recap:

- **View an RSS feed.** Any time you're at a website that offers an RSS feed, you can click the RSS button in Safari's address box to view the feed.
- **Bookmark an RSS feed.** If you want to return regularly to that site, add a bookmark for the RSS page.

- **Check for updates.** Next to the bookmark's name, Safari displays a running total of the number of articles added to the feed since you last viewed it, so if there's no number of new articles shown, you don't have to bother clicking the bookmark.

- **Customize the RSS feeds.** When you do view an RSS feed in Safari, you can adjust article length, sort articles, and filter articles by date, title, or source.

OmniWeb, one of the alternative Mac web browsers discussed earlier in this chapter, can also double as an RSS reader. But if you really want to harness the power of RSS to make your web browsing more efficient, you need a stand-alone RSS feed reader. Here are two stand-alone RSS readers to try:

- **NetNewsWire.** NetNewsWire (free or $14.95 for ad-free version; www.netnewswireapp. com/Mac) is a popular RSS reader. Like most RSS readers, NetNewsWire features a three-pane interface in which the window's three sections display your subscribed sites, the headlines for a selected site, and the article corresponding to a selected headline. The screen on the opening page of this chapter shows NetNewsWire.

Genius

Using a specialized RSS reader enables you to distinguish between what you've read and what you haven't (Safari doesn't remember which articles you've already seen), organize your feed subscriptions into logical groups (for example, Morning News, Work-Related, and Just Wasting Time), save articles in a Clippings category for future reference, and more.

- **Shrook.** Shrook (free; www.utsire.com/shrook) is an RSS reader that can sync all the latest articles in your subscriptions to your iPhone, iPad, or iPod.

Note

You may also see an RSS feed called an *RSS channel*, and RSS readers are often referred to as *RSS aggregators* (because they can collect feeds from different sites and display them all at once).

Web browsers for Dashboard and the Desktop

If you want to monitor the web all the time without switching to your web browser or RSS reader, put your must-see sites in your Dashboard or on your desktop.

To put any web page, or just a piece of it, in Dashboard, use Safari's web Clips feature to create your own widget. Here's how:

1. **In Safari, open the page you want to add to Dashboard.**

2. **Choose File ⇨ Open in Dashboard.** Safari darkens most of the page and displays a highlighted rectangle attached to the mouse pointer.

3. **Move the mouse over the page until the area you want is highlighted, and then click to highlight the area.** Drag the handles at its edges to adjust the size of the area until it contains everything you want.

4. **When you're happy with the widget's size and shape, click the Add button at the upper-right corner of the window.** Your new widget opens in Dashboard.

When you view your new widget in Dashboard, you can click the Info button in its lower-right corner to customize it. Click and drag to move the content around within its frame, or drag the lower right-hand corner to resize the widget, and click a thumbnail image to choose an edge style.

As well as making your own widgets that contain exactly the information you want, you can add widgets other people have created. Take a look at DashboardWidgets (www.dashboardwidgets. com), where you'll find single-use widgets for all kinds of information. Here are three examples:

- **Football.** Display the latest scores and stats for college and pro American football teams.
- **Mount St. Helens Volcanocam.** Keep an eye on the United States' best-known volcano.
- **Gold Price.** Track the price of gold (per troy ounce) and set an alarm to go off if the price goes above or below a set range.

If you want to put your RSS feeds in Dashboard as well, download and install News Reader (free; www.benkazez.com/newsreader.php). This light-weight RSS reader displays as many feeds as you want. You can navigate News Reader using the arrow keys on your keyboard.

Converting your bookmarks from Safari

If you switch from Safari to another browser, you'll probably want to take your bookmarks along with you. Here's how to transfer them:

- **Firefox.** Choose File ⇨ Import. Choose the Safari option button in the Import Wizard dialog and click Continue. Select the check boxes next to the things you want to import: Preferences, Browsing History, Saved Form History, or Bookmarks. Then click Continue.
- **Camino.** Choose File ⇨ Import Bookmarks, choose Safari from the pop-up menu, and then click Import.
- **Opera.** Choose File ⇨ Import and Export ⇨ Import Safari Bookmarks. Opera automatically chooses your default bookmarks file (located in the Library folder in your home folder). Click Open to import the bookmarks.

Note You can also turn your Safari bookmarks file into an HTML file that you can share with others, store on a flash drive as a backup, view in any browser, and import into most browsers. In Safari, choose File ➪ Export Bookmarks, specify the filename and the folder to save it in, and then click Save.

● **Google Chrome.** Choose Bookmarks ➪ Bookmark Manager to display the Bookmark Manager screen. Click the Organize pop-up button, and then click Import Bookmarks. In the Open dialog, select the ~/Library/Safari/Bookmarks.plist file, and then click Open.

● **OmniWeb.** Choose Bookmarks ➪ Import Bookmarks, choose Safari from the Browser pop-up menu, and then click Import.

Genius If you don't want to keep Safari, iChat, and Mail installed just so that you can tell your iMac you don't want to use them, download RCDefaultApp (free; www.rubicode. com/Software/RCDefaultApp) to make these preference settings, and then you can trash the applications you're not using.

Making Non-Apple Applications the Default

If you've switched to a new web browser, email client, or instant-messaging client, you must tell your iMac that you want it to use the new application instead of the Apple application. Here's how to do this for all three types of application:

1. **Start the application you want to replace (Safari, Mail, or iChat).** Open the application's menu (for example, the Safari menu) and choose Preferences to open the Preferences window.

2. **Click the General tab to display its contents.**

3. **Open the Default pop-up menu (for example, the Default web browser pop-up menu in Safari) and choose the new application from it.** If the new application doesn't appear, choose Select, and then navigate to the Applications folder and locate the application.

4. **Close the Preferences window and quit the application.** From now on, any time that type of application is invoked from elsewhere in the system (when you click a web link in an email, for example), your new application starts instead of the Apple one.

Choosing a Suitable Email Application

Mail, the email application that comes with Mac OS X, is plenty powerful enough for many people — but you may be the exception. If you need greater automation, more powerful search features (for example, the ability to restrict a search to particular folders), or a cleaner interface, check out the email applications this section introduces.

Email clients for organization freaks

If you need to keep your email tightly organized, try these six powerful email applications:

- **PowerMail.** PowerMail ($65; www.ctmdev.com) has a clean, flexible interface that's much less cluttered than Mail's. Searching is extremely fast due to PowerMail's FoxTrot search technology, and you can also filter messages within a folder quickly by typing text in a field at the top of each window (like the way you can filter iTunes content). PowerMail's powerful filters can trigger lots of actions, such as modifying Address Book entries, moving attachments, or executing an AppleScript script, which lets you take almost any action on your iMac in response to an email message. You can buy PowerMail together with SpamSieve, one of the best spam-filtering programs available (more on this later in this chapter).

- **Thunderbird.** Thunderbird (free; www.mozilla.com/thunderbird) is Mozilla's own email client and comes in versions for Mac OS X, Windows, and Linux. Thunderbird lets you save searches so that you can repeat them at any time; you can navigate back and forth in a message thread's history just as you would with web pages; and it's got built-in support for Gmail and MobileMe accounts. Also like Firefox, Thunderbird is very extensible, so you can customize the program with all kinds of features, including appearance themes.

- **Mailsmith.** Mailsmith from Stickshift Software (free; www.mailsmith.org) is unlike most other email clients. Mailsmith was originally developed by Bare Bones Software, which concentrates on text processing, so it offers powerful filters and automatic message creation using stationery and a glossary for storing frequently used text snippets. Its pattern-based search-and-replace feature, multiple clipboards, and quoted-text cleanup ability make it a good choice for detail-oriented power users. On the downside, Mailsmith displays only text email, not HTML email.

- **GyazMail.** GyazMail ($18; www.gyazsquare.com/gyazmail) specializes in speed, stability, and data protection. The GyazMail program stores each email message in an individual file so it can't be affected by corruption in any other messages. As anyone who's ever lost an entire email database due to corruption can attest, that's a good thing.

- **SeaMonkey.** The SeaMonkey browser (free; www.seamonkey-project.org) is based on the same code as Firefox, which means it can use the same extensions to add to its capabilities. SeaMonkey comes with a combo email and UseNet newsreader that's similar to Thunderbird, an HTML editor, and the ChatZilla IRC (Internet Relay Chat) client.

- **Opera.** Opera (free; www.opera.com) includes its own Opera Mail client along with a basic contact manager and a similarly bare-bones IRC client. Opera Mail can classify both received and sent messages by type, such as whether a message was addressed to a mailing list or whether it had an attachment.

Converting your email from Mail

Getting your existing email messages out of Mail and into your new email client isn't too much trouble, because all the applications discussed in this chapter support either Mail's native format or the universal standard mbox format, or both. Here's what you'll need to do with each of the email clients discussed:

- **Thunderbird or SeaMonkey.** Choose Tools ⇨ Import, select the Mail option, and click Next. On the following screen, select Apple Mail, and then click Next.

- **Opera.** Choose File ⇨ Import and Export ⇨ Import Mail. On the Select the program to import from screen of the New Account Wizard, click Import from Apple Mail, and then click Next.

Genius
To get your mail into some email apps, you may need to create mbox files — standard mailbox files. You can also use mbox files when you need to import only some mailboxes rather than all of them. From Apple Mail, click a mailbox and choose Edit ⇨ Select All, and then choose File ⇨ Save As to save the messages in Raw Message Source format. Give the file a name that reflects the folder or mailbox you're exporting.

- **Mailsmith.** When you first set up Mailsmith, it will scan your hard drive for Mail messages and ask if you want to import them. In the Mailsmith Setup dialog, select the Apple Mail option, and then click Continue. If you skip this step, you can import messages later by creating mbox files as explained in the nearby Genius, and then dragging and dropping them into either the folder list or a message list, depending on whether you want the messages in a separate folder or added to an existing folder.

- **PowerMail.** To import Mail messages directly, choose File ⇨ Database ⇨ Import. Choose Email messages, click Next, and then choose Mac OS X Mail, and click Next again. Choose whether you want to import all the email in your Mail folder or just one mailbox (if the latter, select the mailbox), and click Go Ahead.

● **GyazMail.** When you choose File ⇨ Import ⇨ Mail in GyazMail, the application finds your
Mail folder and asks you which mailboxes to import. All you need to do is select the
check boxes next to the ones you want to transfer.

Exporting your Address Book

When you switch from Address Book to a different contact manager, usually the easiest way to get
addresses from Address Book into that application is to export them as vCard (.vcf) files. Open
Address Book, select the contacts you want to transfer, and then click and drag them to the desktop or to another folder to create a vCard file containing the data.

Genius

Dragging contacts out of Address Book to the desktop produces a single vCard file containing all the selected contacts' information. If the program you're switching to can't
handle multiperson files, create a new folder to store the files in. Then press Option as
you drag the cards into the folder. This creates an individual file for each contact.

If you're moving to an application that can't import vCard files, create a tab-delimited text file or a
comma-separated values (CSV) file instead:

● **Tab-delimited text file.** Use the free Address Book Exporter application (www.gwenhiver.
net/address-book-exporter.html) to convert your Address Book database.

● **Comma-separated values file.** Create a single vCard file from your contacts, as
described previously, and then visit http://labs.brotherli.ch/vcfconvert. This website
accepts your vCard file and converts it to CSV for free. Choose CSV in the Format pop-up
menu, and then click Convert.

You can then import the tab-delimited text file or CSV file into your new contact manager.

Moving appointments from iCal to another calendar application

When you switch from iCal to another calendar application, export your iCal data as an iCalendar
file like this:

1. **Open iCal.** For example, click the iCal icon on the Dock.

2. **Click the Calendars button on the toolbar to display the Calendars pane, and then
click the calendar or calendar group you want to export.**

3. **Choose File ⇨ Export ⇨ Export to display the Export dialog.** If you selected a calendar
group, choose File ⇨ Export ⇨ Export as Calendar rather than File ⇨ Export ⇨ Export.

4. **Specify the filename and the folder in which to store it.**

5. **Click Export.** iCal exports the file and gives it the .ics filename extension.

You can now import the file into your new calendar application.

Improving your spam filtering

Given more than 85 percent of all email sent is spam, ISPs are continually struggling to filter out spam messages and prevent them from reaching our inboxes. To help, most email clients include spam filtering, such as the Junk Mail controls that Mail provides (discussed in Chapter 7).

If you're still getting too much spam in your inbox, consider getting a third-party add-on to help weed out spam. At this writing, the best example is SpamSieve ($30; www.c-command.com/spamsieve). SpamSieve uses blacklists and whitelists to help determine what's spam and what's not, but it also uses Bayesian filtering, in which the software learns from your responses to its actions.

After your email client (for example, Apple Mail) retrieves your messages, SpamSieve applies its own filtering methods to each message. SpamSieve's methods include its Bayesian filters, a black-list and a whitelist that you can edit yourself to deny or allow messages from particular senders; the Habeas Safelist, which indicates messages that are not spam; and the ADV subject tag, which is supposed to be used in commercial email to indicate that it's advertising and most likely spam.

One of SpamSieve's best points is that you can train it with existing messages, so you don't neces-sarily have to continue dealing with spam during the few days it might otherwise take to get up to speed. It works with Mail, Outlook, GyazMail, Mailsmith, PowerMail, and Thunderbird.

Finding the Ideal Chat Application

As you saw in Chapter 7, iChat is a capable chat application. But if you need to chat with users of services to which iChat can't connect, or if you need features iChat doesn't provide, you have to look to third-party software. You can either use a different chat application or add the missing features to iChat.

Chatting with MSN, IRC, and Yahoo! users

If you want to chat with MSN, IRC, or Yahoo! chat users, consider these chat clients:

- **Microsoft Messenger.** If you want to talk to friends who use Microsoft's Windows Live Messenger service, download Microsoft Messenger for Mac (free; www.microsoft.com/mac/messenger).

- **Yahoo Messenger.** Use iChat in Mac OS X Lion (10.7), or download the Mac version of Yahoo! Messenger (free; http://messenger.yahoo.com).

- **Adium.** If you want to handle all your instant-messaging needs with one program, download Adium (free; http://adium.im). Adium can handle a wide variety of chat accounts — including AOL Instant Messenger, Jabber (which includes Google Talk and Facebook Chat), Microsoft Messenger, Yahoo! Messenger, and MySpace IM — in the same window. Adium also features encryption, tabbed message windows, file transfer, and more; better still, you can extend its capabilities with plug-ins.

- **Snak.** If you want to chat on IRC, try Snak ($29; www.snak.com) or one of the web browsers that supports it (Firefox and Opera). IRC is primarily used for group chats; it features channels (similar to chat rooms) that you can join at any time by connecting to a network such as EFnet, IRCnet, QuakeNet, or Undernet.

Adding extra features to iChat

If you use iChat but want to make it more useful, try the add-ons discussed in this section.

Improving video chat quality

Somehow, video chats never look quite as bright and crisp in real life as they do in Apple's promotional images. But you can greatly improve the picture from your iMac's built-in iSight camera using iGlasses ($10; www.ecamm.com/mac/iglasses). iGlasses works with iChat and other programs including iMovie, Photo Booth, Yahoo! Messenger, Skype, and web-based chat. You can improve image color, brightness, and contrast; add fun special effects; and even simulate pan and zoom actions.

Marking up a video chat feed

If you've tried sharing a file, web page, or iPhoto with iChat Theater (as discussed in Chapter 7) but found you need to share other items, have a look at ShowMacster ($20; www.showmacster.com). ShowMacster lets you include photos, movies, sketches, and screenshots in an iChat video chat. You can display and transfer files via drag and drop, and ShowMacster has a built-in slide show function as well. You can use the Sketchboard to explain your ideas visually, either as a stand-alone sketch or as markups on a photo.

Giving iChat superpowers

If you don't get any of the other software mentioned in this chapter, download Chax (free; www.ksuther.com/chax). Chax provides a slew of helpful additions for iChat, including the ability to

- Keep a single buddy list for all your accounts that automatically resizes to fit the number of visible buddies

- Auto-accept text chats without you having to click the Accept button in the new message notification dialog
- View message senders' buddy icons in the Dock
- Automatically set your status to Away when your screen saver turns on

Choosing Office Applications

Mac OS X's TextEdit application is good for working with documents that consist largely or entirely of text, but if you have to create many documents, you'll need a full-on word-processing application. And if your projects include spreadsheets, you'll need a spreadsheet application as well. In the same way, if you must give presentations, a presentations application is a must. This section points you to the leading office applications, both paid and free.

Microsoft Office for Mac

Microsoft Office for Mac is the market-leading office suite for Mac OS X. Microsoft Office for Mac comes in two editions, Home & Student Edition and Home & Business Edition. Each edition includes the word processor Microsoft Word, the spreadsheet application Microsoft Excel, and the presentations application Microsoft PowerPoint. Home & Business Edition also includes the email and desktop-management application Microsoft Outlook, which Home & Student Edition doesn't provide.

The choice between the two editions is pretty clear: If you need Outlook, buy Home & Business Edition; if not, buy Home & Student Edition.

To decide whether to buy Office at all, and (if so) whether to get Outlook, start with the free 30-day trial of Office that Microsoft offers (www.microsoft.com/mac/default.mspx). This gives you plenty of time to decide whether you want to pay for a full version (with Outlook or without) or go with an alternative.

iWork

Your iMac most likely included a 30-day trial version of Apple's iWork suite, which includes the Pages word-processing and page-layout application, the Numbers spreadsheet, and the Keynote presentations application. If not, you can download it from www.apple.com/iwork/download-trial.

The iWork applications have many attractive features and a thoroughly Mac-like interface, and they're more than adequate for creating many types of documents, spreadsheets, and presentations. Overall, the iWork applications offer fewer features than the Microsoft Office applications, but many of the missing features are ones that most people use seldom or never.

Note

Instead of running office applications on your iMac, you can use an online tool such as Google Docs for creating documents, spreadsheets, and presentations. This is a good solution if you have an Internet connection all the time and if you need to work on your files from multiple computers or devices (for example, an iPad).

Genius

If you use iWork, be aware of this drawback: While the applications can open the equivalent Microsoft Office document formats and can export to them, they cannot save directly to them. For example, you can open a Microsoft Word document in Pages, save it as a Pages document, and then export a version of that document as a Microsoft Word document. But you cannot open a Microsoft Word document in Pages, edit it, and save it back in the same Word document.

LibreOffice

If you need a full-powered office suite but you prefer not to pay, download the LibreOffice suite from the LibreOffice website (free; www.libreoffice.org). LibreOffice contains modules for creating word-processing documents, spreadsheets, presentations, drawings, and databases, and has advanced features including a macro language.

The LibreOffice modules don't include every single feature that the Microsoft Office applications have, but they have the vast majority of widely used features — so it's well worth seeing if LibreOffice meets your needs before you lay down the money for Microsoft Office.

Making different office applications work with each other

The office applications discussed in the previous sections save their documents in a variety of formats. This is fine as long as you're the only one working on a document — but when you share a document with other people, you need to make sure it's in a format they can use.

Genius

Microsoft has complicated the issue of sharing files by changing the Office formats. In Office 2011 (Mac), Office 2010 (Windows), Office 2008 (Mac), and Office 2007 (Windows), the applications use new XML-based file formats. For example, Word 2011, 2010, 2008, and 2007 use an XML-based document format (with the .docx file extension) rather than the binary document format (.doc) Word has used since about 1997. The binary document format is a better choice for sharing, as many other applications do not yet support the XML-based format.

At this writing, the Microsoft Office formats — Word document, Excel spreadsheet, and PowerPoint presentation — are the most widely used formats for office documents. When you share your documents, you will typically need to use either these formats or an industry-standard format, such as the Rich Text Format (RTF) files that almost all word-processing applications can create and open.

Making Microsoft Office create compatible files

If you're using the Microsoft Office 2011 or 2008 applications, check whether the people you work with can use the new file formats. If not, either save each file back to an older format before sharing it, or set the application to use the older format. For example, in Word 2011, choose Word ⇨ Preferences, click the Save icon, and then choose Word 97–2004 Document (.doc) in the Save Word files as pop-up menu.

Genius

Microsoft provides a utility called the Microsoft Office Open XML File Format Converter for Mac that lets Office 2004 for Mac and Office v.X for Mac (the version before Office 2004) open the new file formats. You can find it at www.microsoft.com/downloads (search for "Open XML File Format Converter for Mac").

If the people with whom you work aren't using Office, choose a common format for your projects. For example, for word-processing documents, you might choose the Rich Text Format (.rtf), which is available on almost every known word processor and text editor.

Making iWork create compatible files

The iWork applications create documents in different ways than the Office applications. As a result, you need to translate files when you move them from an iWork application to an Office application, or vice versa.

Here's how to translate iWork files to Office formats:

1. **With the file open in the appropriate iWork application, choose File ⇨ Export.** The Export dialog appears. Figure 10.3 shows the dialog for exporting documents from Pages.

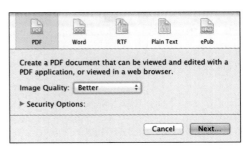

10.3 Use the Export dialog to export an iWork document in a format compatible with the office applications your colleagues are using.

2. **At the top of the dialog, click the format you want to use.** For example, the Pages dialog offers you PDF, Word, RTF, Plain Text, and ePub.

   - Select the PDF option if the recipient needs only to view the document, not edit it.

   - Choose the Office file format (for example, Word) if you want to include as many features of the original file as possible.

   - Choose RTF if you need only the text and major formatting, or if your colleagues need RTF files.

   - Choose Plain Text if you need only the text.

   - Choose ePub if you want to create a document for reading in iBooks.

3. **Click Next, specify the name and folder for the exported file, and click Export.** The iWork application exports the document to the file you specified.

Note

If the person for whom you're exporting the iWork document needs only to view the document rather than edit it, export the document as a PDF. This format is pretty much guaranteed to display correctly on almost all known operating systems, as long as the operating system has a PDF reader application.

Making LibreOffice create compatible files

LibreOffice is so good at opening and saving files created in different formats that it offers you the option of using those file formats throughout. For example, you can set LibreOffice to save text documents in Word format or RTF by default.

Here's how to set the default formats that LibreOffice uses:

1. **Choose LibreOffice ⇨ Preferences to open the LibreOffice Options dialog.**

2. **In the left pane, expand the Load/Save category by clicking its disclosure triangle.**

3. **Click the General item to display the General pane of preferences (see Figure 10.4).**

4. **Open the Document type pop-up menu and choose the document type you want to affect.** For example, choose Text document.

5. **Open the Always save as pop-up menu and choose the format you want to use.** For example, choose Microsoft Word 97/2000/XP.

6. **Repeat Steps 4 and 5 for each other document type you want to affect.** For example, set LibreOffice to save Spreadsheet documents as Microsoft Excel 97/2000/XP format and Presentations as Microsoft PowerPoint 97/2000/XP format.

7. **Click OK to close the Options dialog.**

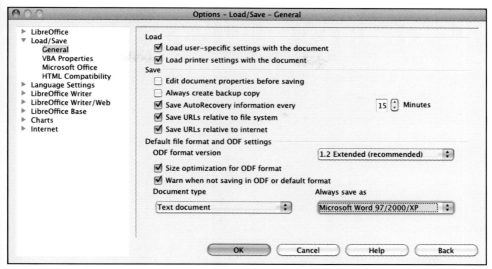

10.4 In LibreOffice's Options dialog, use the Document type pop-up menu and the Always save as pop-up menu to set the default formats for the documents you create.

Note

When you choose a format other than LibreOffice's own Open Document format (ODF), the Options dialog warns you that "not using ODF may cause information to be lost." But usually, unless you create highly complex documents, presentations, or spreadsheets, your data should be fine. Experiment with a sample document to make sure.

Making other applications create compatible files

Many word-processing applications can create files in the Word document format, either by using the Save As command or the Export command. If not, use RTF instead.

Some spreadsheet applications can create files in the Excel spreadsheet format. Again, you usually use the Save As command or the Export command. Otherwise, use either the tab-delimited text format or the CSV format to export spreadsheet data so that you can import it into another spreadsheet application.

Genius

RTF is an effective format for transferring most of the information in word-processing documents, although you may lose complex formatting. Tab-delimited text format and CSV format transfer only the text data from a spreadsheet, not objects (such as charts or graphics).

How Can I Run Windows Programs and Games on My iMac?

Mac OS X is a great operating system, but from time to time you may need to use Windows — either running the Windows operating system itself directly on your iMac's hardware or using a virtual machine application to run Windows and Windows programs alongside your Mac OS X applications. Both capabilities are useful, but which one is best for you depends on what you need to do with Windows. Running Windows directly on your iMac is best for demanding programs such as games, while using a virtual machine is usually the best choice for business needs.

Choosing How to Install Windows on Your iMac

If you need Windows on your iMac, you have two choices:

- **Install Windows directly on your iMac.** Mac OS X's Boot Camp feature gives you an easy way to create a separate partition on your hard drive and install Windows on it. You can then boot your iMac into Windows instead of Mac OS X. When you need to return to Mac OS X, you restart your iMac and boot Mac OS X. Dual-booting in this way is like having two separate computers — your Mac OS X iMac and a PC version of your iMac — of which you can run only one at a time.

- **Install Windows in an application on your iMac.** Use virtual machine software to run Windows on top of Mac OS X. The virtual machine application emulates a PC, fooling Windows into thinking it's running on a real PC. You can then run Windows programs right alongside your Mac applications. To use a virtual machine, you don't need to change the partition structure of your iMac's hard drive, and you can easily back up a virtual machine and its contents by backing up the entire file that contains the virtual machine.

Note If your iMac has enough RAM, you can run two or more virtual machines at the same time — for example, you can run two different versions of Windows, or run Windows and another operating system such as Linux.

Using Boot Camp gives you the full performance that your iMac can deliver in Windows, so it's usually the best choice for playing Windows games that have heavy hardware requirements (for example, Crysis or Halo). By contrast, a virtual-machine application runs Windows more slowly than Boot Camp does. But if your iMac has a dual-core or quad-core processor and 4GB or more RAM, you will probably find performance acceptable.

Genius Choosing between Boot Camp and a virtual machine can be difficult — but in fact you don't have to choose. There's nothing to stop you from installing Windows using Boot Camp and installing a virtual-machine application on Mac OS X and loading Windows in it. Once you decide which approach suits you better, you can get rid of the other — or simply continue to use both.

Choosing the Best Version of Windows for Your Needs

Your iMac or your virtual-machine application can run pretty much any version of Windows that you can lay your hands on. At this writing, your best bet is to install one of the versions of Windows 7, because it's not only the latest version of Windows but it also runs much better than its immediate predecessor, Windows Vista. Now that Windows 7 is available, Vista is not worth running unless you need it for testing purposes, but you may want to consider running Windows XP, which has much more modest hardware demands than Windows 7. Table 11.1 compares the hardware requirements for Windows XP and Windows 7.

Whether you choose Windows XP or Windows 7, you also need to choose which edition of Windows you want. Table 11.2 explains the three main editions of Windows XP. Table 11.3 explains the six main editions of Windows 7.

Table 11.1 Hardware Requirements for Windows XP and Windows 7

Operating System	Windows XP	Windows 7
Disk Space (Minimum)	2GB	16GB
Disk Space (Recommended)	20GB or more	40GB or more
RAM (Minimum)	128MB	1GB
RAM (Recommended)	512MB or more	2GB or more
Processor	Any Intel Mac	Dual-core Intel Mac
Optical Drive	CD or DVD	DVD
Graphics	4MB	128MB

Table 11.2 Windows XP Editions

Windows XP Editions	Explanation	Choose This Edition for Use
Home Edition	For home users who don't need TV and multimedia features.	At home or in a small business on networks that don't have a Windows server.
Media Center Edition	For home users who need TV and multimedia features.	At home when you want TV viewing and recording features.
Professional	For business users who need encryption.	In businesses on networks that do have complex networking and Windows servers.

303

Table 11.3 Windows 7 Editions

Windows 7 Editions	Explanation	Choose This Edition for Use
Starter Edition	Minimal edition for first-world countries.	On underpowered computers and netbooks. Lacks the highly graphical Windows Aero interface and TV viewing and recording. Only available preinstalled on PCs.
Home Basic Edition	Stripped-down version for "emerging markets" to discourage piracy of more-expensive editions.	Available only in certain countries.
Home Premium Edition	Main edition for home users.	At home when you want TV viewing and recording features. Includes the Windows Aero interface and TV viewing and recording.
Professional Edition	For business users who need encryption.	In businesses on networks that have complex networking and Windows servers.
Enterprise Edition	For large corporations only.	Available only to corporate customers.
Ultimate Edition	For business users who need networking, encryption, and TV viewing and recording.	At home or in businesses when you need all available Windows features. Includes all the features of Home Premium and Professional editions.

Compared to getting Mac OS X, where you choose the latest version and have no choice of different editions unless you want the Server edition, the choice of Windows versions is confusing. In most cases, though, you'll probably want to get one of the editions of Windows 7, depending on what you're planning to do with it. Here are my suggestions:

- **Business use.** Choose Windows 7 Professional Edition if you need to connect to Windows networks. Choose Windows 7 Ultimate Edition if you need every feature in sight.

- **Home use.** Choose Windows 7 Home Premium Edition if you have a dual-core or quad-core iMac and want the full graphical interface and TV features. If you have an older iMac with a single-core processor, choose Windows XP Home Edition.

- **Light use.** If you just need to run the occasional Windows application, run Windows XP Home Edition or Windows XP Professional in a virtual machine.

- **Gaming.** Choose depending on the game's requirements. For example, if the game is designed to run on Windows 7, choose Windows 7 Home Premium Edition or a better version.

Installing and Using Windows with Boot Camp

Even the most die-hard Mac enthusiast may need to use Windows programs sometimes, either for work or for play. Because Apple has designed your Mac as a kind of super-PC, you can easily install Windows on your iMac and run those programs without getting rid of Mac OS X.

Genius   Before installing Windows using Boot Camp, connect a USB mouse to your iMac. The Magic Mouse and Magic Trackpad don't work during the beginning of the Windows setup process, so you'll need another mouse.

Performing the installation

To install Windows on your iMac, follow these steps:

1. **Get a suitable copy of Windows.** You need either one of the mainstream versions of Windows 7 (Home Premium, Professional, Ultimate, or Enterprise) or Windows XP with Service Pack 2 or Service Pack 3. (Windows XP can be either Windows XP Home Edition or Windows XP Professional.)

Genius   Usually, the least-expensive way to get a legitimate copy of Windows 7 is to buy an OEM version or system builder version. (OEM is the abbreviation for Original Equipment Manufacturer, which in the PC world means a company that builds the PCs it sells.) Most online stores will sell you an OEM version of Windows 7. For some versions, you will need to buy a system component to confirm that you're building a computer. This system component can be any major internal component of a PC, such as a RAM chip or a hard drive. To find a copy of Windows XP at a competitive price, use eBay (www.ebay.com).

2. **Create a Mac OS X recovery drive.** Download the Lion Recovery Disk Assistant and create a USB recovery drive. If you downloaded Lion and installed it as an update to an earlier version, you can also burn Mac OS X to a DVD. See Chapter 12 for details.

Genius   Your iMac has a recovery partition that you can use to repair or reinstall Mac OS X if it gets corrupted. But because it's possible for your iMac's recovery partition to get scrambled too, it's a good idea to burn a DVD containing the Lion installation files so that you can reinstall from DVD if necessary. See Chapter 12 for instructions on this.

3. **Click the Finder button on the Dock, and then choose Go ⇨ Utilities to open the Utilities folder.**

4. **Double-click the Boot Camp Assistant icon.** The Assistant starts.

5. **On the opening screen, click Print Installation & Setup Guide to print the documentation.** Make sure you have this documentation in case you run into any issues this book doesn't cover.

6. **Click Continue.** The Download Windows Support Software screen appears.

7. **Select the Download the Windows support software for this Mac option button.**

Note

If you have already downloaded the Windows support software for your iMac and stored it on a CD, DVD, or removable disk, select I have already downloaded the Windows support software for this Mac to a CD, DVD, or external disk option. You will then need to provide the CD, DVD, or optical disk when Boot Camp is setting up your iMac's hardware for Windows.

8. **Click the Continue button.** Boot Camp Assistant downloads the Windows support software for your iMac. This may take anywhere from a few minutes to an hour or more, so be prepared to step away from your iMac or entertain yourself for a while.

9. **When the Save Windows Support Software screen appears, save the software in one of these ways:**

   • **Burn to CD or DVD.** Select the Burn a copy to CD or DVD option button. Insert a blank CD in your iMac's optical drive, click the Continue button, and then click the Burn button in the Burn Disc dialog.

   • **Copy to an external drive.** Select the Save a copy to an external drive option button. Connect an external drive format to your iMac, and then click the Continue button. In the dialog that opens, select the drive, and then click the Copy button.

Caution

When you copy the Windows Support Software to an external drive, that drive must be formatted with the FAT file system rather than the Mac OS Extended file system. If necessary, use Disk Utility to reformat the external drive. Follow the instructions in the section on formatting an external drive in Chapter 1.

10. **If a dialog (see Figure 11.1) appears telling you that Boot Camp Assistant is trying to add a new helper tool, type your password and click Add Helper.**

11. **On the Create a Partition for Windows screen (see Figure 11.2), click and drag the divider bar to increase or decrease the size of the Windows partition.** Boot Camp Assistant suggests

11.1 Type your password and click Add Helper to allow Boot Camp Assistant to add a new helper tool.

5GB, which is enough for a modest installation of Windows XP but not enough for Windows 7 (which needs at least 16GB). If more than half of your iMac's hard drive is free, you can click Divide Equally if you want to devote half the iMac's hard drive.

Genius

Windows 7 needs at least 16GB to install and run. Windows XP needs at least 4GB to install and run. 32GB is plenty of space unless you plan to install large games or store many audio and video files. Use the Divide Equally button only if you're certain you want to use Windows a lot on your iMac.

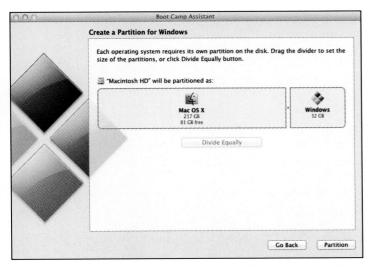

11.2 Click and drag the divider bar to set the size of the Windows partition.

12. **Click Partition.** Boot Camp Assistant creates the partition for Windows, and then prompts you to insert your Windows disc.

13. **Insert the disc, and click Start Installation.** Your iMac restarts and automatically launches the Windows installation routine.

Caution

In Windows 7, click the Custom (advanced) button on the Which type of installation do you want? screen. If the Upgrade button is available, don't click it.

14. **Choose the installation partition.** The partition is labeled BOOTCAMP and set to the size you chose, so it's easy enough to find.

15. **Format the installation partition with NTFS.** This is required for Windows 7 but optional for Windows XP. NTFS is the NT File System that most desktop versions of Windows use. NT itself stands for New Technology, which is what Windows NT 3.1 was in 1993 (compared to Windows 3.1).

    - **Windows 7.** Click the Drive Options (Advanced) link, click the Format link, and then click OK.

    - **Windows XP.** Choose Format the partition using the NTFS file system (Quick).

16. **Complete the rest of the installation, and set up a user account when prompted.** Windows then starts.

Prevent Windows from Activating Itself Automatically

Windows uses a tool called activation to discourage software piracy. Windows will run only for a set period (usually 14 or 30 days, depending on the version) before requiring activation.

The setup routines for Windows XP and Windows 7 include automatic activation, but I strongly suggest you wait until you've had a chance to check how well Windows suits your iMac (and yourself) before tying this copy of Windows to your iMac.

When installing Windows 7, deselect the Automatically activate Windows when I'm online check box on the Type your Windows product key screen. When installing Windows XP, skip the Activate Windows Now prompt near the end of the setup routine. Windows reminds you aggressively that you need to activate it, so there's no risk you will forget.

Genius

If your Windows partition is 32GB or smaller, you can use the FAT32 file system for Windows XP. The advantage is that you can then save files to the Windows partition directly from Mac OS X (which you can't do if the partition uses NTFS). The disadvantage is that Windows XP doesn't run as well on FAT32 as on NTFS.

Getting your iMac's hardware to work in Windows

The first time Windows starts, your screen may look wrong because the resolution is set too low. Other hardware components may not be working because the drivers they need are not yet installed.

You can fix this easily after you install the drivers needed to tell Windows how to work with the iMac's hardware. Here's how to install the drivers:

1. **Click Start, and then click Computer (on Windows 7) or My Computer (on Windows XP).** A Computer window or My Computer window opens.

2. **Right-click the DVD drive and choose Eject.** Remove the Windows disc when your iMac ejects it.

3. **Insert the Windows Support disc you burned, or connect the external drive.** The AutoPlay dialog opens.

4. **Click the Run setup.exe link.** On Windows 7, you then need to click Continue in the User Account Control dialog that appears. The Boot Camp Installer window then opens.

Note

User Account Control is a Windows 7 feature that double-checks each time someone tries to install software or change an important system setting. This check is to ensure that you have requested the action rather than a malevolent software program requesting it.

5. **Click Next, and follow the steps of the installation process.** This takes several minutes, and you'll see pop-up messages and hear audio tones as various components spring to life.

6. **When you see the Boot Camp installer completed screen, click Finish.** Boot Camp then prompts you to restart your iMac (see Figure 11.3).

7. **If you used a Windows Support disc, eject it.** In the Computer window or My Computer window, right-click the DVD drive, and then choose Eject. Remove the disc from the drive and stow it safely. Click the Close button to close the Computer window or My Computer window.

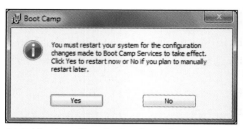

11.3 After installing the Windows drivers, you must restart your iMac.

Note If you used a removable drive to install the Windows drivers, you can either eject it or leave it connected. To eject the drive, right-click it in the Computer window or My Computer window, and then click Eject on the shortcut menu.

8. **In the Boot Camp dialog, click Yes.** Your iMac restarts. After you log in, Boot Camp automatically sets the display resolution to match your iMac's screen, so Windows now displays correctly if it didn't before. Boot Camp also displays the Boot Camp help window to help you get started using Windows.

Windows is a fact of life for hardware manufacturers, so most third-party hardware that works with Macs also has Windows drivers. These are the three main sources for Windows drivers for hardware:

- **Windows Update.** Windows Update provides drivers submitted by hardware manufacturers for Windows compatibility testing. If Windows finds a nonfunctioning device attached to your iMac, follow the prompts in the wizard (which starts automatically) to search automatically for drivers.

- **Hardware manufacturer's website.** If Windows Update can't provide a driver, go to the hardware manufacturer's website and search for a driver.

- **Third-party driver sites.** Sites such as DriverGuide (www.driverguide.com) provide a wide range of drivers, including ones for older equipment whose manufacturers are no longer supporting the devices (or no longer in business). Some sites charge for downloads or require you to become a member. You may be able to bypass membership requirements by searching for the driver on a search engine (for example, Google) and then going directly to the driver's page on the driver site rather than using the driver site's search tool.

Switching between Windows and Mac OS

Because you can run only one operating system at a time using Boot Camp, you must restart your iMac to move between Windows and Mac OS X.

First, tell Boot Camp whether to start in Mac OS X or in Windows by default. From Windows, follow these steps:

1. **Click the Boot Camp icon (a gray diamond) in the notification area at the right end of the status bar, and choose Boot Camp Control Panel.** On Windows 7, you need to click Continue in the User Account Control dialog that appears. The Boot Camp Control Panel window opens (see Figure 11.4).

11.4 Set your preferred operating system on the Startup Disk tab in Boot Camp Control Panel.

2. **In the Select the system you want to use to start up your computer box, click the operating system you want to use by default: Macintosh HD Mac OS X or BOOTCAMP Windows.**

3. **Click OK.** The Boot Camp Control Panel window closes.

To shut down Windows and restart your iMac using Mac OS X, click the Boot Camp button in the notification area, and then click Restart in Mac OS X. In the confirmation dialog (see Figure 11.5), click OK. Your iMac then restarts with Mac OS X as the default operating system.

Here's how to shut down Mac OS X and restart in Windows:

1. **Choose Apple menu ⇨ System Preferences.** The System Preferences window opens.

2. **Click Startup Disk (in the System section) to display the Startup Disk preferences (see Figure 11.6).**

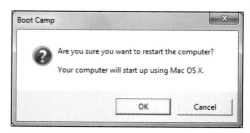

11.5 You can quickly shut down Windows and restart in Mac OS X.

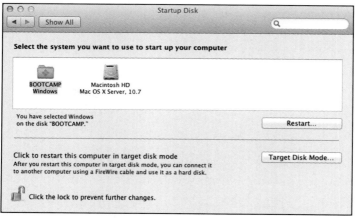

11.6 Use the Startup Disk preferences to set your default OS and to restart your iMac with Windows.

3. **In the Select the system you want to use to start up your computer box, click the operating system you want to use by default.**

4. **To restart in Windows, click Restart, and then click Restart in the confirmation dialog that appears.** Otherwise, choose System Preferences ⇨ Quit System Preferences.

To override your default operating system when you start your Mac, press Option when you hear the startup chime. Hold Option down until the various startup disks appear. Click the one you want to use, and then click the arrow button to start it.

Protecting and updating Windows

Windows is the online world's main target of malware, so you must protect it with an antivirus program. Many programs are available depending on your needs. Here are four examples, two paid and two free:

- **Norton security products.** Symantec (www.symantec.com/norton/internet-security) sells several Norton-branded security products. Norton AntiVirus ($40) provides adequate protection for savvy users. Norton Internet Security ($70) adds extra features, such as protecting against phishing messages and parental controls for keeping kids safe online. Norton 360 ($60) has almost all the features of Norton Internet Security but adds features for optimizing Windows and backing up (and restoring) your files.

- **Kaspersky security products.** Kaspersky (www.kaspersky.com) offers various security products. Kaspersky Anti-Virus ($40) provides protection against virus and malware, scans websites to see if they contain malicious software, and provides phishing protection. Kaspersky Internet Security ($65) adds extra features such as parental controls and spam control.

- **AVG AntiVirus Free Edition.** This free antivirus program (http://free.avg.com/us-en/homepage) provides plenty of protection if you use the Internet sensibly.

- **Avast Home Edition.** Also free, this antivirus program (www.avast.com) gives you solid protection against viruses and malware without providing extra features like phishing protection.

After installing antivirus software, choose Start ⇨ All Programs ⇨ Windows Update to run Windows Update. Follow the prompts to download and install any updates available for Windows.

Caution

Make sure the antivirus program you get is genuine. A favorite means of attack by online malefactors is fake antivirus programs and fake antispyware programs. Such programs typically display a pop-up message on a web page claiming that your computer has a virus infection. If you accept the offer to download and install a program to fix the problem, you actually install the malware on your PC.

Installing and running programs on Windows

Windows comes with various programs built in, but you will probably need to install others to get all your work (or play) done.

To install a program

- **Install a program from a CD or DVD.** Insert the program's disc in your iMac. Windows normally opens an AutoPlay window offering to install the program. If not, choose Start ⇨ Computer or Start ⇨ My Computer, double-click the optical drive's icon, and then double-click the setup.exe file for the program.

● **Install a program you've downloaded.** Normally, Internet Explorer prompts you to run a program file you're downloading; click the Run button to proceed with the installation. If you have already downloaded the program file, open a Windows Explorer window to the folder that contains the file, and then double-click the file to launch the installation.

To run a program, click the Start button, find the program's icon on the Start menu, and then click it.

Removing Boot Camp from Your iMac

If you decide that you don't want to keep Windows on your iMac, you can remove it quickly. Here's what to do:

1. **If you're currently using Windows, boot to Mac OS X.**

2. **Back up your Mac using Time Machine.** See Chapter 13 for instructions.

3. **Click the desktop, choose Go ➪ Utilities, and then double-click the Boot Camp Assistant icon.** Boot Camp Assistant displays the Introduction screen.

4. **Click Continue.** Boot Camp Assistant displays the Download Windows Support Software screen.

5. **Select the I have already downloaded the Windows support software for this Mac to a CD, DVD, or external disk option.**

6. **Click Continue.** Boot Camp Assistant displays the Select Task screen (see Figure 11.7).

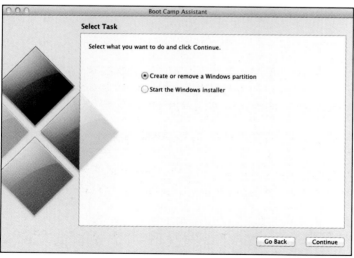

11.7 To remove Boot Camp, select the Create or remove a Windows partition option on the Select Task screen of Boot Camp Assistant.

7. **Select the Create or remove a Windows partition option.**

8. **Click Continue.** Boot Camp Assistant displays the Restore Disk to a Single Volume screen (see Figure 11.8).

9. **Click Restore.** Mac OS X removes the Windows partition, and then displays the Partition Removed screen.

10. **Click Quit to quit Boot Camp Assistant.**

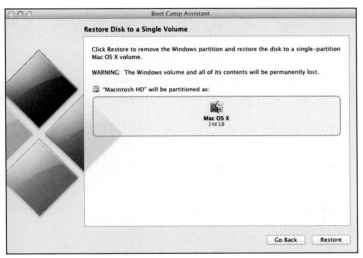

11.8 On the Restore Disk to a Single Volume screen, confirm that you want to remove the Windows partition.

Recovering from the "No bootable device" error

Boot Camp Assistant normally does a great job, but if it messes up it may leave your iMac unable to start correctly. If this happens, you see the message "No bootable device — insert boot disk and press any key" over a black screen when you try to start your iMac.

If this happens, follow these steps to make your iMac's disk bootable again:

1. **Restart your iMac.** For example, press and hold down the power button until your iMac turns off. Wait a few seconds, and then press the power button again to turn the iMac back on.

2. **When the startup chime rings out, press ⌘+R.** Keep holding these keys down until the Apple logo appears on screen, and then release them.

Genius

If your recovery partition cannot restart your iMac to recover from the Boot Camp problem, and you have burned a DVD containing your Lion installation files, insert that DVD now. Press and hold down the power button until your iMac turns off. Wait a few seconds, and then turn it back on. As it starts, press and hold down the C key until you can tell Mac OS X is starting from the DVD. (Usually, you can hear the DVD whirring.) On the Install Mac OS X screen, go to the menu bar and choose Utilities ▷ Disk Utility to launch Disk Utility.

3. **When the Mac OS X Utilities screen appears, click Disk Utility.** Disk Utility opens (see Figure 11.9).

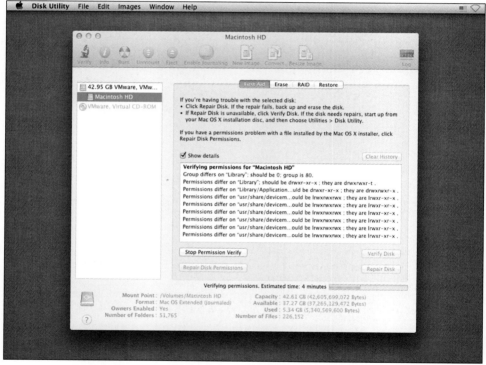

11.9 If Boot Camp prevents your iMac from booting, use Disk Utility to verify the permissions on the hard disk. You may need to repair the permissions; you may also need to verify and repair the disk itself.

4. **In the left pane, click your iMac's hard disk.**

5. **Click the First Aid tab to display the First Aid pane.**

6. **Verify and repair your disk permissions:**

   ● **Click Verify Disk Permissions.**

- **If Disk Utility tells you that you need to repair disk permissions, click Repair Disk Permissions.**

7. **Verify and repair the disk:**

   - Click Verify Disk.

   - If Disk Utility tells you that the disk needs repair, click Repair Disk.

8. **Quit Disk Utility.** For example, choose Disk Utility ⇨ Quit Disk Utility.

9. **Choose Mac OS X Installer ⇨ Quit Mac OS X installer.** The Are you sure you want to quit Mac OS X Installer? dialog opens (see Figure 11.10).

11.10 In the Are you sure you want to quit Mac OS X Installer? dialog, click Choose Startup Disk to open the Choose Startup Disk dialog.

10. **Click Choose Startup Disk.** The Choose Startup Disk dialog opens (see Figure 11.11).

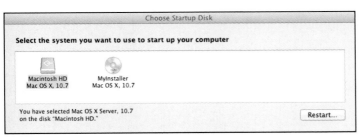

11.11 In the Choose Startup Disk dialog, select your iMac's hard disk as the startup disk, and then click Restart.

11. **In the Select the system you want to use to start up your computer box, click your iMac's hard disk.**

12. **Click Restart.** Mac OS X displays a confirmation dialog.

13. **Click Restart.** Mac OS X restarts your Mac from the hard disk, and you can log in as usual.

Installing and Using Windows in a Virtual Machine

Instead of using Boot Camp to repartition your Mac's hard drive, you may prefer to install a virtual-machine application and install Windows in it. This approach enables you to run Windows programs at the same time as your Mac applications, exchanging data between them as needed.

317

The first step is to choose which virtual-machine application you will use. You then install the application, after which you install Windows in it.

Genius

By using a virtual machine, you can run several versions of Windows at the same time. This capability can be useful when you're developing or testing software, providing customer support, or writing documentation. You can also run other operating systems, such as Linux.

Choosing a virtual machine

There are three main virtual machine program applications for the Mac:

- **Parallels Desktop for Mac ($80; www.parallels.com).** The package includes Acronis disk-imaging software, which you can use to keep a backup of your Windows installation. The chapter-opening figure shows Windows 7 running on Parallels Desktop.

- **VMWare Fusion ($80; www.vmware.com).** VMWare Fusion includes highly automated setup routines that take the work out of installing many versions of Windows.

- **VirtualBox (free; www.virtualbox.org).** VirtualBox is a free virtual machine application that can run many operating systems. VirtualBox doesn't offer as many advanced features as Parallels Desktop or VMWare Fusion, but it's more than adequate for light use.

Both Parallels Desktop for Mac and VMWare Fusion have a trial version available for download, so you can try installing Windows and decide which works best for you. Both these applications also let you run an installation of Windows that you've installed using Boot Camp as a virtual machine instead.

Installing the virtual machine

After downloading the virtual machine application, open its disk image in a Finder window (Safari may do this for you) and then double-click the installation file to launch the installer. Follow through the installation process, accepting the license agreement and choosing to install the application on your iMac's hard drive if the installer offers you a choice.

Installing Windows in the virtual machine

Once the virtual-machine application is installed, launch it from Launchpad (or click and drag its icon from Launchpad to the Dock, and then launch it from there). The application then launches an Assistant or wizard to walk you through the process of setting up a virtual machine. For example, VirtualBox displays the Create New Virtual Machine wizard (see Figure 11.12), in which you first name your virtual machine and choose the operating system to install.

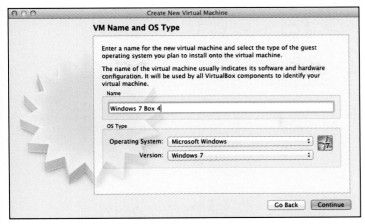

11.12 Each virtual-machine application provides an Assistant or wizard to help you create a virtual machine.

After you provide your Windows disc, you get to choose options for installing Windows. The names of these options vary depending on the virtual-machine application, but you have three main choices to make:

● **Where to store the virtual machine.** To get good performance, store the virtual machine on your iMac's hard drive or on a Thunderbolt external drive. While you can use a FireWire or USB drive, performance will suffer. Whichever drive you use, make sure there's plenty of space for the virtual machine. Allow at least 16GB for Windows 7 and 4GB for Windows XP.

Genius

If you need to share the virtual machine with other people who use your iMac, store the virtual machine in the /Users/Shared folder or another shared folder.

● **How many processors to give the virtual machine.** If your iMac has a dual-core processor, allocate one processor (one core) to the virtual machine. If your iMac has a quad-core processor, allocate two processors unless you need to run multiple virtual machines at once (in which case, allocate one processor to each virtual machine).

Genius

You can adjust the number of processors and the amount of RAM later as needed, so it's not vital to get them right the first time.

● **How much RAM to give the virtual machine.** If possible, give Windows XP 1GB of RAM and Windows 7 2GB, as long as your iMac contains at least double that amount. Otherwise, use 512MB for Windows XP and 1GB for Windows 7.

After making these decisions, you sit back and let the installation roll.

Note

If you choose to pick up the Boot Camp partition, the virtual-machine application needs only a short time to set the partition up to work as a virtual machine.

Installing tools or additions on your virtual machine

After your virtual machine has started Windows for the first time, you need to install drivers to enable Windows to make the most of the machine's virtual hardware. Some of the virtual-machine applications call these tools; others call them additions.

Note

Some virtual-machine applications install the tools or additions automatically.

Here are the commands to use to install the tools or additions manually:

● **Parallels Desktop.** Choose Virtual Machine ➡ Install Parallels Tools.

● **VMWare Fusion.** Choose Virtual Machine ➡ Install VMWare Tools.

● **VirtualBox.** Choose Devices ➡ Install Guest Additions.

Protecting and updating your virtual machine

To keep your virtual machine in good shape, you need to protect it against malware and keep it updated. So after you set up Windows on your virtual machine, install antivirus software on it immediately:

- **Parallels Desktop.** Choose Virtual Machine ⇨ Install Parallels Internet Security to install the Internet Security package.

- **VMWare Fusion.** Choose Virtual Machine ⇨ Install McAfee VirusScan Plus to install the version of McAfee VirusScan Plus that VMWare integrates in Fusion.

- **VirtualBox.** Download and install a third-party antivirus program such as AVG AntiVirus Free Edition (free; http://free.avg.com/us-en/homepage) or Avast Home Edition (free; www.avast.com).

Next, use Windows Update (choose Start ⇨ All Programs ⇨ Windows Update) to download and install any updates.

Installing and running programs on your virtual machine

Once you've protected and updated the virtual machine, you can install programs and run them just as you would do on an actual PC. For example:

- **Install a program.** Insert the program's disc in your iMac and double-click the setup.exe file if Windows does not launch it automatically, or download a program file from the Internet and double-click it to launch the installation.

- **Run a program.** Click the Start button to open the Start menu, find the program's icon, and then click it.

Closing or suspending the virtual machine

When you have finished using the virtual machine, you can simply shut down Windows by opening the Start menu and choosing the Shut Down command from it.

Alternatively, you can suspend the virtual machine by issuing the Suspend command from the toolbar or the menu bar (for example, Virtual Machine ⇨ Suspend). The Suspend command puts the virtual machine to sleep in its current state, so that you can reawaken it later with all your applications still running, and resume work (or play) where you left off.

How Can I Make My iMac Run Faster and More Reliably?

Software Update

New software is available for your computer.

If you don't want to install now, choose Apple menu > Software Update when you're ready to install.

Install	Name	Version	Size
☑	iWeb Update	3.0.4	187.4 MB
☑	GarageBand Update	6.0.4	51.5 MB
☑	iPhoto 9.1.5	9.1.5	232.1 MB
☑	iMovie 9.0.4	9.0.4	79.9 MB
☑	iDVD 7.1.2	7.1.2	37.6 MB

About iWeb 3.0.4

This update improves overall stability and addresses a number of minor issues.

This update is recommended for all iWeb 3 users.

Note: Use of this software is subject to the original Software License Agreement(s) that accompanied the software being updated. A list of Apple SLAs may be found here: http://www.apple.com/legal/sla/ .

Hide Details   Not Now   Install 5 Items

If you use your iMac extensively, as most iMac users do, you'll soon find that it's indispensable to your life — and that goes double if you use your iMac for work as well as for fun and home stuff. To make your iMac run as fast as possible, you need to give it plenty of RAM, make the most of your hard drive space, and squeeze every modicum of speed out of your network connection. To keep your iMac running reliably, you need to use Software Update to keep your Mac's software up to date and also update third-party applications. You should consider buying AppleCare so that you know your iMac's covered for disasters that occur after the warranty has expired. And finally, even though your iMac will likely prove a reliable beast, you will need to know how to troubleshoot problems when they rear their heads. So I'll show you how to figure out what's wrong, deal with network and Internet issues, fix hard drive problems, and summon extra one-on-one help when severe problems occur.

Making Your iMac Run Faster

How fast your iMac runs depends on the speed of its processor and the number of cores the processor has, the number of tasks you load on the iMac, how much RAM it has, and how much available hard drive space it has to work in. You choose the processor speed when you buy the iMac (you can't sensibly upgrade it), but you can affect the other three variables, as discussed in this section. You can also take steps to make your network connection run as fast as possible, so that a network bottleneck doesn't act as a brake on your iMac's speed.

Maxing out your RAM

The world keeps changing — but some things remain the same. Even though celebrities have now proved conclusively that you can be too thin or too rich (or, in certain spectacular cases, both), you still can't have too much RAM in your computer. Macs are no exception to this rule, and the 27-inch iMac's capacity for 16GB of RAM is as welcome a boost to its power as it is an unwelcome kick in the wallet.

The more RAM your iMac has, the more data it can hold in memory at once — and the faster it can crunch through the tough tasks you throw at it. So if you haven't yet maxed out your iMac's RAM, you have a strong motivation to max it out now — or at least to stuff into your iMac as much RAM as you can afford now.

Checking how much RAM your iMac has

If you're not sure how much RAM your iMac has, choose Apple menu ⇨ About This Mac, and then look at the Memory readout in the About This Mac dialog. This gives you the amount of RAM and its type — for example, 4GB 1333 MHz DDR3 SDRAM.

Checking which RAM modules your iMac has

To see which RAM modules your iMac has, click the More Info button in the About This Mac dialog to open the System Information utility. At first, System Information appears as a larger version of the About This Mac window. Click the Memory button in the toolbar to display the details of the RAM that's installed.

Figure 12.1 shows the About This Mac window in System Information for an iMac that has two memory slots. The first slot contains a 1GB memory module. The second slot contains a 2GB memory module.

From the Memory pane in the About This Mac window, you can click the Memory Upgrade Instructions button to open a Safari window to a page on Apple's website that gives instructions for removing and installing memory on iMacs. This RAM upgrade is one of the changes that Apple permits you without voiding your warranty, which is good news.

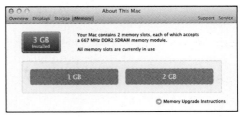

12.1 Use the Memory tab of the About This Mac window in the System Information utility to see which memory modules your iMac contains.

Getting RAM for your iMac

You can buy RAM for your iMac either from Apple or from third-party vendors. RAM is a big buy, so it's well worth comparing prices before making the purchase. Vendors such as Crucial (www.crucial.com), Kingston (www.kingston.com), and Other World Computing (www.otherworldcomputing.com) provide tools that make it easy to find exactly the memory your iMac needs. Other World Computing offers a small rebate if you turn in your old RAM, which saves you from having to try to find a buyer for it.

Installing RAM in your iMac

Installing RAM in the last few generations of iMac models is an easy six-step process:

1. **Shut down Mac OS X and unplug your iMac's power cable.**

2. **Lay the iMac face down on a soft cloth you've placed over a flat surface, such as a table.**

3. **Unscrew the screws in the access doors at the bottom of the screen, and open the doors.**

4. **Touch a metal object, such as the iMac's case, to discharge any static you've built up in your body.**

5. **Remove any RAM modules you need to replace, and slide in the new modules firmly.** You should feel them click into place, but you shouldn't need to apply serious force.

6. **Replace the doors, screw in the screws, and set your iMac upright again.** Connect the power, and you're on your way.

After installing the RAM and starting your iMac, choose Apple menu ➪ About This Mac. Check the Memory readout in the About This Mac dialog to make sure that all the RAM is present and correct.

Maximizing hard drive space

To keep Mac OS X and your applications running well, keep plenty of free space on your iMac's hard drive. This not only makes it easy for Mac OS X to use virtual memory, augmenting your iMac's RAM by writing extra memory data temporarily on the hard drive, but it also gives Mac OS X a better chance of writing large files to disk in neighboring sectors, where the disk head can retrieve them quickly, rather than scattering them all over the disk.

Genius

There's no hard-and-fast minimum amount of space that you must leave free on your iMac's hard drive, but aim for keeping 10 to 20 percent of the drive free. Below this threshold, your iMac may slow down or exhibit odd behavior. For example, if your iMac has a 1 terabyte (TB) drive, try to keep at least 100–200GB free.

Understanding your options for getting more free space

There are three main ways to increase the amount of free space on your iMac's hard drive:

- **Remove some of the existing data.** With the iMac, this is the best bet. I cover your options in a moment.

- **Replace the hard drive with a larger one.** The iMac's all-in-one design means that a hard-drive replacement involves major surgery. Unless you're both skilled and dexterous, leave opening your iMac's case and replacing the hard drive to trained technicians.

- **Add an external hard drive.** An external hard drive is a great option for adding storage, but because it's slower than the internal hard drive, don't plan to keep frequently needed data on it. Most external hard drives also spin down (or go to sleep) when you're not using them, and the delay they take to spin back up when you awaken them can be frustrating.

Cleaning out files that you don't need

Two great utilities that will ferret out unnecessary files and delete them for you are OnyX (free; http://www.titanium.free.fr/download.php) and IceClean (free; www.macdentro.com/MacDentro. Each of these programs can (among other useful tasks) clean out the many cache files and related temporary data files that your iMac generates every day. Figure 12.2 shows the Cleaning pane in OnyX.

Each provides a graphical way to execute commands that you could give your iMac using Terminal; this means they do exactly the same things, and which one you use is a matter of preference. You can free scores or hundreds of megabytes by using the cleaning function of either tool. You'll need to run the tool regularly, because your iMac continues creating the cache files and temporary files.

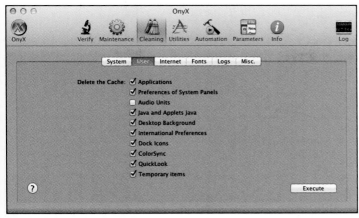

12.2 By cleaning up cache files and temporary files, OnyX can free up large amounts of space on your hard drive.

Genius

OnyX is great for cleaning out cache and temporary files because you can access its cleaning functions from the toolbar. IceClean's cleaning commands are on the Cleanup menu, which is less handy, but IceClean includes some network functions that aren't part of OnyX, and its documentation is excellent.

If your iMac's internal hard drive is still short on space after you've run OnyX or IceClean, you have several options:

- Add an external hard drive or two, as discussed in this section.

- Archive old files you no longer need, as discussed next.

- Remove applications you no longer need (as discussed after that).

Adding an external hard drive is the quick-and-dirty fix to your iMac's storage blues. You want to look for the following specs:

- **Thunderbolt interface or FireWire 800 interface.** The 2011 and later iMac models include Thunderbolt ports, which give by far the highest file transfer speeds. If you need speed, Thunderbolt is the way to go, but you'll pay a price premium over other drives. The next best choice is a FireWire 800 port. While USB 2.0 drives are more widespread than FireWire and work fine, FireWire not only delivers much greater speed than USB but is also better at sustained transfers of the type you'll run into when accessing video and large sound files on a drive.

- **High spindle speed, preferably 7200 RPM.** Using a faster-spinning hard drive can increase disk performance by a surprising amount.

- **A large cache, ideally 32MB or larger.** This is RAM within the hard drive set aside to hold data that's being written to or read from the disk, in order to speed up access to the data you're using right now.

Genius When setting up a drive to be used primarily for gaming, turn off journaling. For gaming, you shouldn't need the backup that journaling provides, and it slows down disk access. To disable this feature, start Disk Utility, choose your new drive from the list, and choose File ⇨ Disable Journaling.

Archiving old files

Clearing out old and unneeded system files can reclaim some space on your iMac, but if you're still short of space after running cleanups, you'll need to tackle your own files as well. Chances are that these are the files that are occupying most of the space you want to get back.

Note Don't forget to clean out your Downloads folder. It's likely stuffed with disk images and reference materials you no longer need or could move to an external drive or DVD.

If you work on separate projects on your iMac, archive your older projects by burning them to DVD, checking that the contents are all present and correct, and then deleting the projects from the hard drive.

Reclaim space from your mailbox by removing attachments from old Mail messages. If you make a habit of removing all attachments before you file each message, as recommended in Chapter 7, your mailbox won't gradually build up with attachments; but if you leave attachments in place, your mailbox can quickly balloon to an impressive size.

Genius To see how much space your email folders are taking up altogether, click the desktop, click the Go menu, hold down Option, and then click Library to open a Finder window to your ~/Library folder (the Library folder inside your home folder). Control+click or right-click the Mail folder, choose Get Info, and look at the Size readout in the General section. If the size is several (or many) gigabytes, go into Mail and look through your mailboxes for large attachments you can dispose of.

Songs, photos, and movies tend to take up a huge amount of space on hard-used iMacs, so a careful purge can often take care of your iMac's space problems for a while. Here are some suggestions:

- **iTunes.** If you've rated all the songs in your music library, create a Smart Playlist for the lower-rated songs — for example, the one-star and two-star songs. Burn the playlist to DVDs so that you have the songs safe. Then sort the whole library by its rating, and delete the one-star and two-star songs. Repeat the procedure for videos, TV shows, and other content.

- **GarageBand.** Cull all the loops you don't need — for example, if you don't need 63 different Club Dance Beat loops, delete them. When you finish a song project, export it to iTunes or share it online, and then move the project files to an external hard drive or burn them to DVD.

- **iPhoto.** If you've rated your photos, create a Smart Album containing the lower-rated photos — for example, the one-star and two-star photos. Review the photos to find any you've misjudged, and then export the photos for safekeeping and delete them from your iMac.

- **iMovie.** Archive your finished projects to DVD so that you can remove them from your iMac. For projects you may still need to refer to, click and drag them in the Project Library window from your iMac's hard drive to an external hard drive. Move your rejected clips to the Trash, and use Space Saver (choose File ⇨ Space Saver) to delete all rejected footage. Empty the Trash.

- **iDVD.** Delete old project files you no longer need.

Removing software you no longer need

If you install all the applications that pique your interest, you'll probably end up with several gigabytes of applications that you don't actually use.

The simple way to get rid of an application is to click and drag it from the Applications folder to the Trash (or click the application in the Applications folder and press ⌘+Delete). This removes all the files and folders in the application's package file but leaves in place two types of files related to the application:

- **The application's preference files.** These files, stored in your ~/Library/ Preferences folder, take up a minimal amount of space. You may want to keep the preference files in case you reinstall the application.

● **The application's supporting files.** Some applications include many supporting files stored in other folders rather than inside the application's package file. For example, GarageBand puts several gigabytes of files in the /Library/Application Support/ GarageBand folder. If you get rid of GarageBand, you'll want to remove these files too.

Note If an application includes an Uninstaller utility, run that utility to remove the application rather than simply clicking and dragging the application to the Trash.

You can go into the ~/Library/Preferences folder and prune your preference files manually, or visit the /Library/Application Support folder and evict any folders that have outstayed their welcome. But if you don't know exactly which files the application creates, you may prefer to get help from a third-party tool. Here are a couple of examples:

● **AppTrap.** AppTrap (http://onnati.net/ apptrap) is a free preference pane that installs in System Preferences. When you move an application to the Trash, AppTrap asks if you want to move the preferences files as well. If you choose to move them, AppTrap identifies them for you.

● **AppCleaner.** AppCleaner (see Figure 12.3; http://download.cnet.com and other sites) is a free utility that identifies associated files when you delete an application.

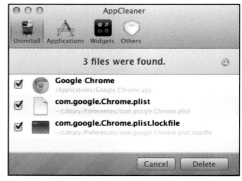

12.3 AppCleaner helps you identify associated files that you may want to delete along with an application you're trashing.

Apart from applications you no longer need, you can reclaim space from Mac OS X itself by deleting any localizations that you don't need. The free utility Monolingual (http://monolingual.source-forge.net) enables you to remove any unused languages (from Afrikaans and Albanian to Welsh and Yiddish). Figure 12.4 shows Monolingual.

Caution If you use Microsoft Office, be careful about removing localizations. Sometimes Office refuses to update correctly if you've removed languages.

Speeding up your network connection

Networks are vital to both business and pleasure these days, so I bet you want to speed up your network as much as possible. This section shows you four ways to improve performance.

Replacing a hub with a switch

If your network uses a network hub to connect the cables, replace it with a Gigabit Ethernet switch. A switch gives much better performance than a hub because it transmits the data to only the cables that need it rather than blasting out the data indiscriminately on all the cables.

12.4 Monolingual removes languages you don't need on your iMac.

Note The speed of your Internet connection typically depends on the grade of Internet service you pay for and how far your place is from the telephone central office or cable connection point — plus how good a connection your ISP has to the Internet and how well the ISP manages traffic. Check out customer forums to see if the speed you get is typical for your ISP and whether other available ISPs offer better performance.

Making sure all your network uses the same standard

Next, make sure that all your network components can run at the same speed. If you connected your iMac's Gigabit Ethernet port to a 10 Mbps switch (or hub), you're choking the network.

Similarly, if you have a wireless network, make sure that it's not holding your iMac back by using a slower standard. Most iMacs have 802.11n AirPort cards, so you'll want an 802.11n-capable wireless router rather than an 802.11g or 802.11b router. Most recent models, including Apple's AirPort access points, can support multiple standards at different speeds at the same time, but older access points may drag the whole network down to the slowest speed — so a single 802.11b device can bring even 802.11n devices down from 300 Mbps to 11 Mbps.

Taking your wireless network out of the crowded 2.4 GHz band

Most wireless networks use the 2.4 GHz spectrum band, which can get crowded if your neighbors also have wireless networks. If your wireless network seems suspiciously slow, try switching to a dual-band router that also uses bandwidth in the 5 GHz band, which is less susceptible to interference.

For any wireless network, place your router as centrally as possible to provide even coverage throughout your place. Try to keep the router away from walls, the floor, and large metal objects.

Check to make sure you're not using any 2.4 GHz cordless phones, which can interfere with wireless networks, and confirm that your router's firmware is up to date. For an AirPort, check for updates by running Software Update — just choose Apple menu ⇨ Software Update.

Note   If your wireless network's signal strength is poor, you may be experiencing interference from another network. Try changing the channel that your network uses. First, run iStumbler (free; www.istumbler.net), which lists all the wireless networks it can detect and shows which channels they're using. Then, start AirPort Utility from the Applications/Utilities folder. Select your AirPort base station and click the Wireless tab. Choose a channel no one else is using from the Channel menu, and then click Update.

Using IPv6 for local networking only

At this writing, the world is very gradually moving from Internet Protocol version 4 (IPv4) to Internet Protocol version 6 (IPv6). IPv4 has now run out of IP addresses (if only technically, as ISPs are hoarding them), while IPv6 has enough IP addresses for everybody's Internet-enabled refrigerator to have thousands of addresses of its own — not to mention other advantages. But most of the Western world is still using IPv4. China, Korea, and other countries with less legacy infrastructure are going straight to IPv6.

By default, Mac OS X turns on IPv6 addressing, which allows your iMac to connect to other devices it may encounter that use IPv6. But unless your Internet connection actually uses IPv6, you should set your iMac to use IPv6 only for local networking — contacting computers and devices on your network —to prevent Mac OS X from wasting time by trying IPv6 first on each Internet connection before falling back on IPv4.

First, check whether your iMac is using IPv6 for Internet connections. Open your web browser (for example, Safari), and go to the IPv6 Test site, www.ipv6-test.com. The site automatically analyzes your connection and displays the results. If the "When both protocols are available, your browser uses" readout shows IPv4 and the "Your Internet connection is not IPv6 capable" message appears, you're using IPv4 only for Internet connections, and you should set your iMac to use IPv6 only for local networking.

Here's how to set your iMac to use IPv6 only for local networking:

1. **Choose Apple menu ⇨ System Preferences.** The System Preferences window opens.

2. **In the Internet & Wireless section, click the Network icon to open Network preferences.**

3. **In the left list box, click the first network interface that's active — for example, Ethernet.** Each active network interface has a green light on its left.

4. **Click Advanced to display the Advanced dialog.** Make sure the TCP/IP tab is at the front; click it if it's not (see Figure 12.5).

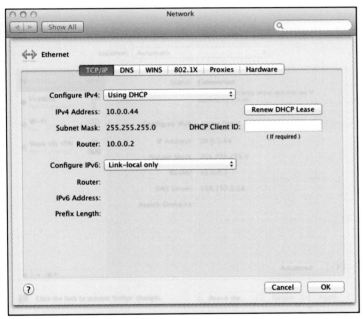

12.5 Setting your iMac to use IPv6 only for local networking may speed up network access.

5. **Open the Configure IPv6 pop-up menu and choose Link-local only.**

6. **Click OK to close the Advanced dialog.**

7. **Repeat Steps 3 through 6 for each active network interface.**

8. **Click Apply to apply the changes you make.**

9. **Quit System Preferences.** For example, press ⌘+Q.

Keeping Your iMac Up and Running

Later in this chapter, I cover how to deal with trouble when it occurs, but first take a look at ways of staying out of trouble in the first place. To keep your iMac in shape, you normally want to run Software Update automatically and update your third-party software. You may also want to buy AppleCare to cover hardware problems, and you may need to clean your iMac's outside as well as clean up its insides.

Running Software Update automatically

To make sure your iMac has the latest updates, fixes, and added features, run Software Update automatically. Software Update checks for Apple's updates not only to Mac OS X and the applications that come with it (such as iChat and iTunes) but also to other Apple software (such as the iLife and iWork applications).

You can run Software Update manually by choosing Apple menu ⇨ Software Update, but to save time and effort, set it to run automatically. Here's how to do that:

1. **Choose Apple menu ⇨ System Preferences.** The System Preferences window opens.

2. **In the System section, click the Software Update icon to open Software Update preferences.** Make sure the Scheduled Check tab is at the front (see Figure 12.6).

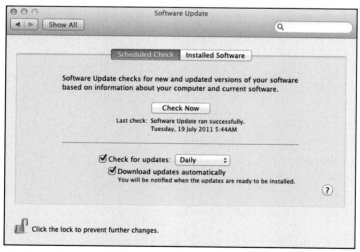

12.6 Set Software Update to check automatically for updates either daily or weekly.

3. **Select the Check for updates check box, and then choose the frequency in the pop-up menu.** Daily is the safest choice, Weekly is more or less okay, and Monthly is much too rare unless you frequently check manually.

Note If you don't have an always-on Internet connection, deselect the Check for updates check box. Instead, check for updates manually at times that suit you.

4. **Select the Download updates automatically check box if you want Mac OS X to get the updates for you when it discovers them.** This feature is great if you have an always-on Internet connection that's not permanently busy, as it means you can install the updates much more quickly. But if you and your family thrash your Internet connection most of the time, you'll probably want to deselect this check box so that you can download the updates when things are quiet.

Note From Software Update preferences, you can click Check Now to check manually for updates. But usually it's easier simply to choose Apple menu ➪ Software Update.

5. **Quit System Preferences.** For example, press ⌘+Q.

Whether you check manually or Software Update runs automatically, it lets you know when updates are available (see Figure 12.7).

The first thing to look for here is the message, "You must restart your computer after the updates are installed." If you don't see this message, you can install the updates immediately without restarting your iMac; otherwise, you'll need to plan a shutdown, for which you may prefer to install the updates at a more convenient time.

12.7 When Software Update tells you there are updates, check whether you'll need to restart your iMac.

Note If you check for updates manually and there are none, Software Update displays a dialog telling you it came up dry. If Software Update checks automatically and finds nothing new, it displays no messages.

335

To see the details of the updates, click Show Details. You see the full list of updates, as in the picture shown on the opening page of this chapter. Here you can deselect the check box for any update you don't want to install, and then click Install Items to start downloading the updates (unless Software Update has automatically downloaded them for you) and installing them. If Software Update prompts you to restart your iMac to complete the installation, save your open documents and close all your applications, and then allow the restart.

If you don't want to install the updates right now, click Not Now to close Software Update.

Genius

If an update appears in the list that you know you'll never want, such as a new version of an application you never use, click that list entry and choose Update ⟡ Ignore Update, and then click OK in the confirmation dialog. If you then want to see the updates you've ignored, choose Software Update ⟡ Reset Ignored Updates.

If you click the Installed Updates tab of Software Update preferences, you can see a list of everything Software Update has installed, going back months. This is a great way to quickly find out your installed versions of Apple software; just click the Name column header to sort the list by program name and scroll through to find the application you're interested in.

Checking for third-party software updates

Software Update makes it so easy to keep your Apple software up to date that keeping third-party software updated seems like a chore by comparison.

Many applications include a Check for Updates command (or simply an Updates command) on the Help menu. Start by looking here to see if you can quickly force a check for updates.

If the Help menu doesn't provide a way of checking for updates, open the app's menu and click Preferences to display its Preferences window or Preferences dialog. You'll then need to look for the update options and choose suitable settings.

For example, in Firefox, click the Advanced button in the Preferences window, and then click the Update tab (see Figure 12.8). In the Automatically check for updates to area, select the Firefox check box, the Add-ons check box, or the Search Engines check box as needed. In the When updates to Firefox are found area, select the Ask me what I want to do option to keep your freedom of choice or select the Automatically download and install the update option if you want to install updates automatically. If you choose the latter option, you can select the Warn me if this will disable any of my add-ons check box to make sure you learn about any add-on functionality the update will remove.

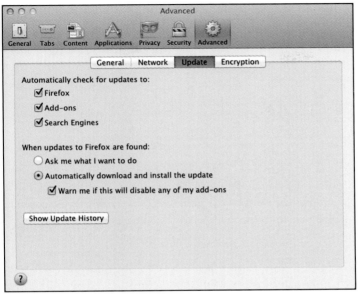

12.8 Many applications include an Update tab or section in the Preferences window or Preferences dialog. For example, Firefox lets you choose which updates to check for and whether to download and install them automatically.

Having each application check separately for its updates works pretty well, but you may also want to try tools that check for updates to all the third-party applications you have installed. Here are two candidates to try:

- **TechTracker.** TechTracker (www.cnet.com/techtracker-free) is a free application from CNET Downloads that tracks all your installed software and lets you know whenever a new version is available.

- **MacUpdate Desktop.** The MacUpdate website (www.macupdate.com) provides applications and lists software updates. The MacUpdate Desktop application ($20 per year) notifies you of updates to the software installed on your iMac.

Buying AppleCare: Is it worth the money?

Apple would like you to buy an AppleCare three-year extended warranty for every Mac, iPod, or other Apple product you purchase. But like most extended warranties, AppleCare isn't cheap ($170 for an iMac), and many people feel it's not worth the price. This is a tough call, because if anything does go wrong with your iMac in those three years, even a single repair will probably cost you more than $200.

Note

One of the best things about AppleCare is that you don't have to buy it when you buy your Mac. You can wait till your first 90 days of free service is almost up and buy it then, to extend your warranty even more. And if you're comfortable buying on eBay (www.ebay.com), you can save a bundle — iMac AppleCare plans go for as little as $120 on the online auction site. If you're not comfortable with eBay, you can also save by buying on Amazon and other online sites.

But if your iMac is vital to your life or work (or both), or if you're prepared to pay for the peace of mind that comes from knowing you can get your iMac fixed if it breaks, AppleCare is well worth considering. Similarly, if you suspect your iMac is starting to go wrong, and you're nearing the end of the one-year limited warranty, you may want to get AppleCare to make sure you're covered. Or if you want telephone support beyond the 90 days that Apple provides, AppleCare can be a good buy.

Cleaning your iMac's screen and case

If your iMac's case or screen gets grubby, clean it with a microfiber cleaning cloth. Dampen the cloth with either water or a special screen-cleaning solution such as iKlear (www.klearscreen.com/iKlear.aspx).

To prevent disagreements with electricity, Apple recommends shutting down the iMac and disconnecting all its cables before cleaning it. If you're careful with the cloth, you may decide these precautions aren't necessary.

Caution

Never use glass cleaner to clean your iMac's screen because the alcohol or ammonia in these cleaners can damage an LCD screen. Don't spray anything on your iMac's screen or case — just dampen the cleaning cloth a little.

Troubleshooting Problems

Even if you update and maintain your iMac, you'll probably run into problems sooner or later. You may find things just don't work as expected, that an application — or your iMac — keeps crashing, or that you can't open a vital file.

Don't panic; you can figure out what's going on, and there's a good chance you'll be able to fix it.

Figuring out what's wrong

Your first step is to work out what's going wrong. To do this, you need to be able to reproduce the problem consistently. So work out what you were doing just before the problem occurred — for example, were you printing a particular document, viewing a certain web page, or running an application you've just installed? Take the action again and see if it produces the same problem.

If it does, investigate these possibilities:

- **System error.** Most system and application updates are released to fix known problems, but sometimes updates can introduce unexpected problems in features or applications that were working fine before. To fix system errors, use Software Update to check for system updates, and check the latest news and forum posts about problems other Mac users have run into at MacFixIt (www.macfixit.com).

- **Software conflict.** When two pieces of software don't play well together, you're going to need to turn one off, at least for the time being. But which one? Start by disabling everything you suspect may be involved — quit other applications, deactivate fonts, uninstall plug-ins — and see if the problem goes away. If so, put things back one at a time until one triggers the issue again. This is likely to be the source of your issue if you've added any new software recently or changed anything significant in your iMac's system.

- **Software bug.** You could be running into a known bug in your third-party program. Check the developer's website for news and updates, and read any user forums you can locate in search of known issues and workarounds. If you don't find any useful information this way, try emailing the developer to find out whether others have reported the same problem.

Genius You can use Safe Boot mode to track down a problem. Shut down your iMac, and then press the Shift key and keep holding it as you reboot the iMac. Safe Boot disables third-party system utilities, extra fonts, login items, and other "extras," and it forces the iMac to check the hard drive. If you don't experience the problem you're troubleshooting in Safe Boot mode, you've narrowed down the places you need to look for it.

- **Hardware problem.** Have you added any new devices lately? How about a new external hard drive or memory? If you think one of your hardware devices may be causing the problem, double-check the power cords and cable connections for the devices. For USB,

FireWire, or Thunderbolt connections, try using a different port if you have one available. If all the connections are shipshape, try removing the devices. If the problem goes away, put things back one at a time, testing after each replacement, until the problem recurs. Watch out for odd sounds coming from your peripherals, especially hard drives; they often let you know they're about to fail, if you're paying attention. Use Disk Utility or a third-party disk repair program to check hard drives.

Note If your iMac struggles to access data on a particular CD or DVD, odds are that the disc is damaged; see if another computer's optical drive can read the disc successfully. To make sure that your iMac's drive is okay, try another CD or DVD in it.

- **File corruption.** The particular document you're working with, or one of its components such as a font or image, may be damaged. If the problem occurs when you're printing, identify the part of the document that causes the problem: Try printing just the first half; if that works, try the second half. Within the half that causes the problem, print shorter sections or individual pages until you identify the problem. If you have a virus scanner, run it just in case. Log out of your account and try the same sequence of actions in a different account — this will tell you if something in your user folder is causing the problem. Run Disk Utility and verify the disk, as discussed later in this chapter. If Disk Utility reports any problems, back up the disk before attempting to repair it.

Note If you don't yet have a good backup of all your important files, now is a good time to create one. See Chapter 13 for details on how to arrange and manage backups with Time Machine.

Working out network and Internet issues

These days, email and the web are so vital to everyday life and work that you don't have to be an Internet addict to find connection problems a severe and immediate headache. This section shows you how to identify the exact problem and deal with it quickly and efficiently.

Distinguishing between Internet and LAN issues

If you have a local area network (LAN), the first thing to do when your Internet connection goes down is determine whether the problem lies between you and your ISP or on your LAN. You won't get far trying to troubleshoot one when the other is the problem (and vice versa).

First, check whether your DSL router or cable router thinks it has a connection to the ISP. Most models have a light that shows whether the router has a connection to the Internet and another light that shows whether the connection is transferring data. For example, your router's connection light may blink while it's connecting (or trying to), stay on if there's a steady connection, or go out completely if the router is severely confused.

If you can see that the router doesn't have a connection but it's trying to establish one, give it a minute to try to do so. Failing that, turn the router off, wait for 10 seconds, and then turn it back on. Give it another minute to dust itself down and make the connection. If it can't connect, fire up your web browser or configuration utility (depending on the router), connect to the router, and check its configuration. You may find that it has mysteriously forgotten its connection password or that there's some other straightforward problem you can fix in moments.

If the router thinks the connection is okay, the problem lies between your iMac and the router. If this is a wired network, make sure that your network switch (or hub) hasn't lost power and that the cables are plugged in firmly at each end and haven't been chewed through in the middle. Simple connection problems can easily occur on a LAN, but usually they're easy enough to solve.

If the network switch and the cables are okay, the problem may lie with your iMac. Open Network preferences on your iMac (choose Apple menu ⇨ System Preferences, and then click the Network icon in the System area) and see if anything is obviously wrong — for example, that your iMac is set to connect to the Internet through AirPort rather than through the Ethernet connection you normally use.

If you can see a problem in Network preferences, fix it, and see if that solves the connectivity issue. If it doesn't, open Network Utility and try to ping your router like this:

1. **Click the desktop, choose Go ⇨ Utilities, and then double-click the Network Utility icon to open Network Utility.**

2. **Click the Ping tab to display the Ping pane (see Figure 12.9).**

3. **In the Enter the network address to ping text box, type the network address of your router — for example, 10.0.0.2 or 198.162.0.1.**

4. **Select the Send only *N* pings option, and type a small number such as 5 in the text box.**

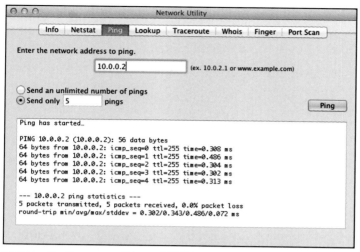

12.9 Use the Ping pane of Network Utility to test whether your iMac can communicate with your router across the network.

5. **Click Ping to send the pings, and check the responses you get:**

- A response such as "64 bytes from 10.0.0.2" (followed by details of the time the response took) shows that your iMac can communicate with the router.

- A response such as "Request timeout" and "5 packets transmitted, 5 packets received, 100.0% packet loss" indicates that your iMac can't reach the router.

If your iMac can reach the router, try pinging a site on the Internet — for example, ping www. yahoo.com. (Yahoo! is a site that responds to pings. Some sites don't respond to pings, so they're not good for testing.) If you can reach it, your iMac has recovered from its connectivity problem.

If your iMac can't ping the router, but you're able to ping the router from another computer that's connected in the same way (for example, via Ethernet), restart your iMac to see if Mac OS X has become confused by a bad network setting. Restarting takes a minute or two, but it often solves network problems.

Locating wireless problems

If you use a wireless network, try these diagnostic techniques:

- **Make sure you're connecting to the right AirPort network.** If your signal strength isn't what it should be, check your AirPort menu or the AirPort interface in Network preferences (choose Apple menu ⇨ System Preferences, and then click the Network icon in the

Internet & Wireless section) to find out what network you're connected to. If your regular wireless network has to restart itself, your iMac may connect to another network that you've connected to before — which may cause connectivity problems.

- **Check your router to make sure it has the most recent firmware version.** If your router is one of Apple's AirPort models, you can do that by running Software Update (choose Apple menu ➪ Software Update).

- **Check for device interference.** Other wireless devices, including 2.4 GHz cordless phones, can interfere with your wireless network. If you have anything of that description around, try turning it off to see if your problem goes away.

- **Turn on interference robustness.** You'll shorten the range of your wireless network but make its connections stronger with this optional setting. Follow these steps:

  1. **Open AirPort Utility.** Click the desktop, choose Go ➪ Utilities, and then double-click the AirPort Utility icon.

  2. **In the left column, select your AirPort.**

  3. **Click Manual Setup to enter manual setup.**

  4. **In AirPort settings, click the Wireless tab to display its contents (see Figure 12.10).**

12.10 From the Wireless tab of AirPort settings, you can open the Wireless Network Options dialog or change the channel or security type the wireless network is using.

343

5. Click **Wireless Network Options** to display the Wireless Network Options dialog (see Figure 12.11).

6. Select the **Use interference robustness** check box.

7. Click **Done** to close the Wireless Network Options dialog.

8. In the main AirPort Utility window, click **Update** to update the AirPort. Wait for the AirPort to restart, and then see if you can connect.

12.11 To make your wireless network more resilient against interference, select the Use interference robustness check box in the Wireless Network Options dialog.

● **Change wireless channels.** Wi-Fi networks can operate on any of several different channels, and if there are nearby networks using the same channel as your network, you may get interference. Open AirPort Utility and follow the steps listed previously until you reach the Wireless tab, then open the Channel pop-up menu and choose a different channel. Click the Update button to update the AirPort, and then wait while it restarts.

● **Change the security type you're using.** Open AirPort Utility and follow the steps in the preceding instructions until you reach the Wireless tab. Choose a different security type from the Wireless Security pop-up menu. For example, if you were using WPA/WPA2 Personal, try switching to WEP 128 and test whether that allows you to connect again. As before, click Update to apply the change.

● **Reset your AirPort.** If you can't sort out the AirPort's configuration problems, you may need to perform a hard reset on it. The hard reset restores the AirPort's default values, so you need to set up the wireless network again from scratch. The exact steps depend on the AirPort model, so look either at the instructions or the resetting article on Apple's website (http://support.apple.com/kb/HT3728).

Using Mail's Connection Doctor and Network Diagnostics

When Mail can't connect to the mail server, choose Window ⇨ Connection Doctor to see if it can tell what's happening. Connection Doctor checks all your mail accounts to see if you can connect and log in (see Figure 12.12). If at least some of them work, you have an Internet connection. If not, then the Network Diagnostics button becomes available.

If the Network Diagnostics button is available, click it to have your iMac check the different components of your network: the interface, your Network preference settings, your connection to an ISP, the ISP's connection to the Internet, and your DNS server's ability to translate URLs into IP addresses so the data you're sending can get to the right place (see Figure 12.13).

You can also open Network Diagnostics in these ways:

- **From Safari.** If Safari can't connect to the web, it will show you a Network Diagnostics button that you can click to open Network Diagnostics.

- **From System Preferences.** In the Internet & Wireless area, click the Network icon to display Network Preferences. Click Assist Me, and then click Diagnostics in the Do you need assistance setting up a new network connection or solving a network problem? dialog.

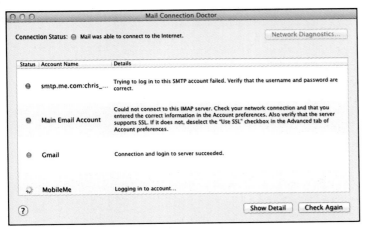

12.12 Mail's Connection Doctor feature shows that one of my SMTP servers seems to be taking an extended lunch hour and my main email account has fallen over.

- **From the Finder.** You'll find Network Diagnostics in the /System/Library/CoreServices folder. You can either run it from there or click and drag it to somewhere more convenient, such as your Applications folder or the Dock.

Note In theory, Network Diagnostics can tell you exactly where the problem lies; in reality, it may not tell you anything you couldn't have figured out yourself using the techniques described earlier, but it's always worth a try, just in case you've been overlooking something. Sometimes simply running Network Diagnostics gives Mac OS X enough pokes and prods to sort out problems even without your needing to make changes.

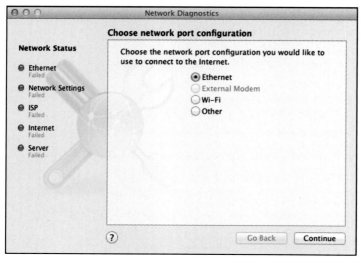

12.13 Network Diagnostics indicates that there's no connection at all. In this case, the first thing to check is the Ethernet cable.

Dealing with disk problems

If you think the hard drive is causing problems, back it up, and then run Disk Utility. Your first step is to repair permissions on the disk.

Repairing permissions

Each file or folder on your iMac has a set of permissions that controls who can read the file, change it, or open it (if it's an application or folder). Installing new applications can modify those permissions, sometimes incorrectly, as can file corruption. Sometimes these errors lead to crashes; most of the time they just slow things down.

When these permissions problems occur, you can easily fix them with Disk Utility like this:

1. **Click the Desktop, choose Go ⇨ Utilities, and then double-click the Disk Utility icon.**

2. **Choose your startup disk in the list on the left side of the window.**

3. **Click the First Aid tab to display its contents.**

4. **Click Repair Disk Permissions.** Disk Utility repairs the permissions on the disk (see Figure 12.14).

5. **Quit Disk Utility.** Choose Disk Utility ⇨ Quit Disk Utility.

When Disk Utility finishes, each permission is back in its default state, and things should work smoothly again.

After repairing permissions, you may need to modify permissions for an individual file or folder to which you need special access. Here's how to change the permissions:

1. **In the Finder, Control+click or right-click the file or folder you want to change, and then choose Get Info to open the Info window.**

2. **If the Sharing & Permissions area of the Info window is collapsed, click the disclosure triangle to expand it.**

3. **Click the padlock button to unlock the file's permissions.** When Mac OS X prompts you for your credentials, type an administrator name and password, and then click OK.

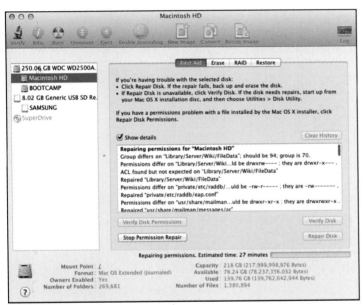

12.14 Repairing permissions takes a few minutes but it is a good way to start fixing a puzzling problem.

4. **Use the Privilege pop-up menus next to each Name entry to change the permissions for that person or group (see Figure 12.15), as follows:**

- **Me.** This is the account you're currently using.

- **Staff.** This group includes all nonadministrator users of your iMac.

- **Everyone.** This group includes every user and any application other than those specified previously.

5. **If you're changing permissions for a folder, and you want those changes to apply to all the folders within that folder, click the Action button and choose Apply to enclosed items from the pop-up menu.** Click OK in the confirmation message box.

6. **When you finish changing permissions, close the Info window.**

Repairing the formatting

Before you can use any storage device (hard drive, thumb drive, CD, or DVD), you must format it. Formatting sets up the disk with storage slots in which you can store data. If the formatting goes wrong, you may have trouble accessing the files you want, or your system may just feel slow. To deal with this problem, use Disk Utility to check your drive's formatting and fix any problems that you find.

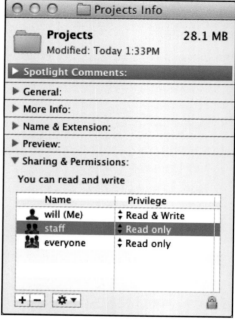

12.15 Use the Sharing & Permissions area of the Info window when you need to change the permissions on a file or folder.

Here's how to repair the formatting on a drive:

1. **Click the Desktop, choose Go ⇨ Utilities, and then double-click the Disk Utility icon.**

2. **Choose the problem drive in the list on the left side of the window, and then click the First Aid tab (see Figure 12.16).**

3. **Click Verify Disk.** Wait while Disk Utility checks the disk.

4. **If Disk Utility finds problems, run a backup of the disk, and then click Repair Disk in Disk Utility.** Don't skip the backup part of this step — the disk can fail while you're repairing it.

5. **When the repairs are complete, click Verify Disk again.** Repeat Steps 4 and 5 until no problems are found.

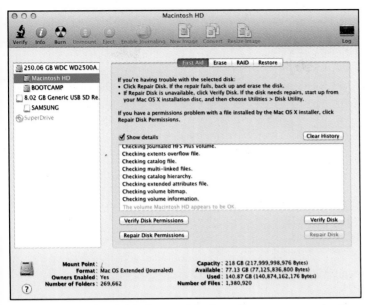

12.16 Always verify a disk before repairing it, so that you can run a backup before the repair if you do find any problems.

Note

If the drive you need to repair is your iMac's boot drive, you must boot into the recovery partition in order to fix it. Restart your iMac. At the startup chime, hold down ⌘+R until the Apple logo appears on screen. When the Mac OS X Utilities screen appears, click Disk Utility to launch Disk Utility so that you can run the repair.

If Disk Utility isn't able to fix some or all of the problems it finds with your disk, it's time to turn to a third-party utility. Keep reading to learn more.

Genius

To get some warning of imminent hard drive failure, get SMARTReporter (free; www. corecode.at/smartreporter), which taps into the SMART (Self-Monitoring Analysis and Reporting Technology) technology built in to most modern hard drives. You can always check the status of your drive in the SMARTReporter menu, and if a drive shows signs of failing, SMARTReporter can email you, show a warning dialog, or even run a specific program (such as your backup software).

Using third-party utilities

Some disk problems are too complex for Disk Utility to handle, but they may be manageable for third-party utilities such as the following:

- **DiskWarrior ($100; www.alsoft.com).** This utility can rebuild the directory of a damaged drive by creating a new directory based on the drive's contents and then comparing the new directory to the old one.

Genius To make sure you always have your disk-fixing tools available, don't just install them on your iMac's hard drive; install them on any external boot drive that you use (for example, a FireWire drive) — and keep them available on an optical disk as well.

- **TechTool Pro ($100; www.micromat.com).** TechTool Pro has many functions, not just disk-related ones. It can still zap your PRAM (resetting a portion of your Mac's memory that contains vital system info), and it can check your RAM for flaws. One of the coolest features of TechTool Pro is its eDrive, a small partition of your hard drive that you can use to boot when your system software is damaged.

- **Drive Genius ($99; www.prosofteng.com).** Apple uses this product to defrag hard drives at its Genius Bars. As a disk fills up, files are broken into fragments that may be stored far away from each other on the drive. Putting all the pieces back together, so they're stored in adjacent locations, can speed up disk access to those files. Drive Genius can also repair directories, clone disks, and more.

All three of these products cost about the same, so you'll want to choose based on features. If you buy only one, DiskWarrior is usually the best choice — if you have to use it to repair a trashed hard drive even once, it will have been worth the money.

Caution Before running any of these programs, or before using Disk Utility to repair your permissions, always run a full backup. Some disk problems can be bad enough that trying to fix them causes more trouble. If worse comes to worst, you'll be able to recover files from your backup.

Creating a Mac OS X Lion installation DVD or recovery disk

Earlier versions of Mac OS X came on a DVD from which you could install or reinstall them as needed, but Lion comes only preinstalled on Macs or as a download for Macs running earlier versions of Mac OS X. Preinstalled versions of Lion include a recovery partition that includes tools for fixing problems with the operating system. And when you install Lion on a Mac running an earlier version of Mac OS X, the installer creates a recovery partition.

For anyone who has one of the Macs from which Apple has removed the DVD drive, such as the MacBook Air and the Mac mini, providing the operating system in these ways makes a lot of sense. But given that your iMac has a DVD drive, and that it's possible for the recovery partition to get corrupted, it's a good idea to burn a DVD containing Mac OS X Lion so that you can recover your iMac if it develops severe problems. You can do this only if you've downloaded and installed Lion as an update to an earlier version of Mac OS X.

Whether Lion came preinstalled or you downloaded it, you can create a USB Recovery Disk that works like the recovery partition on your iMac's hard drive but which will work if the recovery partition is damaged. In this section, I'll show you how to do this too.

Creating a Mac OS X Lion installation DVD

To create a Mac OS X Lion installation DVD, follow these steps:

1. **Click the desktop to activate the Finder, and then choose Go ⇨ Applications.** A Finder window opens showing the contents of the Applications folder.

2. **Control-click or right-click the Install Mac OS X Lion item, and then click Show Package Contents on the context menu.** A Finder window opens showing the contents of the file.

3. **Open the Contents folder.**

4. **Open the SharedSupport folder.**

5. **Control-click or right-click the InstallESD.dmg file, click Open With on the context menu, and then click Disk Utility on the submenu.** Disk Utility opens, and the InstallESD.dmg disk image file appears in the sidebar.

6. **Click InstallESD.dmg in the sidebar to select it.**

7. **Click the Burn button.** The Burn Disk In dialog opens.

8. **Insert a blank recordable DVD in your iMac's optical drive.**

9. **Click the Burn button.** Your iMac burns the DVD.

10. **When the burn finishes, eject the DVD and label it.**

Creating a Mac OS X Lion recovery disk

To create a Mac OS X Lion recovery disk, follow these steps:

1. **Get a USB drive that you can dedicate as the recovery disk.** Normally, you'll want to use a USB key drive with a 1GB capacity. You can use a bigger drive, or an external hard drive that connects via USB, but there's no benefit.

Caution

The Recovery Assistant erases any data on the USB drive you provide, so make sure the drive contains no data you care about.

2. **Connect the USB drive to your iMac.**

3. **Open Safari and download the Lion Recovery Disk Assistant from the Apple Support website (http://support.apple.com/kb/dl1433).**

4. **Click the Downloads stack on the Dock, and then click RecoveryDiskAssistant.dmg to mount the disk image.** A Finder window opens showing the contents of the disk image.

Note

If your iMac automatically mounts the disk image, skip step 4.

5. **Double-click Recovery Disk Assistant.** A dialog opens warning you that it is an application downloaded from the Internet.

6. **Click Open**. The license agreement appears.

7. **Read the license, and then click Agree if you want to proceed.**

8. **In the Recovery Disk Assistant window (see Figure 12.17), click the drive you want to use, and then click Continue.** Mac OS X prompts you to authenticate yourself.

9. **Type your password (and an administrator name if you're not logged in as an administrator), and then click OK.** Recovery Disk Assistant copies the data to the disk and then verifies it.

10. **When Recovery Disk Assistant displays the Conclusion screen, which tells you that it has created the recovery drive, click the Quit button.**

11. **Remove the USB drive from your iMac, label it, and store it somewhere safe.**

Note To use your recovery disk, connect it to your iMac. Restart the iMac if it's running, or start it if it's not. When the startup chime sounds, press and hold Option until the Apple logo appears, and then release it. Mac OS X displays a screen showing all available disks. Double-click your recovery disk to launch Mac OS X Utilities and start the recovery.

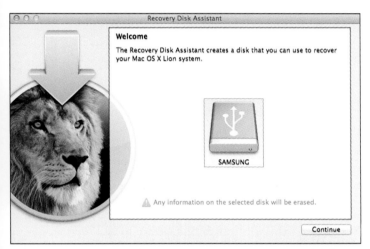

12.17 Use the Recovery Disk Assistant to create a USB recovery disk from which you can repair Mac OS X if disaster strikes.

Getting one-on-one help via screen sharing or VNC

If you need to get help from someone who's not physically present, use screen sharing or Virtual Network Computing (VNC). With screen sharing, you can either let someone else view what's happening on your iMac's screen (while you control it) or allow that person to take control of your iMac so that he or she can fix the problem for you.

Note See Chapter 9 for details on how to set up screen sharing on your iMac.

If your helper is running Lion, Snow Leopard, or Leopard on a Mac, have him connect to your iMac via screen sharing. If your helper has an older version of Mac OS X or is running another operating system, select the VNC viewers may control screen with password check box in the Computer Settings dialog and type a strong (unguessable) password in the text box. You'll then need to communicate this password securely to your helper so that he can connect to your iMac.

How Can I Keep My iMac and My Files Safe?

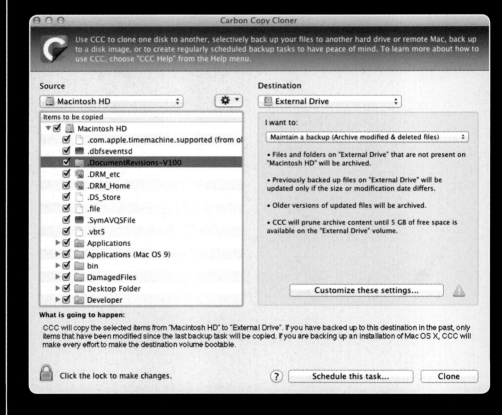

In the previous chapter, you saw how to keep your iMac running smoothly by looking after it and troubleshooting problems that occur. You also need to keep your iMac secure — secure from viruses, from threats that come from the Internet or other networks, and from the threats that other users of your iMac can pose. Beyond this, you almost certainly want to keep your files safe by backing them up automatically with Time Machine, by making online backups of files you simply can't afford to lose, and by backing up your entire iMac so that you can restore it in minutes. You can also use Lion's ingenious feature to restore an earlier version of a document even after you've saved changes to it.

Keeping Your iMac Secure

A big part of maintaining your iMac's overall health is making sure that outside people and applications can't affect it. That means using a firewall to protect against unwanted access from outside your network, taking appropriate precautions against viruses and other unwanted software, and controlling access to your iMac over your local network and at the keyboard.

Note

If your account isn't an administrator account, you need to type an administrator username and password to change any Security or Sharing settings.

Setting up the firewall

A firewall is a program that inspects all the data coming into your computer via a network connection and blocks any type of data that is not permitted to pass the firewall — for example, attempts to connect to your iMac from the Internet.

Mac OS X includes a built-in firewall that you can configure to protect your iMac from attacks across the network; in this section, you look at how to configure this firewall. Your Internet router most likely also has a firewall for protecting the network as a whole from attacks across the Internet. You learn how to configure your Internet router's firewall later in this chapter.

Genius

Compared to some other operating systems, Macs provide good protection against external threats right out of the box. Even so, it's a good idea to turn on the firewall.

To turn on the firewall, follow these steps:

1. **Choose Apple menu ➪ System Preferences.** The System Preferences window opens.

2. **In the Personal section, click the Security & Privacy icon to display Security & Privacy preferences.**

3. **Click the Firewall tab to display its contents (see Figure 13.1).**

4. **Click the lock icon in the lower-left corner of the Firewall tab, type your username and password in the authentication dialog, and then click OK.** Mac OS X makes the controls active.

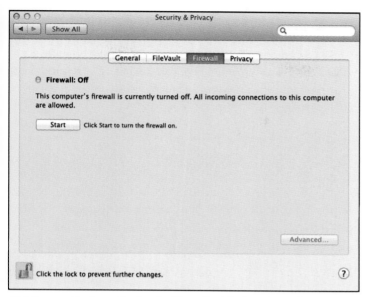

13.1 Turn on the firewall using the Firewall tab in Security preferences.

5. **If the Firewall readout in the upper-left corner says Off, click Start to turn the firewall on.**

6. **Click Advanced to display the Advanced dialog (see Figure 13.2).**

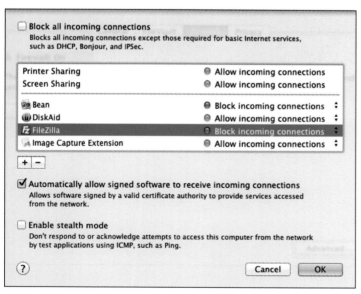

13.2 Use the Advanced dialog to tell the firewall which connections to allow and which to block.

357

7. **If you want to give your iMac as much protection as possible, select the Block all incoming connections check box.** You will normally want to do this only when connecting to public networks — for example, in coffee shops or hotels. This is a setting you're more likely to need on a MacBook than on an iMac (unless you take your iMac traveling).

Genius

Selecting the Block all incoming connections check box makes all the other controls in the Advanced dialog unavailable, except for the OK button and Cancel button. Mac OS X automatically selects the Stealth mode check box for you, as blocking all incoming connections also turns on Stealth mode.

8. **To get a moderate level of security while allowing most software to connect through the firewall, select the Automatically allow signed software to accept incoming connections check box.** Mac OS X then allows any application with a digital certificate signed by a recognized certificate authority to accept incoming connections. You can also allow other applications to accept connections, as described next.

Note

A certificate authority is an organization that provides digital certificates to companies, organizations, or individuals. A digital certificate is encrypted code that identifies the holder. The holder can use the digital certificate to apply a digital signature to a file such as an application. The digital signature verifies that the file comes from the certificate's holder and that the file has not been changed since the signature was applied.

9. **To specify exactly which applications to allow through the firewall and which to block, use the list box in the middle of the Advanced dialog.** Here's what to do:

- **Add an application.** Click the Add (+) button, select the application in the dialog that opens, and then click the Add button.

- **Remove an application.** Click the application in the list box, and then click the Remove (–) button.

- **Allow or block the application.** Click the pop-up menu, and then choose Allow incoming connections or Block incoming connections.

Note

If you've turned on any sharing services in Sharing preferences, these services appear in the list box in the Advanced dialog. You can't remove these services by using the Advanced dialog. Instead, you need to go back to Sharing preferences and turn off the services there.

10. **If you want to prevent your iMac from responding to electronic prods from other computers on the network, select the Stealth mode check box.** Stealth mode stops Mac OS X from answering ping requests and similar requests (which are used to test whether the network is working).

11. **Click OK to close the Advanced dialog.**

12. **Quit System Preferences.** Press ⌘+Q.

Protecting your iMac from viruses and malware

To keep your iMac safe, you also need to protect it against viruses and malware (malevolent software). Even though most virus writers target Windows PCs because Windows has the greatest share of the market, some create viruses that work on Macs. Your iMac can also suffer from macro viruses (which can be hidden in Microsoft Office documents) or from other attack code, such as scripts attached to web pages.

Mac OS X includes several features for protecting your iMac from malevolent software. For example, Mac OS X has a built-in list of malware that it automatically protects the iMac against, and it updates this list automatically when an Internet connection is available. Safari also has a Safe Downloading feature that attempts to prevent you from downloading dangerous software. Even so, you need to remain on your guard while online.

You can avoid many problems by following these safety guidelines:

- **Turn on any spam filtering and antivirus protection that your ISP provides.** Most ISPs provide spam filtering, and many offer to scan email attachments for viruses. If you use a free email service, make sure it provides this protection, as Gmail, Yahoo! Mail, and Windows Live Mail (Hotmail) do.

- **Use Firefox with the NoScript plug-in.** This add-on intercepts any web page script or plug-in that could pose a danger to your system.

- **As much as possible, avoid the following:**
  - **Installing unfamiliar software from shady sources, such as websites you've never heard of or applications posted to forums.**
  - **Installing social networking plug-ins.** Incompetently programmed plug-ins can harm your iMac just as badly as malevolent ones.
  - **Online gambling.** This can be as bad for your iMac as it can be for your wallet.
  - **Illegal file sharing (or legal file sharing on the same networks).** Apparently attractive files can contain malevolent code, and even file-sharing clients may include software that you wouldn't install knowingly.

● **If you use Windows on your Mac, whether with Boot Camp or with a virtual-machine application, install virus protection on your Windows system.**

What's Malware?

Everyone talks about viruses, but there are actually several different kinds of damaging software out there, collectively referred to as "malware." Here's a primer:

- **Virus.** A computer program that can distribute copies of itself by being attached to or embedded in an infected file. A virus may try to delete or modify data on your computer or damage it in other ways, or it may try to use your computer to spread itself further. Some viruses let you know they're present (for example, by displaying a message or by deleting data), but the most widespread viruses tend to be the ones that remain hidden and simply spread themselves.

- **Worm.** A worm is a program that can spread by itself, without needing to be attached to another file. Often worms cause damage simply by clogging up a network.

- **Trojan.** A program that appears to be harmless or even beneficial, such as a fake "security checker" or "speed enhancer," is considered a Trojan horse if it causes harm or attempts to deceive the user when run. For example, the Imunizator and MacSweeper programs detect nonexistent system and security problems on your Mac and offer to fix them — but only if you pay. Another Mac Trojan, OSX.RSPlug.A, masquerades as a video codec that's supposedly required to view content on web porn sites. When you download and run the file, it changes your DNS server to one that hijacks your web browser to phishing sites and ads for more adult sites.

- **Scareware.** A program that tries to scare you into paying for an application. For example, MacDefender advertises itself as a program for keeping Macs safe, but it displays fake alerts to try to persuade you to pay a registration fee. (This approach is similar to the Trojan approach described in the previous paragraph, but MacDefender doesn't disguise itself as another type of program.)

- **Spyware.** This term refers to programs that don't duplicate themselves, but do subject you to unsolicited pop-up advertisements, steal your personal data, monitor your web activity, or hijack your web browser to advertising sites instead of the sites you were trying to view.

- **Keyloggers.** Programs that record your every keystroke (including passwords, private emails, and credit card numbers) are called keystroke loggers or keyloggers. A virus or Trojan may install a keylogger, which then sends the intercepted data back to the program's creator via the Internet. Many antivirus applications are designed to run in the background all the time, checking pretty much everything that happens on your iMac in the hope of detecting a virus or other malware. This constant checking can slow down even powerful iMacs noticeably, so if you install an antivirus application, you may prefer to turn off automatic scanning and instead scan incoming and outgoing files manually. This greatly reduces the performance hit from the antivirus application, but it does reduce the protection you get.

Because viruses are so rare on Macs, there are relatively few antivirus applications. Here are three to consider:

- **Norton AntiVirus.** Norton AntiVirus, which you can buy from the Symantec website (www.symantec.com), costs $50 for the basic edition. This is all you need for Mac-only use, but if you also run Windows on your iMac, get the Dual Protection edition, which includes antivirus software for Windows as well. Symantec also sells Norton Internet Security Dual Protection for Mac, which includes extra features such as filtering for spam and phishing sites.

- **Intego VirusBarrier.** VirusBarrier X6 from Intego (www.intego.com) costs $50 and protects your iMac against the most important threats. If you run Windows on your iMac, check out VirusBarrier X6 DP, which includes BitDefender Antivirus for Windows. Intego offers a free downloadable trial of VirusBarrier, which lets you see how VirusBarrier works and how well your iMac can run it. Keep the trial disk image for the time being, because it contains the uninstaller that you'll need if you decide to remove VirusBarrier.

- **ClamXav.** ClamXav, which you can download for free from www.clamxav.com, is a graphical interface for the ClamAV open-source antivirus engine. ClamXav doesn't offer the extra features that the commercial antivirus applications do, but it's good at detecting viruses and easy to run. Figure 13.3 shows ClamXav rounding up email Trojans.

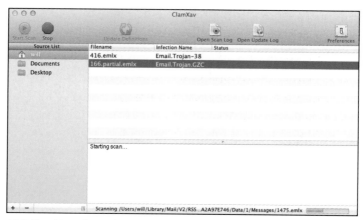

13.3 ClamXav is basic, but it works, and it's a real bargain.

Configuring your Guest user account

If you let other people use your iMac, you must make sure that they don't mess up your files and settings.

As you've seen earlier in this book, you should create a separate user account for each person who will use your iMac regularly, so that each person has her own space and settings. And anyone who needs to use your iMac just occasionally can use the Guest user account. The Guest user account is an account that Mac OS X automatically clears at the end of each user session, wiping out any files the user has created and resetting the settings to the defaults. As a result, the Guest user account appears fresh and unused each time someone logs on to it.

Mac OS X creates the Guest user account for you automatically but leaves it disabled until you enable it like this:

1. **Choose Apple menu ⇨ System Preferences.** The System Preferences window opens.

2. **In the System area, click the Users & Groups icon to display Users & Groups preferences.**

3. **If the padlock is locked, click the padlock, type your administrator name and password, and then click OK to unlock it.**

4. **In the accounts list, click the Guest User entry to display its preferences.**

5. **Select the Allow guests to log in to this computer check box (see Figure 13.4).**

6. **If you want guests on other Macs to be able to mount shared folders over a network, select the Allow guests to connect to shared folders check box.**

7. **To limit what a guest can do once logged in, select the Enable parental controls check box, and then click Open Parental Controls.** See Chapter 2 for instructions on setting Parental Controls to restrict the Guest user account as needed.

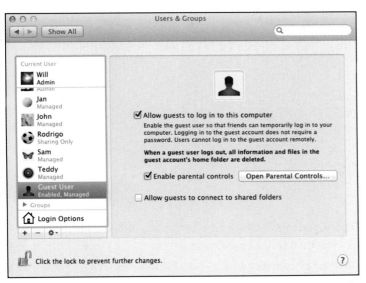

13.4 Enable the Guest user account to allow visitors to use your iMac, and then choose whether to apply Parental Controls to restrict the actions guests may take.

Note

The Guest user account has no password, so after you enable the Guest user account, anyone can log in to your iMac by clicking the Guest entry in the list of accounts on the login screen. (If you have set your iMac not to display the list of accounts, the user must type the word *guest* on the login screen.) When a guest logs out, any new files created or downloaded by that user are deleted. Be sure to warn guest users that they need to copy files off your iMac before logging out, or they'll lose them.

Genius

The Mac OS X Guest user account is pretty generic, but if you're prepared to put in a little effort, you can set custom options, such as your preferred desktop image and Dock setup. You do this by changing the user template that Mac OS X uses for new accounts. Check out the tutorial here: www.michaelsmac.com/modules.php?name= News&file=article&sid=394.

Keeping Your Network Secure

Just as you've secured your iMac against threats from your network, you must secure your network against threats from the Internet. If you have a wireless network, you must control access to it so that unauthorized people can't attack your computers. And if you take your iMac places, you will also need to know how to connect it securely to other people's networks.

Securing your Internet connection

To protect your network against threats from the Internet, you must secure your Internet connection with a firewall.

Most Internet routers — for example, cable routers and DSL routers — include a built-in firewall that is turned on by default. Open your router's configuration utility or its web-based configuration screens and locate the controls for the firewall. The names and locations of the controls depend on the exact device, so you may need to consult the router's documentation to find the settings you need.

For example, in the web-based configuration screen shown in Figure 13.5, you access the firewall settings by clicking Firewall in the left pane.

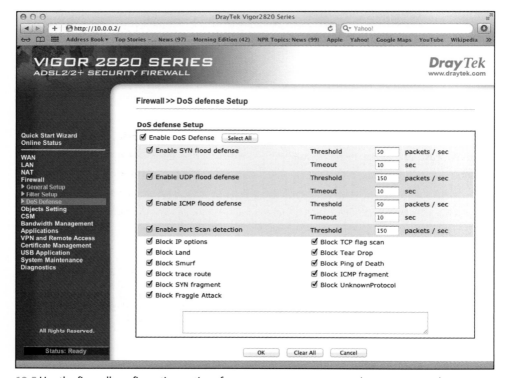

13.5 Use the firewall-configuration options for your router to secure your Internet connection.

You then click the category of firewall settings you want — in this case, DoS Defense, which contains settings for protecting against denial-of-service (DoS) attacks. You can then choose which settings to use — in this case, all of them.

Controlling access to your wireless network

If you have a wireless network, take these five steps to keep it secure:

- **Use WPA encryption.** Encryption scrambles the data sent between your computers and the access point so that anyone eavesdropping on it cannot read it. Most wireless access points offer the choice between Wired Equivalent Privacy (WEP) and WiFi Protected Access (WPA). WEP has security problems and does not provide enough protection to keep your network secure, so use WPA to secure your network.

- **Use a strong password.** Set a strong password for joining the network to prevent anyone within range from connecting to it. A typical access point will broadcast for a short distance outside your dwelling, depending on how many obstacles there are to stop the signal, but anyone determined to access it can do so by pointing an antenna at it from miles away within line of sight — for example, from a tall building or a hill.

Genius If you want to share your wireless network with neighbors or passersby, look for a wireless access point that includes a secondary wireless network designed for public access. Apple's AirPort Extreme is one model that includes this useful feature. The secondary network is separated from the primary network, so outsiders cannot access your private and valuable data on your LAN.

- **Stop the network from broadcasting its name.** Normally, each wireless network broadcasts its name, which is formally known as its service set identifier, or SSID. By turning off the SSID broadcasts, you can prevent your network from showing up when someone is casually scanning for wireless networks. A determined attacker can still detect the network's name by using a "sniffer" tool to capture wireless network packets, but this is a good step to deter casual intruders.

Note To connect to a closed wireless network, you (or your guests) must know the network's name as well as the password. Without the name, your computer will not be able to locate the network.

● **Use a whitelist of MAC addresses.** Each wireless network card has a unique hardware address, usually called the Media Access Control address (MAC address for short, always in capital letters) but sometimes also called the Ethernet address. By telling the wireless access point to allow only specific MAC addresses to join, you can prevent most unauthorized computers from connecting to the network.

Caution Using a whitelist of MAC addresses doesn't give total protection. An attacker can use a sniffer to capture the MAC addresses your computers are using to connect, wait until one of the computers disconnects from the network, and then connect, using a spoofing tool to provide a MAC address on your whitelist rather than the computer's real MAC address.

● **Change the network's default name.** Many people never change the names of their wireless networks from the default settings. This makes it easy for malefactors to find the networks and try to attack them.

How you implement these five measures depends on your wireless access point's configuration screens, but here I'll show you how to set them up on an AirPort, given that there's a fair chance you're using one.

1. **Click the desktop, choose Go ⇨ Utilities to open the Utilities folder, and then double-click AirPort Utility.** AirPort Utility opens.

2. **In the list on the left, click the AirPort you want to configure.**

3. **Click Manual Setup to display the configuration screens.**

4. **Make sure the AirPort button is selected in the toolbar.** If not, click it.

5. **Click the Wireless tab to display its contents (see Figure 13.6).**

6. **If you accepted the default network name when setting up the AirPort, change the name in the Wireless Network Name text box.**

7. **In the Wireless Security pop-up menu, choose WPA/WPA2 Personal or one of the other WPA options.**

8. **Type a password of 12 or more characters in the Wireless Password text box and the Verify Password text box.** As usual, you can click the key icon to have Password Assistant suggest a password or rate the strength of the password you choose.

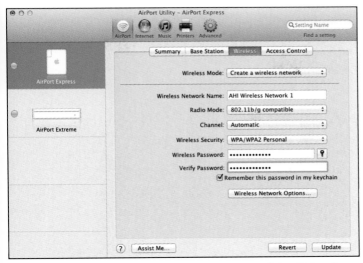

13.6 On the Wireless tab in AirPort Utility, choose one of the WPA options in the Wireless Security pop-up menu, and then type a strong password in the Wireless Password text box and the Verify Password text box.

9. **Click Wireless Network Options to display the Wireless Network Options dialog (see Figure 13.7).**

10. **Select the Create a closed network check box.** This setting prevents the AirPort from broadcasting the wireless network's name.

11. **Click Done.** The Wireless Network Options dialog closes.

12. **Click Update to apply the changes to the AirPort.** When AirPort Utility warns you that the device and its network services will be temporarily unavailable, click Continue.

13.7 In the Wireless Network Options dialog, select the Create a closed network check box to turn off SSID broadcasts.

13. **After the AirPort reappears in AirPort Utility, quit AirPort Utility.** Press ⌘+Q.

Genius

If you find that your wireless network extends farther outside your home than you'd like, you can reduce the power at which the AirPort is transmitting. In the Wireless Network Options dialog, click on the Transmit Power pop-up menu, and then choose 10%, 25%, or 50% instead of 100%.

Connecting your iMac securely to other people's networks

When you connect your iMac to someone else's network, crank up your security settings to the max in case the network isn't as well protected as your own network. This is especially important for a wireless network. Chances are you won't carry your iMac along to the coffee shop, but you may find you need to use it in a hotel, school, or other semipublic setting.

Choose Apple menu ⇨ System Preferences to open the System Preferences window, click the Security & Privacy icon in the Personal section, and then click the Firewall tab. Turn on the firewall as discussed earlier in this chapter, and then click Advanced. In the Advanced dialog, select the Block all incoming connections check box to protect your iMac from all unwanted traffic, and then click OK.

Keeping Your Files Secure

Apple makes iMacs as reliable as possible, but the simple fact remains that your iMac's hard drive could fail at any given point, either from general wear and tear or because of an accident such as your iMac getting knocked over or receiving an electrical spike.

To protect your files from hard drive failure, or from you or other people deleting them accidentally, you must back them up. This section explains how to back up your files easily and effectively. You also learn how to use Mac OS X's versions feature to restore an earlier version of a file.

Genius

To keep your data truly safe, never rely on a single backup. If possible, use two or more backup drives or backup media, and back up your essential files online in case disaster strikes your home.

Making automatic backups with Time Machine

The easiest way to back up your files is to use Time Machine, the automatic tool built into Mac OS X. You tell Time Machine which drive to use and which files and folders to exclude, and then leave it to get on with the job of backing them up. When you need to retrieve a file or folder, you can do so with a minimum of fuss.

Note

Time Machine starts by backing up all the files you don't exclude, which typically takes a lot of space. But after that Time Machine does incremental backups rather than full backups, which means that it backs up only the files that you or the system have changed since your last backup. When your backup drive fills up, Time Machine deletes older backups, but it always keeps the more recent versions of your files.

Setting up Time Machine

To use Time Machine at all, you need an external hard drive. FireWire 800 is usually the best choice; FireWire 400 is fine (if your iMac has a FireWire 400 port); otherwise, USB 2 is fast enough. You can also use Thunderbolt, but usually it's not worth the extra cost, given that Time Machine doesn't need extreme speeds. For best results, devote this hard drive entirely to Time Machine rather than using it for other purposes.

Note Ideally, the Time Machine drive should be much larger than your iMac's drive, as Time Machine will then be able to keep more past versions of your files. This means that when you discover that not only the current file but also recent versions are damaged, you can go further back into the past to find a version that's usable.

Once you connect the external drive you use for Time Machine, set it up like this:

1. **Choose Apple menu ➪ System Preferences.** The System Preferences window opens.

Note When you connect the external drive to your iMac, you may find that Mac OS X automatically suggests using it for Time Machine. If you accept the offer, Mac OS X opens Time Machine preferences for you.

2. **In the System section, click the Time Machine icon to display Time Machine preferences (see Figure 13.8).** At this point, if you haven't yet turned Time Machine on, the big Off–On switch on the left will be in the Off position.

13.8 Before turning Time Machine on, click Select Disk and choose the disk on which to store the Time Machine backups.

3. **Click Select Disk to open the dialog shown in Figure 13.9.**

4. **Click the drive you want to use.**

5. **Select the Encrypt backup disk check box if you want to encrypt the backup disk.**

6. **Click Use Backup Disk.** Mac OS X closes the dialog and returns you to Time Machine preferences, where the Off–On switch is now in the On position and the Next Backup readout is counting down from 120 seconds (see Figure 13.10).

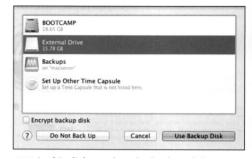

13.9 In this dialog, select the backup disk you want to use for Time Machine.

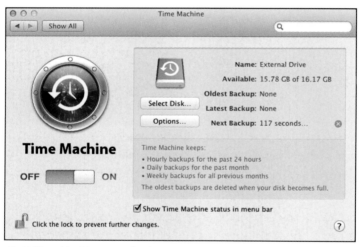

13.10 Time Machine sets a backup to run automatically after 2 minutes, but you may well want to exclude some folders from the backup before it rolls.

Genius

If you have a Time Capsule, Apple's AirPort base station with a built-in backup drive, select it in the dialog for choosing the backup disk. If the Time Capsule isn't listed, click Set Up Other Time Capsule, and then click the Open AirPort Utility button that replaces the Use Backup Disk button. You can then use AirPort Utility to set up the Time Capsule.

7. **Click Options to display the dialog shown in Figure 13.11.**

8. **Add to the Exclude these items from backups list box any drives or folders you don't want to back up with Time Machine.**

   - **Add a drive or folder.** Click the Add (+) button, select the drive or folder in the dialog that opens, and then click the Exclude button.

   - **Remove a drive or folder.** Click it in the Exclude these items from backups list box, and then click the Remove (–) button.

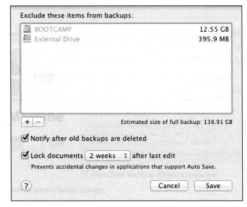

Exclude these items from backups:

BOOTCAMP	12.55 GB
External Drive	395.9 MB

Estimated size of full backup: 138.91 GB

☑ Notify after old backups are deleted

☑ Lock documents 2 weeks ⬍ after last edit

Prevents accidental changes in applications that support Auto Save.

(?) Cancel   Save

13.11 In this dialog, specify any disks and folders you want to exclude from the backup.

Note

You can also add drives or folders to the Exclude these items from backups list box by dragging them to the dialog from a Finder window.

9. **Select the Notify after old backups are deleted check box if you want Time Machine to let you know when it has deleted older backups.** Time Machine automatically deletes older backups when it runs out of space for newer ones; this warning is just a courtesy.

10. **If you want to lock documents automatically after a specific period of time, select the Lock documents after last edit check box, and choose the time period in the pop-up menu: 1 day, 1 week, 2 weeks, 1 month, or 1 year.** The default setting is 2 weeks.

11. **Click Done to close the dialog.** Time Machine resumes its countdown to the first backup.

12. **Select the Show Time Machine status in the menu bar check box if you want to have a Time Machine menulet appear in the menu bar.** This menulet gives you a Back Up Now command and two-click access to Time Machine preferences, so it's usually helpful.

13. **Quit System Preferences.** Choose System Preferences ➪ Quit System Preferences.

You can use the same drive to back up more than one Mac, either by mounting it over your local network on remote Macs or by moving it physically from one Mac to another. If the drive isn't available when Time Machine runs, Time Machine waits for the drive to reappear before starting another backup. Always unmount the drive by clicking the Eject button next to its name in a Finder window sidebar before unplugging it from your iMac. If Time Machine is in the middle of a backup when you put your Mac to sleep or eject the backup drive, Time Machine automatically stops the backup, and then resumes when the backup drive is available again.

Genius

To force Time Machine to do a backup right now, click the Time Machine menulet and choose Back Up Now. Otherwise, Control+click or right-click the Time Machine icon in the Dock and choose Back Up Now.

Restoring individual files with Time Machine

Retrieving files from a Time Machine backup is almost as easy as backing them up in the first place. Here's how it goes:

1. **Click the Time Machine menulet on the menu bar, and then click Enter Time Machine to open Time Machine.** If you chose not to put the Time Machine menulet on the menu bar, click the Launchpad icon on the Dock, and then click Time Machine.

2. **Navigate to the folder that contains the files you want to retrieve.**

3. **Find the older version of the folder:**

   - If you know the date and time from which you want to retrieve the files, click on that point in the timeline at the right side of the screen (see Figure 13.12).

Note

Because Time Machine's interface is just like the Finder, you can open folders, change view options, re-sort list views, and even use the search field at the top right-hand corner of the window. Double-click a file to see its contents.

   - If you're not sure, click the silver arrow pointing away from you next to the folder you're searching to skip to the last time when that folder changed; click again to go further into the past. Click the arrow that points toward you to return to a more recent backup.

4. **When you locate the files you're looking for, select them and click Restore.** Time Machine puts the files back in their previous locations. If this involves replacing the file or files that are there now, Time Machine asks you whether you want to write over the newer files, cancel the restore operation, or rename one of the files so you can keep both of them. Click the appropriate button.

You can also start a search in the Finder, choose a search location, and then click the Time Machine icon on the Dock to look through the search results from various times in your backups.

13.12 Use Time Machine's easy interface to navigate to the version of the file you want to restore.

Note Some Apple applications, such as Mail and iPhoto, work with Time Machine, meaning that you can access Time Machine backups from within the applications themselves. If you're trying to locate a missing photo or email, use this method rather than the Finder.

Restoring all your files with Time Machine

If your entire hard drive crashes, you can restore all your files with Time Machine (assuming you've backed them up). Here's what to do:

1. **Repair or replace the drive.** You don't want to put any files back on it until you're certain the problem is fixed. As mentioned earlier in the book, replacing an iMac's hard drive is normally a professional's job, so don't try it yourself in haste.

2. **Boot from your iMac's recovery partition.** Follow these steps:

   - **Restart your iMac.** For example, choose Apple ➪ Restart, and then click the Restart button.

   - **At the startup chime, press ⌘+R.** Keep holding the keys down until the Apple logo appears on screen, and then release them.

3. **When Mac OS X displays the Mac OS X Utilities screen, click Restore From Time Machine Backup, and then click Continue.**

4. **In the Restore Your System dialog, click Continue.**

5. **In the Select a Backup Source dialog, choose your backup drive, and then click Continue.**

6. **In the Select a Backup dialog, choose which backup snapshot you want to restore, and then click Continue.** If your Mac has just gone wrong, you'll probably want to restore the most recent backup snapshot; if that one turns out to have damage, too, you may need to go farther back in time.

7. **In the Select a Destination dialog, select the hard drive you want your data restored to.**

Restoring an earlier version of a file

Another way to recover lost work is to restore an earlier version of a file. Lion includes a versions feature that enables applications to save different versions of the same document in the same file. You can display the different versions of the document at the same time and go back to an earlier version if necessary.

Note Only applications written to work with Mac OS X Lion can use the versions feature. For example, the TextEdit application and the Preview application included with Mac OS X Lion can use versions, but the Microsoft Office applications cannot.

Here's how to restore an earlier version of a file:

1. **Open the application that you use for working with the file.** This example uses TextEdit.

2. **Open the current version of the file.**

3. **Click the file's name in the title bar to display the pop-up menu (see Figure 13.13).**

4. **Click Browse All Versions to display the screen for working with versions (see Figure 13.14).** The current version of the document appears on the left. Earlier versions appear in a stack on the right, with the newest at the front.

5. **Navigate to the appropriate point in time by clicking the timeline on the right.**

6. **Click the window that shows the version of the file that you want to restore.**

7. **Click the Restore button.** Mac OS X hides the screen for working with versions and displays the version you chose.

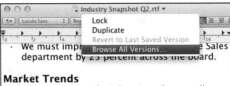

13.13 To access an earlier version of the file you're working in, click the file's name in the title bar, and then click Browse All Versions on the pop-up menu.

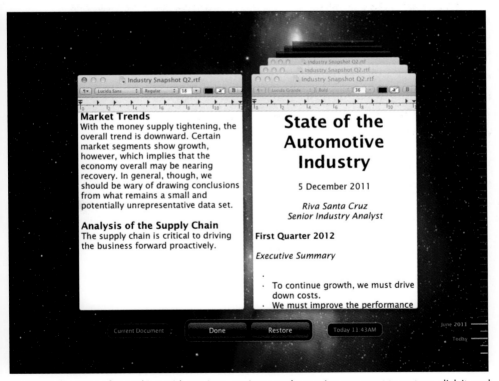

13.14 On the screen for working with versions, navigate to the version you want to restore, click it, and then click the Restore button.

Making online backups

As long as you have a broadband Internet connection, making online backups can be a great way of keeping copies of your most important files where they're safe from any disaster that may befall your Time Machine backups.

Using MobileMe for backups

If you have a MobileMe subscription, you can back up essential files to your iDisk until Apple shuts down the MobileMe service on June 30, 2012. At this writing, iDisk is a reasonable backup solution for backing up modest numbers of files — for example, your most important files.

To use MobileMe for ad hoc backups, click and drag files to your iDisk's Documents or Backup folder. In the Finder, press ⌘+Shift+I to mount your iDisk, and then you can use it just like any drive connected to your iMac.

To back up files automatically to MobileMe, you need the MobileMe Backup application that you can download from the Downloads page on Apple's website (http://support.apple.com/kb/dl1025). After downloading MobileMe Backup, install the application on your iMac's hard drive. You can then run MobileMe Backup from Launchpad and set up a backup plan to back up particular files and folders on a schedule.

Using iCloud for Backups

Apple has announced that iCloud, the service that is replacing MobileMe, will include backup and restore capabilities. If you create an iCloud account, you can automatically sync key data and documents between your iMac and your iPhone, iPad, or iPod touch. The data includes your email, calendars, contacts, and Safari bookmarks. The documents include those you create with the iWork applications — Pages, Numbers, and Keynote — as well as third-party applications designed to use iCloud.

iCloud's focus is on syncing your data across devices rather than backing it up in the conventional sense, but the effect of using iCloud is to create a backup of the files involved. This helps protect you against data loss. But because iCloud doesn't have an area to which you can back up any documents you choose, it's not a complete backup solution in the way that iDisk has been.

Using other Internet backup services

Instead of using Backup and your iDisk, you can use a third-party backup service such as these three:

- **BackJack.** BackJack (www.backjack.com) offers a backup service that ties into Time Machine, running automatically after your Time Machine daily backup completes. BackJack offers a free trial so that you can see how well it works for you before laying down your money.

- **Mozy.** Mozy (www.mozy.com) offers MozyPro for professional users and MozyHome for home users. Mozy also provides a limited free service, MozyHome Free, to encourage you to sign up.

- **CrashPlan.** CrashPlan (www.crashplan.com) provides a low-price version called CrashPlan+ for home and home-office use and a professional version called CrashPlan Pro for business and enterprise users. There's also a free version of CrashPlan that you can use to back up to your own devices or to other computers across a network connection or the Internet. For example, you back up to your friend's computer, and your friend backs up to your iMac, giving both of you off-site protection.

Backing up your entire iMac

Instead of backing up specific folders or files, you may want to clone your entire iMac so that you're fully protected if the hard drive fails. A clone is a byte-by-byte duplicate of your iMac's hard drive that you can either restore to the hard drive (or to a replacement hard drive) or boot your iMac from.

If you want to create a clone, start by looking at Carbon Copy Cloner from Bombich Software, LLC (www.bombich.com). Carbon Copy Cloner (shown on the opening page of this chapter) is dona-tionware — if you like it, you can make a donation toward the developer's costs.

If Carbon Copy Cloner doesn't suit you, try SuperDuper ($28; www.shirtpocket.com/SuperDuper/SuperDuperDescription.html). SuperDuper can not only create scheduled clones but can also update a clone to match your drive's current state (which is much quicker than cloning the whole drive again).

Genius To create a bootable clone, you must make sure the target drive is formatted using Mac OS Extended format with the GUID Partition Table. You may need to repartition the drive using Disk Utility (which you'll find in the /Applications/Utilities folder) before you can create a bootable clone

Index

The Genius is in.

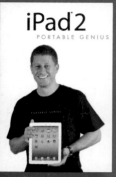

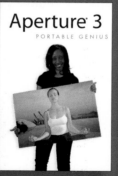